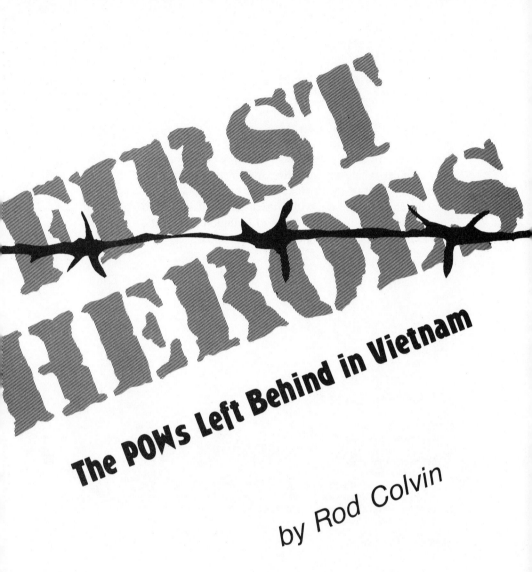

FIRST HEROES

The POWs Left Behind in Vietnam

by Rod Colvin

✳ IRVINGTON PUBLISHERS, INC.
740 Broadway   New York, NY 10003

First Edition

Library of Congress Cataloging-in-Publication Data

Colvin, Rod, 1950–
   First heroes.

   Bibliography: p.
   Includes index.
   1. Vietnamese Conflict, 1961-1975--Prisoners and
prisons.   2. Vietnamese Conflict, 1961-1975--Missing
in action--United States.   3. Prisoners of war--
United States.   I. Title.
DS559.4.C65   1987   959.704'37   87-17268
ISBN 0-8290-2008-X

Frontispiece, map of South East Asia: Isaacs, Arnold R.: *Without Honor: Defeat in Vietnam and Cambodia.* Baltimore/ London, The Johns Hopkins University Press, 1983, p. 14.

Typography by Rivendell Marketing Company
Printed in the United States of America

Dedication

To Those Who Wait

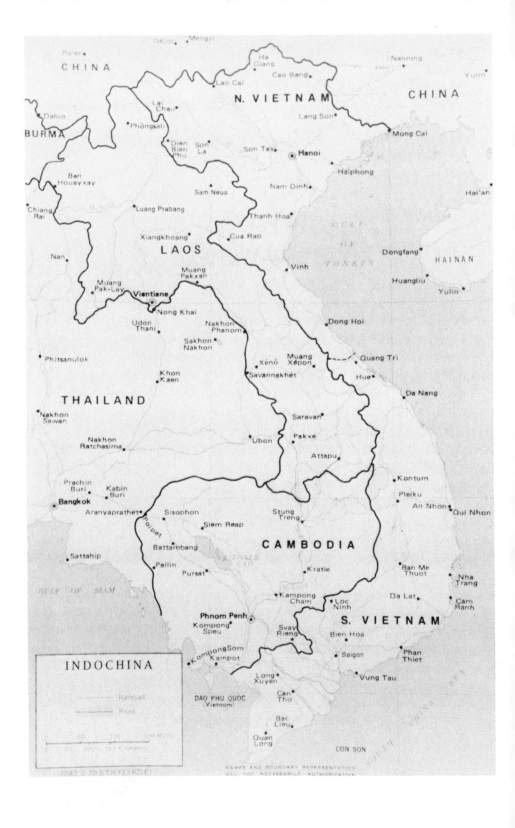

TABLE OF CONTENTS

INTRODUCTION

Back in the spring of 1981, when I was first introduced to the MIA/POW issue at a petition drive on an Omaha mall, little did I realize the seeds for this book were being sown. Although I felt compassion for the families of the missing, initially I was uninformed and believed, like so many Americans, that those who still carried the banner for MIAs were overly emotional and unable to accept the cruel realities of war.

However, after learning enough about the issue to whet my appetite as a reporter, as well as my interest as another human being, I began probing. The more I learned, the more I understood. The Vietnamese have never honored their pledge to provide the fullest possible accounting for America's MIAs. For example, legitimate questions are yet to be answered about men who were known to have been in enemy hands, were seen alive on the ground after parachuting from disabled aircraft or were photographed in captivity.

On the surface, the MIA/POW question seems simple. "Are Americans still being held against their will in Southeast Asia?" The weight of the evidence provides reason to believe Americans were withheld, but the complexity of the problem has precluded verification of these prisoners' existence and any subsequent release or rescue. Diplomatically, the Vietnamese have, for years, steadfastly denied that they detained POWs, despite having strong political and economic motives for so doing. And, given the uncooperative, restrictive nature of the Vietnamese government and the inaccessibility to the region, even U.S. government and military sources concede that proof is elusive.

This book builds a case. It's a case which, when examined in its entirety, leads to a conclusion that American POWs were left behind in Vietnam and Laos.

The strongest evidence, according to the Defense Department, comes from the eye witness accounts of Southeast Asian refugees — the "boat people" who have reported seeing Americans in captivity before they left their homelands in the late 1970s or even early '80s. Since 1975, nearly 5,000 refugees have provided MIA/POW information, with some 800 having reported first-hand sighting information about Americans in captivity. Even though over half of these reports have been determined to pertain to servicemen who have since returned from Southeast Asia, some of the sighting reports are still unresolved. During investigation of these unresolved cases, several dozen refugees have submitted to extensive interrogations, including polygraphs, and many are considered credible by intelligence experts. The refugee reporting, on the whole, has been accurate information. But, unfortunately, the collapse of intelligence capabilities in Southeast Asia after the fall of Saigon in 1975, has made verification of these unresolved reports seemingly impossible.

However, historians have documented Communist governments' long-standing practice of withholding POWs. It is believed North Koreans never released several hundred Americans at the end of the Korean War. It's estimated that the Soviets held back hundreds of thousands of German POWs at the close of World War

Introduction

Two, for reasons ranging from political to exploitation of prisoners' technical expertise. The Vietnamese themselves still held some French forces captive fourteen years after the French withdrawal from Indochina in 1954. The Vietnamese are masterful players of a war game in which prisoners become pawns . . . played only when the move reaps the maximum benefit for the state.

It is the MIA families who recognized early on that their loved ones were the victims of this deadly game, and it is they who first began piecing together details of this story. In fact, the families' quest for information about the fates of missing servicemen kept the issue alive, even during the years when most of the nation wanted to forget about the Vietnam War. And, it's through the eyes of these families that we can best understand the personal, human tragedy of the MIA/POW controversy.

But the issue takes on larger dimensions, raising new questions about the Vietnam War and about national responsibility. Has a super-power, in fact, abandoned its fighting men? What are the implications for the men who will go into future battles? Without the fullest accounting possible, the haunting suspicion lingers that we left American prisoners behind in Southeast Asia and that some, as we cogitate and debate, are still alive . . . waiting. These men, determined to survive and keep the faith, are among our bravest. They are our first heroes.

ACKNOWLEDGEMENTS

Because so little historical data, specifically relating to POWs still being held in Southeast Asia, has been recorded, and because so many government records are classified, I've depended on personal interviews for the greater portion of this book.

I would like to thank the following persons who granted interviews or in some other way shared their experiences or expertise: William Abbot, Samuel A. Adams, Brig. Gen. Herman Aderholt, Everett Alvarez, Carol Bates, Kay Bosiljevac, Dick Childress, Bob Cressman, Walter Cronkite, Carl Daschke, Congressman Hal Daub, Jerome DeBruin, Vince Donahue, Congressman Bob Dornan, John Downey, John Dramesi, Maureen Dunn, Robert Dumas, Myrna Feekin, Gen. John Flynn, Dermot Foley, Clyde Foree, Ralph Gaither, Robert Garwood, Walt Gibbs, Joe Gillaspie, Congressman Ben Gilman, Allen Goodman, Tom Gorgen, Ann Griffiths, Mary Lou Hall, Senator Tom Harkin, Congressman Bill Hendon, Leo Hrdlicka, Charles Hudgel, Edna Jo Hunter, Debbie Lovell Inswell, Steve Johnson, Catherine Joyner, Dr. Henry Kenny, Col. Fred Kiley, Nancy Korenchen, Mike Larsen, John LeBoutillier, Mary Carol Lemon, Rev. Paul Lindstrom, Angus MacDonald, Jean MacDonald, Lt. Col. Paul Mather, Eugene McDaniel, Congressman Sonny Montgomery,

Ambassador John Negroponte, John and Margaret Nevin, Diane Nichols, Dick Ottinger, John Parsels, Lloyd Pate, Rick Rosenthal, Major Keith Schneider, Catherine Shaw, Sarah Frances Shay, Marian Shelton, Major Bob Shields, George and Helen Shine, Frank Sieverts, Calvin Sparks, Carolyn Standerwick, Lynn Standerwick, Hervie Stockman, Sue Sullivan, William H. Sullivan, Virginia Townley, Adm. Stansfield Turner, Adm. Jerry Tuttle, Terry Uyeyama, Mike Van Atta, Bob Vandevoort, LTC Jerry Venanzi, Jim Warner, Lester Wolff, Dr. Jim Yeager and Senator Ed Zorinsky.

A special thank-you to the following persons who granted interviews and who also reviewed portions of the manuscript for accuracy: Le Thi Anh, George and Gladys Brooks, Capt. Jerry Coffee, Glenn Griffith, Laird Guttersen, Col. Earl Hopper, Bill Paul, Roger Shields, Larry Stark and Gen. Eugene Tighe.

A warm word of thanks goes to Susan Acuff Adams, Rosalea Maher, Ramona Scheid and Joe Colvin whose support helped make this book possible.

Finally, I wish to express my deep appreciation to Irving Naiburg Jr. and Editor David Fitzpatrick, of Irvington Publishers, for bringing this book to life.

CHAPTER ONE
TAKING OFF THE BRACELETS

The F-4 streamed like a flaming comet through the thick clouds shrouding the jagged mountain peaks northwest of Haiphong. For Major Laird Guttersen, the pilot and last man on board the fighter escort, the countdown to death was ticking off in seconds. Suddenly the burning aircraft broke through the swirling mist and Guttersen catapulted himself into the air, free of the disabled plane. Before his feet touched earth, the F-4 crashed into the mountainside, spewing its molten metal parts in one last flaming blaze.

Guttersen clambered to his feet, twisting out of the restraints of his parachute. Below him lay a seemingly peaceful valley, a picturesque peasant village nestled against the foot of the mountain. But for him the serenity was a mockery. He was a downed U.S. Air Force pilot in North Vietnam. The natives definitely weren't friendly. He had defied sudden death with a well-timed leap, but the battle for survival was only just beginning.

Impelled by the urgency that began when a MiG heat-seeking missile targeted on the F-4, bursting it into flames, Guttersen scrabbled in the hardpan, digging a hole to bury his 'chute. The frantic shouts of his co-pilot as they'd scrambled to escape the blazing aircraft still sounded in his head. Now they were separated by miles of enemy terrain. The backseater, Lieutenant Myron Donald, was the first to bail out. Donald hadn't waited for the order to jump. He couldn't. The missile had hit just below his seat. He had to get out. He'd parachuted safely to the ground, only to float into the waiting arms of a North Vietnamese Army unit.

As Guttersen stuffed the 'chute into the shallow hole, he wished to God he could bury with it the military secrets stored in his mind. To learn what he knew about the Pentagon's planned offensive maneuvers, his captors would torture him beyond endurance. If he broke under torture — which he feared he would — dozens of his comrades would die needlessly.

Scattering stones over the freshly-mounded dirt to conceal the signs of digging, Guttersen started up the mountain, taking a diagonal course to mask his trail. There was no doubt searchers would soon be in pursuit, drawn to the scene of the fiery plane crash. His hope lay in rescue by a helicopter. He'd commanded the planes in the flight to continue on to the base; their bombing mission completed, they were running low on fuel.

The portable radio in Guttersen's hand crackled to life. "We're sending in a 'copter to get you."

Overhead the murky clouds swirled, obscuring the granite mountain peaks. A rescue attempt was a mission impossible.

"No!" shouted Guttersen. "There's no visibility up here. This stuff's hanging below the tops thick as mashed potato. Later! Get me later when it's moved off!"

Whatever reply was made, the major didn't hear it. He was hearing the voices of villagers already coming up the mountain. In a running crouch, counting on his green and gray mottled flight suit to camouflage his movement, he took cover in a low, sparse thicket. Too late he saw the hazard of his hiding place: it lay beside the only path across the mountain.

Hunkered down in the shrubbery, sweat trickling down his back and leg muscles cramping, Guttersen watched as the excited villagers ransacked the plane's wreckage, triumphantly bearing what they'd salvaged past him as they stumbled homeward.

But not all the villagers had come to scavenge. Some had come in search of the pilot. They were fine-combing the area, shouting instructions to one another and firing warning shots to force him out of hiding. Occasionally, a searcher stood so close Guttersen could have reached out and touched him.

Hour after agonizing hour passed while Guttersen waited, unable to move and hardly daring to breathe. Then in late afternoon he heard the clatter and roar of an incoming 'copter, risking its way through the still low-hanging cloud cover. As the 'copter broke through the cloudbank, too distant for Guttersen to break and run for it, the searchers' guns were trained on it. They had known where to expect the bird's landing because they had guided it in, setting up a homing beacon on the radio frequency used by Guttersen. The helicopter rose into the clouds. There could be no more rescue attempts for that day; dusk was closing in fast.

It was going to be a long night, but not a hopeless one. Guttersen knew the searchers would leave at sundown, fleeing the evil spirits believed to haunt the tops of the mountains at night. He would move under cover of darkness, away from the path and to a more remote area, praying the rescue 'copter could find him again in the morning.

The last band of searchers was getting ready to leave. Led by a teenager in the uniform of a reservist, the searchers chattered and laughed as they peered behind rocks and beat the bushes, playing their deadly game of hide-and-seek. Guttersen saw two young girls leave the group, giggling and glancing furtively around. They were walking toward the bushes where he was concealed.

With a terrifying premonition, he knew what was about to happen. Of all the bushes scattered around the area, the girls had selected Guttersen's place of concealment to relieve themselves. He was about to be found.

Guttersen fumbled in his shirt pocket for the packet of high-potency vitamin capsules he carried and quickly swallowed them.

The vitamins would give him the strength and stamina to take him through the coming seventy-two hours.

Inches away from Guttersen, one girl squatted and reached behind her to push aside a protruding branch. Her hand touched Guttersen's face and she jumped to her feet, screaming.

In seconds Guttersen was surrounded. He stood, warily eyeing a young boy nervously gripping an AK47 in both hands, so frightened he was swinging the weapon wildly, threatening not only the captive but everyone in the group. At that instant a rock the size of a baseball struck Guttersen's groin. Another followed and Guttersen ducked. The possibility of being stoned to death loomed in his mind, but as he turned, bouncing the rocks off his back and hip, he saw that there was but one rock-thrower — a boy pitching rocks as rapidly as he found them.

The uniformed youth, no more than fourteen, stepped forward and Guttersen was looking into the muzzle of a .45. Behind the lad, a white-haired old man with gnarled features aimed a single shot .50 caliber rifle of a vintage dating back almost to America's frontier days.

"Surrender or die!" the young commando ordered in English.

Guttersen surrendered. In weeks to come there would be times he wished he'd chosen death, times in which he would look for ways to commit suicide. But on the day of his capture — February 23, 1968 — he chose life.

A rope around his neck, his hands tied behind him, Guttersen was hauled, stumbling and falling, down the rock-strewn mountain path, and in the dark, over the slippery stones of a creekbed to a neighboring village where a military intelligence team awaited, forewarned of his coming.

Stripped of his wet clothes, Guttersen stood naked before his interrogators. One of them, holding a coil of rope in his hands, threatened that if the major did not cooperate in the beginning, his suffering would be infinitely worse. But to each question, Guttersen gave the same response. He recited his name, rank, serial number, and date of birth. A fist crashed into his face each time, sending him sprawling to the floor. And each time, on command, he struggled to his feet for the next round.

When he felt the rope being fastened around his arms behind him, Guttersen knew the worst was to begin. But the worst was beyond what even his torturors had planned.

Kneeling on the stone floor, the rope looped around his upper arms, Guttersen's agony began. Two guards held the rope ends, one foot braced against his shoulders. Each time he refused to answer a question, the guards increased the rope's tension, gradually wrenching his arms from the shoulder sockets.

But with insane ineptness, his tormentors had looped the ropes wrong. As Guttersen's arms separated from the sockets, his back broke — the vertebrae snapping like knuckle bones.

"It was like having a massive heart attack," he recalled later. "I couldn't breathe for the stabbing pain."

The major had triumphed, however. He had not broken under torture. And the interrogators had not come close to discovering the military secrets he held. They were only trying to coerce him into summoning a rescue helicopter for them to shoot down.

"I hurt over every inch of my body. And they had tied my hands so tightly that when they untied them next day, they were black and swollen like sausages. I figured I'd lost them..." said Guttersen.

In the morning Guttersen's clothes were returned to him, still wet, and he was taken to a waiting truck for the trip to the base camp north of Haiphong.

Overnight the temperature had dropped near the freezing mark. A chilling wind had risen, bringing the threat of icy rains. Huddled on the truckbed, shivering in his wet clothes, and his body racked with pain, Guttersen learned he was not going to the base camp. His captors, bundled in blankets and feather quilts against the biting cold, announced a change of orders. He was to be taken to the infamous Hoa Lo Prison in Hanoi — a twenty-four-hour trip.

Along the route, Guttersen was the source of a sadistic entertainment. At every village his blindfold was removed and he was pushed roughly off the truck to have his picture taken, kneeling at the feet of laughing villagers who held his ropes, pretending they had captured him.

Guttersen arrived at Hoa Lo feverish with pneumonia and was flung into a torture chamber — one of several the POWs bitterly dubbed "New Guy Village" because it was where all incoming prisoners were interrogated. For five days he was given neither food nor water, and allowed no sleep while the questioning and beatings continued relentlessly. In the next room he could hear the screams of a fellow prisoner. He thought it was Donald, his backseater who'd been on his last mission before going home when their F-4 was shot down.

Guttersen lay on the floor, aware that he was dying. Through the feverish haze he heard the interrogation team come into the room, felt the group of hands hauling him to his feet.

A paper was thrust at his face. "Sign this!" a voice hissed, "and maybe we can find you some penicillin."

"I'm allergic to it," mumbled Guttersen.

"Better yet! Sign or we'll give you penicillin!"

Guttersen shook his head. "No."

A hand cracked across his face, sending him crashing into the wall. His knees buckled and he slithered to the floor.

"Get up!"

He stared dumbly at the wall, inches from his face. He blinked and blinked again to clear the mist from his eyes. Scratched in the blood and muck, in letters almost too small to read, was a message: "Keep the faith baby."

For Guttersen, as for all the POWs at Hoa Lo, the enemy's persistence in obtaining signed statements resulted in beatings. The statements were often words quoted from Bobby Kennedy or Senator William Fulbright to which the prisoners were commanded to copy and sign their names.

"I learned early on that if you refused to anything, it led to beatings and torture," Guttersen recalled. "The trick was to refuse at first, then act as if you'd changed your mind and were ready to cooperate."

Consequently, the POWs made up their own statements — nonsensical words to which they signed fictitious names, such as "Ima Bullshitter."

"It aggravated them," said Guttersen, "but not as much as if you didn't write anything at all."

Still uppermost in Guttersen's mind was the fear of divulging secrets the Communists had not learned he knew. If the day came when they did know, Guttersen would have to take his own life because "they would go after it and they would get it." His plan, he said, was to run and dive headfirst into a wall, hoping the impact would kill him or, at least, fracture his skull, driving it into his brain.

In the beginning, Guttersen reacted in anger toward his captors until he realized anger was a cover-up for fear and that it was, in his words, "unproductive." His anger then became hatred, but that was self-destructive. "It tears you to pieces over the long term."

As a last measure he resorted to love. Guttersen created a "love symbol," filling his mind with thoughts of his seven-year-old daughter Karen, her arms around his neck, saying, "I love you, Daddy." It served him well the five years he was held prisoner — teaching him to pity instead of hate his torturers and freeing him from the burden of hate so many captured men brought home with them.

There was much to hate at Hoa Lo. Held in solitary confinement, severely punished if caught talking, the men found one way to communicate. Tapping on the walls of their cells, using a kind of Morse code, they exchanged information and the names of other POWs.

The season in hell ended March 14, 1973, for Guttersen and thirty-one other men at Hoa Lo. They were the ninth group released during Operation Homecoming. On that day they were flown to freedom and home from the Gia Lam Airport. For many, those who could forget, the long ordeal was ended. Laird Guttersen was ready to move on with his life, but he was not ready for the government resistance he encountered when he inquired about the POWs whom he feared had not made it into the system and who may have been left behind.

A classified debriefing troubled Guttersen most of all. "We were given a direct order in writing not to become involved with any MIA/POW organizations such as VIVA and the National League of Families."

What bothered him was the manner in which the order was issued. "It was given to us in writing. We were asked to acknowledge that we understood it and give it back. Then the paper was destroyed...right there in the room!"

To Guttersen it seemed as though "it was not a security problem but rather something they didn't want to go any further." He concluded the motivation was political, "That the administration wanted the whole prisoner release thing to hit a crescendo and then go out of existence really fast."

MAY 24, 1973: White linen tablecloths fluttered in the breeze stealing under the huge red and yellow striped canopy set up on the south lawn of the White House where the romantic airs of the Air Force Strolling Strings mingled with the clinking of crystal goblets.

The menu included roast sirloin of beef and strawberry mousse, washed down with California wine — heady fare for men long accustomed to thin rice gruel, watery pumpkin soup and chunks of hard bread eaten in the stench of dark, dingy cement cells.

The honor guests were the recently returned prisoners of war; the White House gala was a joyous, official celebration of their return. They'd made it. Lining row after row of banquet tables, their Navy whites, Air Force and Marine Corps blues and Army greens contrasted with the bright-hued gowns of their wives and sweethearts accompanying them.

Earlier in the day, their host, President Richard Nixon, had said this was the largest sit-down dinner ever catered by the White House staff: 1,300 guests including 587 returned POWs.

Among the guests were Colonel Laird Guttersen, just promoted, and his wife Virginia. Surrounding them were many of his former comrades-in-arms — some he was meeting again for the first time since he was captured and others, meeting face-to-face for the first time, fellow prisoners known only by their names telegraphed by tapping on cell walls.

Sitting at a table near the Guttersens was Secretary of State Henry Kissinger. From time to time, Guttersen furtively eyed the ranking cabinet member; when there was an opportune moment, the colonel had a question to ask.

Words spoken by the nation's commander-in-chief during an afternoon reception still rang in Guttersen's ears. Nixon had been talking about foreign negotiations and classified documents being leaked to the press when he said:

> "...we must have confidentiality, we must have secret communications. It isn't that we are trying to keep anything from the American people that the American people should know...."

But these same words held different meaning to Guttersen.

Like his guests, the President was enjoying himself on this night, basking in the warmth of hero worship, for to these men he was a hero. He was the man who had secured their release and brought them home. On all other sides he was under increasing attack in the aftermath of the discovery of the Watergate break-in.

Guttersen was also under attack. He believed the Communists were still holding American prisoners and he was being told to keep quiet about it. Both Air Force and Pentagon officials were refusing him permission to speak out on the subject. "Negotiations are ongoing," they said, "for any men left behind."

But Guttersen was being besieged by organizations like VIVA, the California-based group calling themselves Voices in Vital America who had originated the idea of wearing bracelets — each bracelet inscribed with the name of someone missing in action or held prisoner of war. VIVA and the National League of Families represented the hundreds of men still listed as missing or captured and they could find no answers to why their sons and husbands were yet unaccounted for.

Suddenly Guttersen's moment to speak with Kissinger arrived. As applause for the last dinner speaker died away, he pushed his chair from the table and made his way to the secretary of state — even then bidding good night to his table companions.

"Excuse me, Mr. Secretary," Guttersen interrupted.

Kissinger turned and the colonel introduced himself as one of the returned POWs. The two men shook hands and Guttersen came directly to the point.

"As a returned POW I've been sternly instructed not to speak out in public about the POW issue or about the possibility of other prisoners still being held. I'm wondering if there are, indeed, any talks underway that could be jeopardized if I or others speak out on the subject."

Kissinger stiffened, his face assuming the mask of a dignitary. "I do not choose to discuss that issue now." With a curt nod of his head he moved away from Guttersen to join the departing crowd.

Guttersen was dismayed by the rebuff but not crushed. By now he was accustomed to being humiliated by officials. At least Kissinger had been polite — which was more than could be said for several military men Guttersen had approached.

One three-star general named Chappie James, from the Defense Department, had been downright abusive when Guttersen had asked for clearance to speak out at the annual reserve officers dinner being held in Las Vegas. Sprinkling his diatribe with such epithets as "stupid motherfucker" and "crummy sonofabitch," James had told Guttersen to "stop being a professional POW and get back on the team. Start following orders for a change!"

Both men, Guttersen realized, were reflecting the national mood of relief that the hostilities were ended and a desire to forget an unpopular war. The thought of men still being held captive in the isolated, impenetrable jungles of Southeast Asia was too much to bear.

It had been a divisive war for the country. While servicemen fought the Vietnamese, American civilians fought among themselves. Unlike World War Two, the Vietnam War did not send men and women into factories to turn out defense supplies; it sent them into the streets to protest, riot and burn flags and draft cards. The war was unpopular and so were its warriors. Veterans had not returned to rousing welcome-home parades; they had crept back into their home towns . . . "unwept, unhonored, and unsung."

Moreover, Department of Defense figures showed the number of Vietnam casualties to be far lower than in previous wars. After the second world war, for example, 78,751 men had been listed as missing or unaccounted for, whereas immediately after the Vietnam War only 2,546 men were among the missing in Vietnam.

It was a time to forget, Kissinger and others were, in effect, telling Guttersen. But he knew that for those still wearing their sons' and husbands' bracelets, there was no forgetting.

They were refusing to abandon hope. They had prayed, with each planeload of returning POWs, that there had been a glitch in the reporting — a glitch that meant their missing relative was aboard, but not previously identified. They had watched telecasts of returning POWs in anguish as they saw wives and children racing along airport runways, flinging themselves into the arms of fathers and husbands. They watched and cried to God their time was coming.

Carolyn Standerwick was among them. She wore her bracelet for her husband, Bob. Sitting in the living room of their home in Bellevue, Nebraska, she watched one particular telecast in stunned disbelief.

Reporters were descending on Rose Gotner in Sacramento, wanting her reaction to having just learned her husband Norbert was among the homecoming prisoners.

Carolyn had received no such news; yet Gotner was the backseater in Bob's plane, the day they were shot down. She wondered why the two men would not have been captured together.

Carolyn Standerwick, like other MIA family members, was left to wait and hope against all odds as other Americans went on with their lives. Operation Homecoming had signaled to the nation that all the POWs were home. Another part of the Vietnam experience was history. America breathed a sigh of relief.

As headlines about POWs faded, fresh ones loomed about a burglary at the Watergate Hotel in Washington. As the country became captivated by the seediness of the Watergate scandal, the men left behind in Southeast Asia were only as important as yesterday's news. The MIA/POW issue drifted slowly to the bottom of public awareness as Americans, one by one, took off their commemorative bracelets.

CHAPTER TWO
THE MISSING IN ACTION/ PRISONERS OF WAR

On February 14, 1971, Carolyn Standerwick was officially notified that her husband was missing in action. Lt. Col. Robert L. Standerwick, the flight commander of an F-4, had parachuted from his disabled craft during a combat mission in Laos. Voice contact had been established with him on the ground and there was a possibility that he had been captured.

Reviewing known facts, the Air Force noted that Standerwick had radioed searchers that he "was in good physical condition, on high ground, about 200 meters from a village and that he saw no people." A few minutes later he reported that hostile forces were approaching, firing at him.

Major Norbert A. Gotner, the co-pilot downed with Standerwick, had advised searchers he had suffered a minor back injury and that hostile troops were near his position.

Search and rescue (SAR) units had stayed in contact with Gotner for five days until weakened batteries silenced his radio beeper and during that time he said he had lost contact with Standerwick. Bad weather and the presence of enemy forces thwarted rescue attempts of either man.

Not until Gotner's release as a POW in 1973 would Carolyn Standerwick learn that a jungle-covered hill had separated the two fliers and that after being captured Gotner was told by a North Vietnamese soldier that Standerwick had been shot and killed and was buried. However, a Vietnamese officer had told him Standerwick was captured and assured Gotner that if his friend was wounded he would have been taken to a hospital in Hanoi.

The possibilities are that Standerwick died or was taken prisoner after being wounded, yet no accounting has ever been received from the North Vietnamese government or its allies and his name never appeared in the prisoner communication channels or from any other official or unofficial source.

Standerwick is one of many American men — both military personnel and civilians — known to have fallen into the hands of Communist forces and for whom the Vietnamese should be able to account. But the sad fact is that neither the Vietnamese nor the Lao have honored provisions of peace agreements which called for the fullest possible accounting of missing American servicemen.

Still missing in Southeast Asia are 2,441 Americans. They include 916 Air Force personnel, 702 Army, 490 Navy, 290 Marines, one member of the Coast Guard and 42 civilians, including five journalists. Of these, nearly 1,200 are known to have been killed in action but their bodies were not recovered. Of the remaining missing, a number can be presumed to have been casualties, but in the words of the Defense Department, "there is 'hard evidence' (e.g. post-capture photography, U.S. or indigenous eyewitnesses to capture or detention, intelligence reports)....for which the Indochinese should be able to provide an accounting but have not done so."

A case in point is that of PFC Donald Sparks, an Iowa farm boy, who was twenty two when he was first reported missing and then captured. Sparks was engaged in a search and clear operation when his isolated platoon was ambushed June 17, 1969, near Chu Lai in northern South Vietnam. Fellow infantrymen could see that

Sparks lay severely injured but heavy fire prevented any rescue attempt until the following day. Little hope was held for his being alive since five witnesses — based on their observations from a distance — testified he had died. When rescuers were able to move in they found a companion's body, but Sparks was gone.

Then in May 1970, a letter written by Sparks was found on the body of a Viet Cong soldier killed in Quang Tin province. The letter, addressed to his parents, Mr. and Mrs. Calvin Sparks of Carroll, Iowa, was dated April 11, 1970 — ten months after he'd been presumed dead. The letter was submitted by his parents for a handwriting analysis by a military expert who confirmed it was Sparks' handwriting. His status was subsequently changed from MIA to POW and his rank upgraded to sergeant.

A copy of Sparks' letter to his parents follows:

Everyone at Home!

I hope you have received the letters I have been writing. I have not heard to seen another American in nearly 10 months now, and I am longing for a letter from home. All this time I have continually been treated very well by the Vietnamese people. I can't thank them enough for their care.

I think of home all the time and surely hope you are all well and have been blessed with some happiness. I haven't forgotten your birthday Mom. I hope you took the day off, you truly deserve a rest. Then there is my kid brother. He is probably thinking of the service. He could probably get a hardship deferment and stay home if he wanted to. I don't want to run his life; I have trouble with my own. But I know I would have been encouraged to take over some responsibility if I had worked for a percent in a partnership with Dad. And talked about what crop or corn number to plant, the fertilizer program, whether it was a good time to sell livestock and beans, helped keep records, and pay bills rather than just cash a check.

*I have had a lot of time to think these past months. Often I
am very ashamed of my past. All the times I was provided for
and just took for granted. Good Mom and Dad were always
there to take over when I neglected work, or got into trouble. I
just hope to partially make up for it when I get home. Maybe
you should see a recruiter about my income tax. I have an
account (No. 2700) with the American Express and my pay
vouchers should be sent home. If my records have been kept up
to date I should be an E-5 in relation to time and grade.*

Thank you! May God Bless and keep you all!

Love,

Don

U.S. Navy Commander Harley Hall was shot down January
27, 1973 — ironically on the very day on which the Paris Peace
Accords were signed, signaling the end of U.S. involvement in
hostilities.

Hall and Lieutenant Commander Al Kientzler were in one of
two F-4Js attacking North Vietnamese supply vehicles fifteen miles
northwest of Quang Tri in South Vietnam when their plane was hit
by North Vietnamese anti-aircraft fire.

"I've taken a hit!" Hall radioed the lead pilot, Terry Heath.
Advised to "Get feet wet" — a pilot's term for heading toward the
ocean, Hall replied, "We're trying, Terry."

However, the F-4 was ablaze and moments later was rolling
heavily. At around 4,000 feet the men ejected. Their 'chutes
billowed and the men appeared unhurt as they drifted downward.
They were seen landing 100 feet apart near a village, a mile-and-a-
half west of where their plane nosed into the ground. From the air,
Hall was seen running for cover after disengaging his parachute.
Although emergency beepers were heard intermittently the remainder
of the afternoon and throughout the night, no voice contact was
established with them.

Kientzler was captured and after being repatriated reported he had not seen Hall after they bailed out but that he had been told by one of his Viet Cong guards that his friend was shot and buried near where he died. Was the guard telling the truth? No one knows because there has never been an accounting for Hall as either a POW or a casualty.

Captain David Hrdlicka of Wichita, Kansas, was an Air Force pilot shot down in the Sam Neua province of Laos May 18, 1965. Hrdlicka's case is significant because he was photographed while in captivity and the photo was published in August 1966 in *Pravda*, the Moscow newspaper. Radio Peking also broadcast a statement quoting Lao sources that Hrdlicka was a prisoner, and on May 22, 1966, the Pathet Lao broadcast a letter allegedly written by the captain. Military officials have described Hrdlicka's letter as typical of those POWs wrote after being tortured or promised early release for writing. Yet, both the Vietnamese and the Lao deny having any knowledge of Hrdlicka.

His plane — one of four taking part in a mission — was hit by enemy fire. He was seen to bail out and land in a small valley beside a village. None of the other flight members saw him move or attempt to free himself of his chute but fifteen minutes later villagers were seen rolling up the chute and taking him in the direction of the village. Natives working with American intelligence were sent to inquire and they were told the downed pilot was captured by the Pathet Lao.

A CIA report was based on information supplied by a Pathet Lao who said he had witnessed Hrdlicka's capture and had written the officer's name, birth date and service number in his diary. The source claimed Hrdlicka was one of two pilots still being held in caves northwest of Ban Na Kay Tay when he left the province.

Not all MIAs are military men. In September 1974 an American civilian, Charles Dean, was traveling with an Australian journalist, Neil Sharman. The two were aboard a boat enroute to

Thakhek, Laos, when it was captured at Ban Pak Hin Boun, a checkpoint on the Mekong River.

Numerous reports were subsequently made of the men being held at Ban Phontan and an informant who agreed to be polygraphed said he had seen them there six months later, in February 1975. Photos were given to the Defense Intelligence Agency by a man who said the young men had given them to him.

A personal request for information was made by former U.S. Ambassador Charles Whitehouse to the Lao prime minister and a written communication was sent to him by Secretary of State Kissinger, but the Pathet Lao denied any knowledge of Dean and Sharman.

Roger Shields, Deputy Assistant Secretary of Defense, 1971-1976, was one of several American officials who steadfastly tried to secure Dean's release. Shields became respected as one of the nation's experts on MIA/POW matters as he chaired the Department of Defense's (DoD's) MIA/POW Task Group, having oversight of Operation Homecoming. "When our intelligence diminished so drastically after the fall of friendly governments in the area, that was the last time we heard about Dean. Before that we even had his driver's license, an ID card and a McGovern campaign button smuggled out. We knew where he was and what he was doing.

"We went to the Pathet Lao," said Shields, "...We were confident they would own up to it and release [Dean] since they had released one American, Emmet Kay, an Air America pilot, in 1974. But they didn't release Dean. They stonewalled the whole thing... We did everything for Dean short of carrying on a war. At the time, it was viewed as an area impossible to get into without starting a war."

Of the 569 men captured or killed in Laos, Kay is the only American POW returned. Nine American prisoners captured in Laos who were repatriated during the 1973 Operation Homecoming were seized not by the Pathet Lao but by North Vietnamese forces operating in Laos who moved them to North Vietnam for detention.

Shortly after the Paris Accords were signed, the two Lao parties that formed the provisional government of national union agreed to search for Americans missing from the war, but when the Lao People's Democratic Republic was formed in December 1975, the cease-fire agreement was never fully implemented. Consequently, the pledge to search for MIAs was never upheld. However, the evidence that Americans were held prisoner in Laos is abundant.

Declassified intelligence documents show specific sites, list the land coordinates, and frequently disclose the number and nationality of prisoners being detained. One CIA intelligence information cable, dated November 25, 1970, refers to several dozen Lao prison sites, some in which the presence of Americans was confirmed by "two or more independent sources." The cable report stated that as many as twenty American prisoners were held at the Ban Nakay Neua prison, while forty Americans or other foreign nationals were being detained at the Khamnouane Province prison, consisting of three separate caves.

The presence of American POWs in Laos was also confirmed by the late General Creighton Abrams during an interview in 1970 with Bob Dornan of California who was later elected to Congress. The interview took place at Ton Son Nhut airbase in Saigon and included four MIA wives, one of the first groups to seek international support for the MIA issue.

"We sat there in a meeting with General Creighton Abrams, commander of all the forces in Vietnam, with great authority in Laos and Cambodia," Dornan recalls. "He said to me, 'I have seen photographs from Laos, low-level photography, of Americans — guys in white T-shirts waving to the planes passing overhead. There was one photo from 1968 with men on a *karst* in Laos. They were playing volleyball or football and were clearly Americans.'"

If the location of POWs in Laos was known, why were no attempts made to rescue the men? Abrams explained. "We have some very sophisticated operations being planned by some very sophisticated people to make some rescue attempts on many of these prisons, but we have photographic evidence that these Communist camps, even in the caves of Laos, have automatic weapons pointed at the caves. The prisoners can come and go and dump their sanitary buckets, but if we were to put the best low-level paratroopers to strike in there — like a strike where they take out the guards or guard towers in one blow — they would spray the caves and kill every prisoner. We have to do this surgically."

Statements made by Lao officials, prior to the cessation of hostilities, also indicated the presence of POWs in that country.

In May 1971, Soth Phetrasi, who was at one time the Pathet Lao representative in Vientiane, was asked by U.S. personnel why the Pathet Lao had not released a list of prisoners similar to that released by North Vietnam. Phetrasi replied that in Laos there was no means of communication between villages even under normal conditions and because of U.S. air activity it was often impossible to reach the site of a downed plane to ascertain the fate of the pilot. For these reasons, he argued, it was impossible for the Pathet Lao to compile a complete list but he maintained that prisoners being held in various regions of Laos were well treated. In an April 1972 interview he stated American POWs were being held in liberated areas of Laos but would not provide specific figures.

In that same month, a Swedish correspondent interviewed Prince Souphanouvong, formerly the chairman of the Lao Patriotic Front Central Committee who had been named president of the People's Democratic Republic of Laos. Asked to comment on the Pathet Lao policy toward captured enemy soldiers, Prince Souphanouvong said:

"The LPF [Lao Patriotic Front] has made public a concrete policy toward enemy soldiers or agents

captured or giving themselves up, including GIs. All
the American pilots engaged in bombings or toxic
chemical sprays of Lao territory are considered
criminals and enemies of the Lao people. But once
captured, they have been treated in accordance with the
humane policy of the LPF. The question of enemy
captives, including U.S. pilots, will be settled
immediately after the U.S. stops its intervention and
aggression in Laos first, and foremost, ends the
bombing of Laos territory."

In sharp contrast to these pronouncements, the Lao claimed
to have no knowledge of American POWs by the termination of
Operation Homecoming in 1973. In April 1973, Phetrasi stated that
the Lao People's Forces had released all U.S. prisoners captured in
Laos.

The fact that only one POW captured by the Pathet Lao was
ever returned to the U.S. has, in the past, brought criticism of the
CIA and accusations of making only token efforts to collect POW
intelligence inside Laos. A former senior CIA official who spent fifteen years in Southeast Asia with major responsibilities in Laos,
concedes that POWs were being held but he defends the agency
against critics.

"During and after the war I can assure you that POWs were
not put on the back burner. There was a high degree of concern and
we had a very good book on prison locations and precise fixes on
accidents or shootdowns. But you have to realize that Laos was like
taking a bottle of ink and throwing it at the wall — you had ink
splotches all over the place.

"Most of the country was held by the North Vietnamese,
who had over 100,000 regulars committed to Laos. On our side,
the limited objectives were mainly to have a reasonably stabilized
area — to tie down as many North Vietnamese as possible. So we

never had the resources to 'roll it back' to look for prisoners and that was never the intent."

Explaining that prison locations normally were accessible only by air, he added, "The prisoners were always moved to the centers of the highest concentration of enemy forces; they were never held in isolated areas. There were operations planned to try to recover them, but we didn't have the air mobility — that is, helicopters to go in on that kind of daring operation, attacking strongly-held, fortified points in Sam Neua or elsewhere along the Vietnam border."

It would be nothing short of folly to believe that in any final accounting there will be explanations for all those listed as missing in action. This point was made clear by Roger Shields. "There are many explanations for what happened to a lot of men," Shields stated. "For example, in 1975, we had some Vietnamese woodchoppers who found the wreckage of a helicopter in a thick jungle area. It was almost impenetrable. There were no remains in the wreckage...it looked like the seatbelts had been unfastened, the first aid kit had been taken out of the 'copter. There was a helmet with one of the men's names on it...on the ground close by. It had been lost several years before.

"I'm confident that if anyone had been in that wreck, they would have been injured; this was an area that most people would have had a very hard time surviving in. It could be that the men tried to get away and perished somewhere in the wilderness. We'll probably never know what happened to them."

The discussion of whether the Vietnamese withheld prisoners is a complex one, requiring consideration of common American attitudes which cast doubt on the possibility; it also calls for examination of possible Vietnamese motivation for detaining POWs.

One question that is invariably raised is why POWs haven't succeeded in escaping. Given the mountainous terrain, the expanse of nearly impenetrable jungle, the highly restrictive nature of North Vietnamese society and the relative isolation of small villages, the opportunity to escape and survive is limited, to say the least. In testimony presented in 1976 to the House Select Committee on Missing Persons in Southeast Asia, it was noted that between 1961 and 1973, during the war when American military support was available, no prisoners escaped from captivity in North Vietnam or Cambodia. Only two Americans escaped from Laos and succeeded in reaching freedom; during the same period, twenty-seven succeeded in South Vietnam.

Moreover, about ninety percent of the Navy's POWs were captured within an hour of shootdown, it was reported. Air Force data indicated that sixty-five percent of its POWs were captured within two hours and of 209 Air Force returnees, only six said they had avoided the enemy for more than three days.

Is it possible that some MIAs are in reality deserters? Government officials insist that they have no confirmation of known deserters. Although there's speculation about some men who may have chosen to stay in Vietnam, none of the alleged deserters has been identified. Col. Richard Childress, National Security Council Director for Asian Affairs, admits that reports have been received "of people in a noncaptive status as well as the classic captive status" but, he said, "Our stance is really summed up in one sentence — we will not classify anyone as a deserter until we have evidence gathered after their return."

The reasoning behind this policy, Childress says, is that "if you start calling people deserters [because they appear to be noncaptive] then what you really do is write off the issue."

According to Commodore Thomas Brooks, Assistant Deputy Director for Defense Intelligence Agency (DIA) Collection Management, "We have reports of Americans in a non-prisoner environment — even married to Vietnamese women with families or sighted roaming freely in the cities. Whether or not these are deserters or people who were taken prisoner and later chose to remain...or maybe they're not Americans at all...is totally unclear. We just have no way of judging."

Reasons Vietnamese May Have Withheld POWs

Theories abound but one widely-held belief is based on the so-called Nixon-Kissinger "secret agreement" to pay $3.25 billion in war reparations to Vietnam over a five-year period. Nixon later explained that this commitment was to have been based on congressional approval but the Vietnamese maintained Nixon's pledge was made unconditionally.

Perhaps fearing the U.S. would not follow through, the Vietnamese withheld a number of prisoners as bargaining chips. If this is so, why haven't the men been released during the past decade? Two possibilities have been suggested. One is that the men are being held as pawns for negotiations in the future, only when the Vietnamese decide the time is right. A second but perhaps less likely possibility is that by holding the prisoners, the Vietnamese created a dilemma for themselves and now cannot admit their ploy in the face of international criticism.

Another theory suggests that certain prisoners were detained because of their technical expertise. When the U.S. pulled out of Southeast Asia, over five billion dollars worth of military equipment was left behind. According to the Center for Military History in Washington, a partial list of the equipment includes: 430 Huey helicopters, 36 CH47 medium choppers, 73 F-5 jet fighter/interceptors, 36 A-1 ground attack planes, 10 C-130s, 40 C-119s, 40 C-7s, 36 C-47 cargo planes, 22 T-41 trainers and 144 T-34s.

Also left behind were 42,000 trucks, 940 ships of various sizes, 300 M41 light tanks, 250 M48 medium tanks and 1,200 armored personnel carriers. The list also contains thousands of weapons including 90,000 .45 cal. pistols, 791,000 M16 rifles, 857,580 other assorted rifles and carbines, 50,000 M60 machine guns, 47,000 M79 grenade launchers, 12,000 mortars, 63,000 light antitank weapons and 1,330 assorted cannons.

According to a Vietnam News Agency postwar broadcast, the people of the Socialist Republic of Vietnam were reusing "every salvaged nut and bolt" from war-damaged equipment to repair the thousands of trucks, tanks and other pieces of hardware left behind by American forces. American military men could have been withheld to help maintain the more highly technical equipment as well as instruct the Vietnamese on how to use it.

Still another theory is that American POWs were sent to the Soviet Union for interrogation about U.S. advanced weaponry and technical or intelligence information. Interestingly, of the 591 returned prisoners, none was ever interrogated by Soviets nor questioned about nuclear weapons although the Communist leaders of the region were extremely fearful of the possible use of nuclear weapons by the U.S.

Although many returned POWs were tortured to divulge military secrets, the Vietnamese did not press for sensitive, hi-tech intelligence information. The interrogations were seemingly intended to intimidate rather than elicit anything more than details on combat maneuvers. Many who did possess sensitive information which was not demanded concluded their captors were both unsophisticated and inefficient.

Thus it is plausible that knowledgeable military men were taken to the Soviet Union for more skillful questioning.

It is also conjectured that the Vietnamese have withheld any men disfigured or disabled during captivity or from neglect of serious combat injuries. These could include those seriously burned, who lost limbs or whose mental condition degenerated. The Vietnamese saw to it that most prisoners who returned during Operation Homecoming stepped spritely off the planes, able to snap salutes to their superiors. Only a few were dealing with problem injuries. All had gained weight through improved diet their last weeks in captivity, belying the true facts.

It has also been reported that POWs are being held for use as slave labor, being forced to repair damage done by U.S. bombs.

Refugees have reported seeing Americans on work gangs — doing construction work, building roads and bridges, clearing forests, and even working in rice paddies.

Another possibility, especially in remote areas of Laos, is that some men were taken prisoner by local warlords or chieftains who kept them as status symbols. In an article in *National Review*, returnee Laird Guttersen was quoted as saying, "I know that two of our prisoners were kept in a village and they were right on a truck route, so they could have been taken north to Hanoi anytime. They were kept in a village for a year, primarily, as far as they could figure out, because the head man of the village had done something nice to somebody and so they gave him as a prize a couple of American POWs to keep in a cage in his village for the people to look at. Because it gave him prestige. So there doesn't have to be a logical Western reason..."

Similarly, it's possible that civilians, angered by the casualties inflicted by a bombing mission, might have captured a downed pilot and held him unbeknown to the central government or local military units.

A final theory to consider is that the withholding of POWs is a form of psychological warfare still being conducted by Southeast Asian Communists. Considering that men are missing from every state in the Union and virtually every sizable city, the enemy has, in effect, dropped an "emotional ICBM" into hundreds of American communities. Such conduct, as with more recent terrorist attacks, can foster a public perception that their government has become impotent or that government response is lacking.

Unquestionably, the withholding of prisoners after the U.S. cease fire is in violation of the Geneva Convention to which Vietnam acceded in 1957. But early on, during the war, North Vietnam insisted the convention agreement did not apply because war was not declared by the U.S., a prerequisite for abiding by the Geneva agreement, they said. Thus, they contended, captured Americans were not prisoners of war but criminals and air pirates, subject to punishment according to local laws.

A congressional fact-finding committee in 1972 published numerous Democratic Republic of Vietnam violations it uncovered on treatment of U.S. prisoners. In a report entitled, "Communist Treatment of Prisoners of War, a Historical Survey," prepared by a Senate subcommittee, thirteen violations were cited. A listing of the Geneva requirements and DRV violations included:

Requirement	DRV Performance
POWs must be humanely treated, protected; reprisals against POWs prohibited	Paraded in streets, forced to make statements, some torture
POWs not to be held in "close confinement"	Many POWs held in solitary confinement for years
Mark POW camps so as visible from air, give information on camp locations	No markings on camps; locations concealed
Provide sufficient food, prevent loss of weight, take account of normal diet	Standard fare consisted of: pumpkin soup, rice, bread, pig fat. All POWs underweight and suffered from malnutrition
Adequate medical care	Much evidence of inadequate medical care; many prisoners died in camps
Regular religious services	Only some Christmas services

Requirement	DRV Performance
Write to family within one week of capture	Some not permitted to write for five years
Minimum of two letters and four cards a month	Average of 2-3 letters per year (none at all for some)
Free receipt of parcels	Delivery was irregular
Immediate repatriation of seriously sick and wounded. Release of POWs long held in captivity	No regular release of sick and wounded or long-held POWs
Advise of deaths in captivity, full official information on circumstances, cause, burial, grave identification	Bare assertion of death through unofficial and irregular channels, no details
Advise promptly names of all POWs held	Never released official or complete list
Neutral inspection of all camps, interview of POWs without witnesses	No inspection; propaganda interviews only

This flagrant abuse of the Geneva Convention, in part, spurred formation of the National League of Families. Although families of missing and imprisoned men had been instructed by government representatives to keep a low profile, the families starting banding together once word of harsh treatment and torture filtered out of Vietnamese prisons and into U.S. media reports. An organized effort, bringing greater public attention to the plight of the prisoners might, they decided, create international embarrassment for the Vietnamese and result in better treatment for the POWs. Their efforts yielded some results and coincided with a later decision by the government to launch a "go public" campaign. However, proposal after proposal for release of the American prisoners was rebuffed by the Vietnamese who declared that the POWs would be released only after the U.S. had withdrawn its forces.

Beginning as an informal meeting over a kitchen table in the late '60s, the League was formed by Sybil Stockdale, a California MIA wife whose husband later returned. On May 28, 1970, the National League of Families was incorporated in the District of Columbia. The membership, made up of families from across the nation, was to form a collective, resonant voice, calling for the release of American prisoners of war.

Even after Operation Homecoming, the League continued operating. Its members were committed to finding out what had happened to those men whom they felt should have returned.

In the years immediately following the war, the League members often argued, even among themselves, over whether to continue running the organization. Their travels to Southeast Asia, hours of research and in-depth questioning of experts usually left them with little specific information about their loved ones, but gave them a growing awareness of Communist behavior and history for not returning all prisoners.

The pivotal year was 1977, when the League began to investigate reported sightings of live Americans by Southeast Asian refugees — the boatpeople. The beginning of the refugee sighting program can be traced to an early morning phone call to the home of George and Gladys Brooks.

It was mid-November 1977, when the phone rang at the Brooks house in upstate New York. George Brooks, Chairman of the National League of Families, had just left for work. Gladys set aside the breakfast dishes and made her way to the ringing phone.

The call was from Barbara Kieting, a friend who had lost her husband in the Vietnam war; the Brookses had met her through their League work.

"Gladys, I apologize for calling so early, but I just had to get in touch with you. Last night during a function at the Asia Society in New York City, I met a Vietnamese woman who says she knows someone who has seen live American prisoners in Southeast Asia."

Gladys paused disbelievingly. "Barbara, you've got to be kidding me."

"No, Gladys, I'm not. She has talked to a refugee who says he saw two Americans in Vietnam before he left the country. You must get in contact with her...she lives in Maryland."

Barbara Kieting explained that the woman's name was Le Thi Anh, that she was fluent in English and was the editor of a Vietnamese newsletter. Barbara gave Gladys the woman's phone number indicating that it was all right to call her.

Gladys had barely finished thanking her friend before she was on the phone again, dialing her husband.

George Brooks rushed home. Like Gladys, he could only half believe what he was hearing, but he wasn't going to lose any time hearing the story for himself. Minutes later he was on the phone, talking to Madame Anh.

She willingly told him about the refugee whom she identified as a young man named Trinh Hung. She further agreed to arrange for the Brookses to meet him. They scheduled a date later that month, the day after Thanksgiving, at her home in Cheverly, Maryland, outside Washington.

CHAPTER THREE
REFUGEE SIGHTINGS

November 25, 1977. For much of the five-hour drive to Madame Anh's home in Cheverly, Maryland, George and Gladys Brooks had little to say. After seven years of seeking and praying for word of their missing son, Nick, neither had comforting words that hadn't been said a dozen times before. A dozen times. Perhaps meeting with this Vietnamese refugee, Trinh Hung, would provide a new shred of evidence about their son or others still missing; the parents devoutly hoped so, but to voice any expectations was unthinkable, so they rode without speaking.

George Brooks sat quietly behind the wheel, as if intent on his driving. He was, but part of his mind was replaying events of the past few years — all the trips to Washington, countless League meetings, public speeches and he and Gladys cranking out newsletters from their basement in the wee hours. Now, silently he pondered what he might learn from this refugee.

From the time Nick, a Navy pilot, was shot down over Laos on January 2, 1970, the Brookses had been able to piece together only bits of information...but enough to encourage their belief that he had not been killed, but captured. Soon after Nick's shootdown, a sensitive but reliable source had told them that Nick survived the crash and was able to evade the enemy. Then, during a 1974 meeting of the League of Families in Omaha, Nebraska, they met with Nick's commanding officer, Lou Dittmar, who confirmed that Nick had been alive in captivity and told them about the "road watchers."

The road watchers were Vietnamese villagers paid to report to the U.S. military and one group had given an account of Nick's being captured and tied to a tree. He'd managed to escape once but was recaptured and again tied to the tree. That night, the road watchers reported, they'd gone back to the tree to find that Nick was no longer there but that the ropes that had bound him were lying on the ground. They assumed he'd escaped again.

It was this account that fed George's hope that Nick was alive although he rarely spoke of it to others.

Sitting beside George in the car, Gladys was also apprehensive about meeting Trinh Hung; in fact, she had debated whether to make the trip with George. If she felt anything, it was a sense of bitterness against all Vietnamese...after all it was they who had shot down her son's plane. Images of the Vietnamese, generated by the television news that had brought the war into her living room, were still fresh in her mind. She could see the machine-gun-toting enemy slithering through the jungle grasses and the young, bandaged GIs being carried off the battle fields.

But Gladys talked herself into going; she suppressed the feeling that she was dealing with the enemy — the enemy who captured and tortured her son. It was important to follow up every possible lead. Maybe this man, Trinh Hung, could break the silence that had characterized the years of their agonizing vigil.

"Well, this is Cheverly," George said as they wound slowly through the tree-lined streets of the Washington suburb.

Following the directions Le Thi Anh had given them, the Brookses tracked their way to her address and pulled up in front of an attractive colonial-style house in an upper-middle class neighborhood.

"Can this be it?" Gladys asked in a puzzled tone.

"What were you expecting, a mud hut with a thatched roof?" joked George to relieve the tension.

"Of course not," she replied, "but this?" She hadn't known what to expect, but realized she had associated all refugees with crowded refugee camps or the modest dwellings of their homeland. Le Thi Anh had fled Saigon only three days before it fell.

It was true Le Thi Anh had been an evacuee but her ties with the United States were strong and she was a well- educated woman who came from a wealthy family, owners of a tea plantation in the central highlands of South Vietnam, near Dalat. A published novelist, she was a writer in residence at the University of Michigan from 1964 until 1971, having been the recipient of a UNESCO grant. A Buddhist and a pacifist, in 1945 she was a student activist in the Viet Minh, the anti-French underground movement seeking self-rule for Vietnam. During her seven-year stay in the U.S. she was so deeply involved in the anti-war movement as a writer and lecturer, the Thieu government had demanded her extradition.

None of this Gladys Brooks knew, however, as her husband assisted her from the car. He closed the door and she reminded him to bring the basket from the back seat, containing Thanksgiving pastries — baklava and kourabiedes — and a bottle of French brandy, gifts for Madame Anh. In a sense it was a peace offering and a way of showing their appreciation to their Vietnamese hostess. She tried to conceal her apprehension as they rang the door bell and waited for someone to answer it.

Within moments Le Thi Anh appeared at the door. Smiling politely, her welcome was cordial but businesslike. She was of middle age, her graying black hair drawn back into a chignon, accentuating the outline of her round face of dark olive complexion. She wore the ankle-length sheath favored by Asian women.

Stepping inside from the cold, both George and Gladys noticed the scent of garlic and soy — the lingering odors of Oriental cooking. Le Thi Anh was the first Vietnamese the Brookses had ever met.

For an hour the Brookses and Madame Anh visited until Trinh Hung arrived from Philadelphia, accompanied by three friends who were also refugees. A young man of slight build, he was reserved and somewhat shy but his gaze was direct and his brown eyes friendly.

His three friends withdrew to an adjoining room to chat with other Vietnamese men, relatives of Le Thi Anh's, while Hung remained in the living room with the Brookses and Madame Anh.

At first there was some awkwardness since the language barrier precluded small talk. Trinh Hung's English was all but nonexistent; Le Thi Anh was to translate for him.

George Brooks spoke slowly and deliberately, thanking Hung for agreeing to meet with them, then asking how he had met Le Thi Anh.

Trinh Hung had been a student where she had taught at Hoa Hao University in Long Xuyen from 1972 until 1975, she said. "Earlier this fall I heard he had left Vietnam by boat and was living in Philadelphia," she continued. "Since so few Vietnamese have made it here by boat up to now, I wanted to hear how he'd escaped and what news he had from home.

"It was during our conversation he mentioned having seen two American prisoners near Xeo Ro, Rachgia, in South Vietnam. That surprised me because I didn't think any Americans were in captivity after 1975."

Switching on his tape recorder, George Brooks began questioning Hung — an interview that lasted two hours. When did Hung see the men, Brooks wanted to know. How were they being treated? What did they look like? How were they dressed?

Without reticence Hung answered, Madame Anh interpreting phrase by phrase.

Hung's story was simple. "I have seen two white Americans during the month of October in 1975. One is thin and very tall, another is medium height, also very thin. Both had their heads shaven like monks. They were tied with ropes around the wrists and ankles and lay in a motorized sampan at the Xeo Ro dock. The Viet Communists encouraged the people to come and beat the Americans with bamboo sticks and throw all sorts of accusations and insults. The two men were later transported to a remote area in the U-Minh Forests. The people living around the Xeo Ro dock have witnessed the two men. They can give testimonies if their lives will be protected."

The Brookses were stunned. It was as though reality had caught up with them. Almost as a defense against the frightening truth, Gladys wondered if the refugee were lying. While George asked questions Gladys sat silently, studying Hung's facial expression. He looked sincere and Madame Anh did not appear to be coaching him, but she was wary of being taken in. Could these people be so shrewd as to manipulate them for some self-serving purpose?

George was occupied with asking questions that would prove beyond reasonable doubt the truth of Hung's story. He wanted someway to nail down the facts.

Although George Brooks was chairman of the League board, he had never personally met anyone who claimed to have seen American captives; he had heard only rumors about such refugees. And even now, face to face, all they had to go on was what the refugee was telling them.

At last, he ran out of questions. He had asked everything he could think of. Thanking Hung, he and Gladys stood, preparing to leave.

At that moment the voices of the Vietnamese men talking in the adjacent room prompted him to ask, "When you first came to the United States, were all of you questioned about seeing American prisoners?"

Le Thi Anh translated the question and the replies that followed. "No, no one was."

George and Gladys exchanged startled glances. They had been told by U.S. State Department officials, including Henry

Kissinger, that all incoming refugees were asked about having seen any Americans still in Vietnam. The statements by Hung's friends denied this was so.

George felt that the State Department had lied, "...and that more than anything," he later recalled, gave him the motivation to pursue the truth of Hung's story.

Driving home to New York, the Brookses debated the credibility of Hung's claim. One way to decide, they concluded, would be through a lie-detector test, if Hung would consent to it.

Unknown to the Brookses at the time, the DIA had already considered Hung's story and on November 28, three days after the Brooks' meeting with Hung, issued an analysis discrediting his account.

When Madame Anh had received Hung's letter, she had forwarded it to the League office in Washington, D.C., where the director had read it and routinely forwarded it to the DIA. The League lacked the facilities and resources for conducting its own investigations, serving primarily as a conduit for information it received.

The DIA letter of November 28, 1977, in response to Hung's account, stated:

> "...the report from refugee Trinh Hung contains certain
> elements that are contrary to precedent, and which,
> therefore, tend to cast suspicion on his story.
> Although there is record of American prisoners having
> been abused by an angry populace, such action was
> normally not condoned by those in authority, who had
> directives to assure the safety of captured Americans
> because of their value as political leverage. No U.S.
> returnees reported that their captors ordered that
> their heads be shaved, which description, it is noted,
> is dissimilar to the long hair associated with the
> first refugee's story."

This letter also referred to a 1976 report in which another refugee reported seeing Americans with long, shoulder-length hair, on work details in the U-Minh Forest.

The DIA letter was also critical of Hung's claim that those prisoners in the U-Minh Forest, located in Rachgia and Chuong Thien provinces near the Gulf of Siam in South Vietnam, had been transferred there from North Vietnam. To the contrary, the letter argued, most prisoners in South Vietnam were historically transferred northward.

> "In conclusion, one cannot say with proof positive
> that the reports of Americans being held in the U-Minh
> Forest are true or false because there is no longer any
> way to conduct on-site investigations, but existing
> related information indicates that their veracity is
> quite doubtful," the DIA analysis concluded.

The DIA appraisal of the Trinh Hung report came under immediate fire from the League members and many of the DIA arguments were challenged at a Congressional hearing by Dermot Foley, a New York attorney and legal counsel to the League from 1974 until 1980.

"In fact," argued Foley, "shaving of the head is a traditional punishment for persons whom the Vietnamese wish to humiliate and identify as evil."

As to Hung's allegation that prisoners he saw were subjected to moderate abuse by the public, which the DIA refuted, "Any POW who survived the notorious 'midnight march' in Hanoi knows better," Foley told the Congressmen.

The attorney's reference was to an incident that occurred July 6, 1966. Fifty-two POWs, threatened with war crime trials, were marched handcuffed through the streets of Hanoi. Enraged over the recent heavy bombing of the city and the Haiphong area, the unruly crowd started to attack the prisoners and the Vietnamese military was forced to intervene to avert a tragedy.

In light of the DIA analysis, the suggestion to ask Hung to submit to a polygraph examination gained added emphasis. He indicated his willingness and the test was arranged to take place December 12, at the Golden Chariot Motel in Montgomeryville, Pennsylvania, some forty miles north of Philadelphia.

The services of a licensed polygrapher were obtained by Ray Schrump, a returned POW and friend of the Brookses. Schrump and the polygrapher, Glenn Griffith, flew in from Fayetteville, North Carolina, and George Brooks joined them.

Hung was accompanied by Dr. Le Phuoc Sang, a university professor and Vietnam native who volunteered to interpret.

The testing site was set up in a motel room and at Griffith's recommendation, Brooks did not attend but waited in the motel restaurant.

For two hours Griffith prepared Hung for the examination, explaining how the polygraph machine functioned and the procedure to be followed. Griffith and Hung engaged in a thorough discussion of Hung's account of the two prisoners, Griffith probing for details.

At 6:30 p.m. Griffith was ready to run the first polygraph chart on Hung. As he began to position the polygraph wires, he noticed the young refugee was nervous.

"Will I feel an electric shock?" Hung asked as he eyed the electrodes protruding from the polygraph machine.

"No you won't," assured Griffith, "about all you'll feel is some numbness or tingling in your bicep. That will be caused from the blood pressure cuff I'll be putting on your arm."

Griffith attached the electrodes to the index and ring fingers of Hung's left hand. These would measure the galvanic skin response. He positioned two pneumo tubes, strapping one across Hung's chest, the other across his stomach. They would measure any variation in breathing. Finally, he placed the blood pressure cuff on Hung's upper right arm and signaled for the interpreter to ask the first question.

"Did Mr. Brooks or Mr. Schrump promise you anything for this information?"

"No," Hung replied.

Griffith waited fifteen to twenty seconds before signaling Sang to ask the next question, allowing time for Hung's response to register on the polygraph.

"Are you lying about seeing two white American prisoners in October 1975 at Xeo Ro?"

"No."

Griffith waited again, watching the polygraph's inked needle scribble across the rolling chart paper.

"Are you giving us any false information about seeing those two white Americans?"

"No."

"Are you lying about seeing those two white American prisoners after the fall of Saigon?"

"No."

"Did you hear the Communist guards tell the villagers that the two men were Americans?"

"Yes."

Griffith scanned the erratic lines tracked by the polygraph. He was perplexed. Hung's response to the first question, asking if he'd been compensated for giving information, appeared to be a truthful answer. On the last four questions, the polygram indicated neither deception nor truthfulness but recorded erratic tracing abnormalities, responses that were inconsistent.

Three times Griffith repeated the examination, each time getting the same response patterns. He conferred quietly with Schrump. "My overall opinion is that he's telling the truth," he said. "The way he tells the story and his mannerisms all seem honest. But, I can't give you a complete diagnostic evaluation."

Griffith was saying the official results remained inconclusive. But he attributed the failure to language problems, cultural differences, and Hung's anxiety about the testing.

"We've got a problem with the language barrier," Griffith explained. "The questions I've prepared would take about five seconds to ask in English, but as Sang interprets them, it's taking about ten to twelve seconds. I'm seeing Hung's responses on the chart before Sang finishes the question. I can't be sure what he [Hung] is reacting to."

"Why does the length of the question make a difference?" asked Schrump.

"Well, the insertion of other words in order to make the translation could alter the meaning of the questions. Plus, any variance in voice inflection could be making a difference. I can't be sure the subject is actually understanding what it is that I want asked."

"But do you think he's telling the truth?" Schrump persisted.

Griffith shrugged. "Based on the polygraph, I simply cannot tell you, but based on the three hours I've spent with him this afternoon, my opinion is that he's being honest."

Despite his disappointment at not having official confirmation of Hung's veracity, Brooks was encouraged as to the causes of the failure. He thanked Hung and Sang and offered to pay their expenses for gas, meals and time lost on their jobs. Both graciously refused his offer.

But once back on the highway, Brooks' thoughts returned to the DIA's negative analysis of Hung's reported sighting. He contemplated the agency's unwillingness to speak with Hung or further investigate his report. His puzzlement slowly turned to anger. Why was DIA so unresponsive? Furthermore, in spite of the State Department's claims that all refugees were being asked about encountering Americans in Vietnam, Brooks had come across several who said they were not.

Meanwhile, Brooks and other League members determined their organization should undertake the job they believed the U.S.

Government was failing to do — solicit information from refugees. Hung's credibility as determined by the polygraph was no longer, of itself, relevant. It was Hung's willingness to come forward and speak out that was significant. Other refugees were just as likely to have information, Brooks realized.

In the coming weeks Brooks teamed with fellow League members to expand efforts to solicit information from refugees. A committee was formed consisting of Brooks, Foley, whose brother was missing in Vietnam, and Ann Griffiths, the sister of an MIA. She would later become the executive director of the League.

Le Thi Anh was contacted and asked to develop a system for reaching refugees. Reluctant at first to become involved on a sustaining basis, Madame Anh eventually agreed. Initially the Brookses funded her; later the League hired her as a consultant. Le Thi Anh became the League's link to the refugee communities.

Her first endeavor was to have far-reaching consequences. She placed an advertisement in the weekly Vietnamese magazine, *Trang Den*, which has worldwide circulation. The ad was to elicit hundreds of replies from refugees claiming to have information concerning MIA/POWs.

CHAPTER FOUR
REFUGEE LETTERS

"Attention brothers and sisters and fellow
countrymen who have recently crossed the
border, and those who have departed long ago;
anyone who has any information regarding
American persons who are missing in Vietnam,
especially anyone who has seen living
Americans, please contact Mrs. Le Thi Anh,
5730 Tuxedo Rd., Cheverly, MD 20781, USA.
This work will be of unlimited benefit to our
just cause. Compatriots please be willing to
help. We extend our generous gratitude."

"It was a simple ad," Le Thi Anh recalled. "The publisher
was a friend of mine so I got the ad free for several months. We
just wanted to see how it worked."

The ad worked amazingly well, to the delight of the League
Refugee Committee and Madame Anh. "I thought we might get five
or six replies," she has admitted. Instead, the response was
overwhelming. Between 1978, when the ad first ran, and 1983,
more than 300 letters were received and some sixty contained references to live sightings.

Replies came in from the four corners of the world, and while the veracity of reported sightings was not immediately known, the League had convincing proof for the U.S. government that information on missing Americans could be readily obtained if refugees were solicited.

When Le Thi Anh received replies, she translated them and forwarded them to George Brooks. She then wrote to thank the refugees and asked if they were willing to talk with U.S. government representatives. Most agreed to do so.

In the League's ads, $500 was offered refugees whose accounts of Americans in captivity could be substantiated by a polygraph. None of the refugees asked for the money, according to Madame Anh.

"It wasn't because we thought the refugees wanted money," she explained, "but the League wanted to send a signal to Hanoi that we would have a lot of refugees coming forward with information about American prisoners being held. That way, Hanoi would sense we knew about the prisoners and would not dare kill them."

She theorizes that Hanoi has become hostage to the American POWs. "Even if Hanoi wants to release the prisoners it's not that easy," she insisted. "They've kept them and lied about it, so it's not simple to return them. They're afraid once they admit keeping prisoners they'll be subject to retaliation."

But why should Hanoi want to hold prisoners now that the conflict has ended? There are many things Hanoi wants from the U.S., she pointed out. "If the Vietnamese see they can manipulate the U.S., they will try to continue it forever, like they did with the French."

Although Hanoi has never openly used the prisoners as bargaining chips, "they'll keep them for political or financial leverage," Madame Anh said.

In the beginning, she noted, "they withheld some POWs in an attempt to hold the U.S. to its promise of aid and post-war reconstruction. They knew the U.S. was weary and wanted to wash its hands of the war, and that there was no way the leaders in Hanoi could bring the U.S. back to discuss anything, including aid."

But the prisoners did not become "a conduit to aid and diplomatic recognition," in her words. Instead they became an obstacle. Yet, Hanoi cannot release the prisoners because "theirs is a position of no return," she explained.

Critics of the refugee sighting accounts argue the reports might be self-serving, told to enhance their chances or their relatives' chances of getting into the U.S.

Le Thi Anh disagreed. "On the contrary, refugees are reluctant to mention information about American POWs for fear it will hurt their chances of coming to the U.S. They fear Communist reprisals." Many have not spoken out until they were safely out of Vietnam, she added.

Since 1979, the DIA has kept classified all refugee sighting reports generated by its own staff in posts around the world, and has also kept secret any follow up investigation resulting from refugee reports received by the League and then turned over to the intelligence agency.

Following are eight letters received by the League; the purpose in printing them is to provide examples of characteristic replies. Some of the information contained in them may be reliable and some may not — a determination DIA must make.

Additionally, names and references to some locations have been deleted for security purposes. Many refugees wrote in confidence and this confidence must be kept.

August 1, 1982
West Germany
Dear Mrs. Anh:
   On the question of the U.S. prisoners of war, both the US Government and the POW families want to receive accurate information. I therefore request that you keep this information secret, because my family still in Vietnam would be killed with-

out trace if this information ever leaked out. As you well know, there are a large number of Communist agents infiltrating in the ranks of Vietnamese organizations, religious groups, community, mutual assistance groups, etc. . . . to collect intelligence and report this intelligence to their government. I do not want any reward from the part of the League or the US government when it will be proven that live US POWs are still being held. This is the information given to me by my relatives in Vietnam. You must carefully check it, with the utmost attention, because the Communists are very shrewd, it isn't a simple matter. The US POWs are being held in isolated countryside areas near the seashore.

With my conscience and sincerity, I want to forward this to you, but do not want anything in return.

I know of several areas in the center of Vietnam . . . at these locations, the Vietnamese Communists . . . still hold prisoner a number of US POWs, a small number from eight to ten persons. The local people could see them and mocked them the "long nosed traitors, they have big heads (meaning they are adults) yet they were defeated by the children" (meaning small Vietnamese men). The Communists used to bring the prisoners for the people to heap scorn and insults on them, when they have a celebration, or a victory celebration, etc. . . . in the late afternoon. Because the villagers are afraid of the local Communists, nobody dares to talk about it, they do exactly as they are told. If anyone did otherwise, they would be subjected to self-criticism sessions.

Once more, I ask you to observe strict confidentiality when you verify the location, and also when you try to accomplish what needs to be done to help the POWs return to their country and their families. This is my wish.

My best wishes for good results soon in your endeavor.

Signed,

(Name)

May 26, 1984

Dear Mme Le Thi Anh:

I am happy to receive your letter dated May 20, 1984, regarding the search for the prisoners of war and the missing in action in the Indochinese war. Since 1976, I have organized a clandestine front for the struggle against Marxism-Leninism, in relation with our Indochinese combattants in the Thai refugee camps.

Almost eight months since I arrived in France, I have received two reports pertaining to the situation of the American prisoners of war and their activities inside Laos.

First of all, I can give you information from our Lao-Thai border bases. There exists a holding center for thirty-two old and handicapped prisoners. We can bring you there for a visit; our guide will be a Lao Communist soldier, secretly undertaking the mission.

There is another team of seven prisoners; they are technicians being constantly moved to work in repair service for the old American machineries left over from the war years. They travel in the provinces of Savannakhet, Thakhek and in the region of the Plaine des Jars. And there are three prisoners well locked up in a military garrison in Tchepone.

Fortunately, inside the Lao Communist Army exist our relatives and friends — they are officers and soldiers of every echelons. A Major promises us to evacuate a number of prisoners, with the requirement that after the escape the group would not stay long in Thailand, but should leave immediately, for the sake of his security, after the mission will be accomplished.

For this, we must carefully mount an immediate and precise rescue mission. For all this, it's preferable that the planning for the mission be established in the presence of a person in whom you have full confidence, to avoid risk and the minimum of loss.

If you could arrange a confidential meeting in a location of your choice, we can examine together and consult each other on the very important problems of this operation.

Please accept, Madame, my sincere sentiments and be assured of my devotion.

Signed
(Name)

February 1, 1981
Dallas, Texas
To: Mrs. Le Thi Anh:

[Refugee starts letter with name, military ID number and location where his military unit was stationed].

One of the tasks assigned to our unit was to provide support to a division of the infantry, which was standing face to face with the Viet Cong and North Vietnamese — all aimed toward Pleiku during the month of June 1974. The military events of that period, I am sure you were aware of and can imagine how tough was the battle against the Communists.

I would like to call your attention to the fact that along the front running from Tan Canh to Dac-To to Kontum, during the period from 1970 to 1972, there was a paratrooper brigade defending that front, with replacements and support from a U.S. Cavalry unit which included paratrooper and infantry and the Korean White Tiger, which was a station in An-Khe. But these were under so much pressure from the Viet Cong that the Vietnamese paratrooper brigade was totally defeated.

Only up until 1974, had my paratrooper unit and I got the opportunity to set foot again in the Tan Canh, Dac To area to destroy the enemy's work camps. I met a group of four white men, they were in two working teams, they were tall with blond hair. They were carrying logs to build bridges for the Viet Cong. It was the food-growing area of the military division, which was based in Thuong Duc, Quang Nam. At that time, we did not pay special attention to the white working men on the bridge-building site, mistaking them for Russians. Since in the battle of Pleide, twenty-four km from Pleimoron, I had met personnel from the Russian Engineering Corps bulldozing earth near the manioc farm of the North Vietnam Division. I also saw Russian men manning tanks attacking the base 801 in Le Tanh.

Time went by during October 1973, the Communists transferred me to Tan Cach prison camp where I was forced to do labor. The camp had been in existence since 1970. In that camp, I saw American POWs who were kept separate, more than one kilometer away from the Vietnamese POWs. Those U.S. POWs were transported to an area to labor in building bridges, clearing jungle together with us prisoners from the "puppet Saigon Regime" as they called us.

During that time, I communicated with the Americans in English, using Alpha, Beta, Delta. We learned that Major Johnson was the leader of that group of American POWs. Major Johnson had served in the Cavalry brigade assigned to the defense of Dac To and Tan Cach. Major Johnson was listed as missing in action in 1971. He had served in Thuong Duc earlier. There were two sergeants and a first lieutenant in the group of American POWs. The relationship did not last; I was sent to a prison camp in Binh Dinh, Qui Jhon. Up to the end of 1977, I got permission to go home for a visit with family; I went into hiding and escaped from Vietnam in 1978. I still remember Major Johnson's face quite well, he was thin, short for an American, he had a long face, a bald forehead, brown eyes, long eyebrows, his nose a little flat between the eyes, a dimple in the middle of his chin, teeth distant from one another. I used to be ordered by the Communist guards to bring manioc (sweet potatoes) to the "American pirates;" they had their hands and legs tied up when they were not working, when they were resting. The two sergeants and the first lieutenant were captured during the Mo Duc and Thuong Duc battles.

The exact date I saw him for the last time was during February 1975. At that time, I came back to take my rice ration and to proceed by foot to Binh Dinh, where I was assigned the task of transporting ammunition for the Viet Cong to attack Qui Nhon. At that time, Major Johnson was still building roads, so were the first lieutenant and the two sergeants.

The information I give here is accurate. If the Americans do not find their people, it is their fault. They were not thorough in providing security, not thorough in their search. We sympathize with them, we understand them, they had an opportunity to help the Republic of Vietnam defeat Communism, but to our deep regrets, both them and us are crying in sorrow.

I hope you are pleased with this information. I wish you and the League success.

Signed,
(Name)

July 28, 1981
Dear Mrs. Anh,

For some time, I did not write to you about the American POWs still in Vietnam. The reason was that I wanted to check and make sure that the information I am going to give you is accurate. Following, I shall give you the information regarding the American POWs.

The person who provided me with this information is a Vietnamese second lieutenant by the name of [name deleted]. He was taken prisoner in the Ba Vi Mountain area. At that location, he saw five American survivors. They were imprisoned near his camp. All five were white, one of them was two meters tall.

Everyday, the Communists forced those Americans to draw the plow in place of the water buffaloes in the rice fields under the very eyes of the officers of the ARVN undergoing reeduca - tion there.

[Name deleted, the Vietnamese second lieutenant] was released on July 3, 1981, and returned to the South. Both his legs were paralyzed. He wrote to me and gave me that information. He wrote that the five Americans were still there when he was released. The location is Ba Vi Mountain. He wrote that the photograph of the man two meters tall was taken when he was pulling the plow and was printed in a school textbook for school children.

I am trying to contact my relatives, asking them to clip the photo from the school textbook and send it to me. If I receive it, I would forward it to you.

Signed,
(Name)

July 5, 1982
U.S.A.
Dear Mrs. Anh,

I was a bus driver on the Saigon-Hanoi route for over four years. I used to transport on the top of my bus merchandisesof all kinds for Communist high officials, free of charge. They therefore introduced me to each others; the ranking Communist officials looked for my bus to transport merchandises for them. Those were items they stole from the South after they conquered the South.

The high officials who transported the merchandises on my bus used to eat dinner with me during our night stop at communication checkpoints. They ate their rice mixed with shorghum up to seventy percent shorghum, while I ate my rice unmixed. During dinnertime, I used to ask them about the military feats of our armies, of our nation. All of them lecture me nonstop on those accomplishments. Some samples of what they said: "We have a military genius named Vo Dai Thang. When the Soviet Union provided us with missiles to shoot enemy's B-52s, our military genius decided that those missiles could not reach the planes, he therefore added gunpowder, the result was that many enemy planes were downed, that has caused the American imperialists to flee Vietnam."

By the end of December 1978, I transported merchandises for a Communist Colonel. When he first saw me, he introduced himself as the "Prison Chief," I did not quite know what 'prison chief' meant. He has been introduced to me by Gen. Dao Son Tay, who was the Corps Seven commander. I have transported merchandises for the general earlier. I asked to see the letter of introduction and saw that his name was Nguyen Canh, a prison commander. I agreed to transport the merchandises for him from Saigon to Hanoi. The trip took six days, and as usual he and I ate our dinner together at communication checkposts.

When our vehicle arrived at the Kim Lien bus depot in Hanoi, Canh, like the other high ranking officials before him, he asked me to take the merchandises to his home. Vehicles for transportation were very scarce in N. Vietnam, so he told me, please comrade, help me bring these items to my home, I will not leave you without a compensation.

I was very reluctant, because the roads were very bad. In reality I did not want to go, but he pleaded with me several times. The next morning, I was thinking about unloading his stuff in the bus depot, but I knew they would be stolen, and lots of troubles would happen to me; I therefore had no choice but to transport the merchandises to his home to avoid troubles.

After we arrived in his place, my two aides helped unload the merchandises; we took a bath and we ate dinner in his home. After dinner, the Prison Commander told one of his guards, go and get for me a Bo Doi uniform and a pair of (Ho Chi Minh) sandals, and a Bo Doi hat. He told me to change into these outfits, that he would take me to a tour of his prison camp. During the tour, I saw that the prisoners were Americans, they looked at me coldly, they thought I was a Bo Doi, and were apprehensive not knowing what I was up to. I looked at them, they were in a sorry state, very thin and pale, their clothes were in a faded brown color, they ate part rice part shorghum, the kind previously used to feed hogs. The prison compounds were covered with elephant grass, the walls were made with dirt mixed with grass, earthen floor. Beds were made with bamboo. The prison camp was located in a thick jungle area, quite large, surrounded on all sides by military camps, the armies of the Socialist Republic of Vietnam.

After the prison tour, we returned to the home of the camp commander. I told one of my bus aides to go to the bus to take some dried squids and some liquor, I wanted to drink the whole night with the Chief, I told him, so that I would bid farewell tomorrow to return home.

After a number of drinks, I asked him why did our government keep those people for? Since the war has truly ended, and the US imperialists have withdrawn from Vietnam, why would our government let those men go home too, so that our Party and our State would not have the burden of keeping them and guarding them.

After my question, the Camp commander gave me the following explanation: You see, Our Party and our State are not stupid, we have spent a large amount of money to feed and guard those men, we want to use them to bargain and set a price for their release with the U.S. imperialists. The reason we need to keep those flying bandits is because these bandits have killed many of our comrades. Our people, our Party, and our State will make the claims, in order that our children will enjoy those."

I asked: Thus, how many of those headmen, how many of those "flying bandits" is our Party and our State keeping? His answer was: About 300 of them, the headmen and flying bandits. We keep them here (That was in Son La, formerly Bac Son province. Currently the province is named Cao-Bac-Lang, they, the Communists, lumped three provinces into one), and we keep them in Nho Quah, in former Ninh Binh province, which is today's Ha Nam Ninh province.

It was late, I went to bed, to return to Hanoi the next morning, bringing other comrades to Saigon. I have presented in detail what I know on the subject. I did it following my conscience.

Sincerely
(Name)

Thailand
April 7, 1981
Dear Mrs Anh:

After ten months living in the jungle camp for walk people (NW9) I have been moved to a transit camp to complete formalities for resettlement in the United States. I happened to read in Trang Den magazine the ad from the National League of Families, I wrote this letter and asked the Catholics to mail it for me because I am penniless.

According to a friend of mine, a resistant fighter who operated with me in Tay Ninh province, he told me he saw by the end of July 1976, that he was going to the "reeducation camp" Cay Cay, at the Tan Bien Crossroad (Sa Mat); he went there to try to contact the ARVN officers held at that camp in efforts to get them out of the camp. One day, by happenstance, my friend went by the Tuyen Ngon airfield, my friend saw an RMC truck, covered on every side with a piece of thick cloth, he saw the truck coming out of the airport and heading in the direction of the Cambodian border (New border) in the direction of Ca Tum, Seam Reap. Because of the speed of the truck, the piece of dark cloth was blown by the wind uncovering the inside of the truck. My friend saw two armed guards and about twenty (perhaps more) Americans, the bodies very thin and covered with scabies, sad gaunt faces, their legs were shackled to a long iron bar. They were dressed in black pajamas or in the passe blue.

*All those details went by fast, but through the discerning
eyes of an officer of the ARVN, there was no details that were
not recorded.*

*Those are the information I want to give to you. The friend
who saw the Americans, unfortunately, was arrested in 1980,
after our movement was uncovered; I fear for his life. But, it's
fate....*

*PS. Please answer me as soon as possible, I do not have rel-
atives or friends abroad.*

May 12, 1981
Paris, France
Dear Mrs. Anh,

*My name is [name deleted]. I am sixty years old, a Vietnam-
ese of Chinese descent, presently residing in France. I arrived
here about six weeks ago from a refugee camp in Hong Kong. I
escaped to China by land, across the border from North Vietnam
in early 1978. I went by boat to Hong Kong in 1979. I was
admitted for resettlement in France in late March 1981.*

*Born and educated in North Vietnam, I worked for the
French Military Intelligence from 1947 to 1951. Four years
after the French withdrew from Vietnam, I was arrested in 1958
by the Communists and charged with being a spy. During the
eighteen years inside Communists prisons, I went through the
following camps: Bat Bac, in Son Tay province (the location of
the 1968 U.S. military rescue operation), Yen Tho in Phu Tho
province, Lam Son in Thanh Hoa province, Quyet Tien in Ha
Giang province and Lao Cai on the Chinese border. It was in
Quyet Tien, where I was held from 1972 to 1977, that I saw
more than fifty American POWs. I was in the same prison camp
with these Americans; I saw them from a distance of about fifty
meters.*

*In another prison building, nearer to the Americans, just
about twenty meters away, there were twenty-five Taiwanese*

prisoners. Twelve of those Taiwanese escaped from Lao Cai prison with me in 1978. Among those Taiwanese who saw the Americans at closer range, there were three who could speak English and who talked to the Americans.

Two other former prisoners of Quyet Tien Camp, Vietnamese of Chinese descent, have buried about ten remains of US POWs in a place near the camp.

Quyet Tien prison camp was a high security prison, a for-life compound, located in a high mountain and thick jungle area near the Dong Van village, about forty kilometers from the Chinese border in Ha Gian province.

It is my guess that the Americans are now moved to the South, kept in small jungle camps, and being moved constantly. Probably, they were moved to Thanh Hoa and later to the Ham Tan area.

(Name)

January 17, 1983
Denmark
Dear Anh:

I received your letter 12/29/82, I want to answer you right away to avoid undue delay like the last time.

I am going straight ahead into the question you have been waiting:

1 - One American pilot, named John, Air Force Lieutenant, age around twenty-seven or twenty-eight years old, height around 1.75-1.80 meter, not fat, medium built for an American. His plane went down during a mission in the Hanoi-Haiphong area during December 1970.

This American is currently being employed by the Communists in operating an electric generator (thirty kwh) which belongs to the headquarters of Camp I, 776 Division. This headquarters is located at a location about fifty KM North-West of the city of Yen Bay, along the upper Red River.

I had the opportunity to stealingly talk to him a few times, not much because the Communist soldiers kept a close watch on me. This American told me that the Communists gave the Vietnamese name: Vietnam. I heard the Communists call him "brother Vietnam".

2 - Another American named Smith, a pilot, made sign to me, showed me four fingers and then pointed to his shirt collar, so I supposed he was a Major (Vietnamese name for Major: Officer Four, according to the number of stripes on the collar of French officers). His plane went down in North Vietnam, I don't know in which area, because the Communist soldiers escorting us kept strict surveillance, we therefore could not talk more.

3 - Another American, I succeeded in asking his name, his name is Thomas. He wore eyeglasses, his hair was blonde, slightly leaning on the white. I met him twice, in August and again December 1976, when I was assigned to carry foods at Camp 1, Division 776 in the Yen-Bay area.

4 - In addition, I have also seen several times a group of about thirty American POWs. We were moved into a prison camp immediately after they have been moved out. But they have been moved not far, so when we worked in the field, we could see them quite clearly laboring on the next hill. They also have been doing forced labor.

Above are a few preliminary information I am sending you. Later, if I have a chance to meet with you and the League of Families, I shall provide you and the League members full details of the sightings; I shall also provide you with other information not mentioned in this letter. I shall point out locations on maps, and shall try to recognize them on photographs. All of this I believe to be of great usefulness and importance to the League.

Footnote: Dear sister, I am doing this at the urge of my conscience, and out of a sense of responsibility toward our country, and because of a hatred of the Communists. I am also doing this because of my faith in you. I would like to do this through you only.

I wish you good health, accomplishments for the year 1983. (Name)

The sighting report by a refugee, Ngo Phi Hung, became one of the most extensively investigated refugee reports. He was not only questioned by the League and investigated by the DIA, but testified at a hearing conducted by the House Subcommittee on Asian and Pacific Affairs.

CHAPTER FIVE
NGO PHI HUNG

Ngo Phi Hung came to the League's attention in early 1978 when he wrote Le Thi Anh in answer to the ad in *Trang Den*. He was, he wrote, confined at the Songkhla refugee camp in Thailand, awaiting resettlement in the U.S. A businessman and member of a resistance movement, he said he had knowledge of American POWs but was fearful of writing the details because Communists in the camp could prevent his leaving Southeast Asia.

Through Dermot Foley, contact was made with Larry Stark, a former POW working as a civilian contractor in Bangkok. Foley asked Stark if he would visit Ngo Phi Hung to obtain details of his story.

Gaining admission to the camp, 125 miles south of Bangkok, was not easy but Stark was able to arrange it through a friend, a Vietnamese woman married to a Westerner with diplomatic connections. During the first week of May 1978, Stark flew to Songkhla and took a taxi to the camp located on the outskirts of the city.

A high, barbed wire fence surrounded the squalid camp as a reminder to detainees that although leaving the camp was not forbidden, it was discouraged. Stark and his Thai interpreter entered the wooden guard shack and asked to speak with Mr. Mai, the camp leader who had agreed to allow Stark to meet with Ngo Phi Hung.

The meeting was far from successful. Hung was edgy and unresponsive to Stark's discreet questioning but he agreed to meet Stark for dinner in a downtown restaurant if Stark could arrange it. It was Stark's belief that Hung would be more relaxed and disposed to talk some place away from the camp. Two nights later they met at a popular eating spot.

As they sipped beers after a savory meal Stark said, "I understand you may have some information about American POWs..."

"I cannot say," Hung replied through the interpreter.

"If you have information you could give me we might be able to do something about the prisoners," Stark persisted.

"I may have some information. I cannot say," Hung replied.

The circuitous conversation continued several minutes until Stark was asking himself whether Hung did in fact know anything or if he meant to use the situation as a means of getting to the United States. Stark pushed his chair from the table, indicating their talk was at an end.

Stark's move to leave triggered an admission from Hung. "This information I want to give to your president. I don't want to give it to anyone else..."

"That's not the easiest thing to do...to get to talk with president of the United States," Stark replied, surprised at both Hung's disclosure and his demand. "Can you give me some idea of how many prisoners you're talking about?"

"More than twenty," was Hung's response.

"Do you have names?" asked Stark. Hung did not answer. "Can you tell me where you saw the prisoners?" Hung shook his head.

Realizing he would get no more out of Hung for the time being, Stark wrote down his phone number and handed it to the unwilling informant. "Call me when you get to Bangkok," he said.

But Stark did not hear again from Hung. In June, Hung and his family arrived at a nephew's home in San Diego, a few days before the annual meeting of the League of Families convened there.

Hung immediately contacted Le Thi Anh who notified George Brooks of Hung's arrival. Asking Madame Anh to meet them, Foley and Brooks quietly arranged to interview Hung in San Diego. The night before the League was to convene, they spent six hours questioning Hung who was at last ready to talk. If his story seemed credible, Brooks wanted to take him before the convention where he could tell it to several hundred League members, along with government representatives and journalists attending.

Le Thi Anh was convinced of Hung's credibility. She had also talked with Hung's wife and eldest daughter who confirmed his statements about his business and political affiliations. And she gave her assurance to Earl Hopper, an MIA father and chairman of the League board.

When Hung and Madame Anh arrived at the League session the next day, Hopper apologetically interrupted the speaker, Frank Sieverts of the U.S. State Department, to announce the arrival of a special guest. With Le Thi Anh translating, Ngo Phi Hung told his story publicly for the first time.

Hung described himself as an ethnic Chinese who had operated his own transport and barge business. Until 1975 he contracted with the Saigon government to carry cargo — including military materiel — into the southernmost area of South Vietnam. Later he had contracted with the Communist government as the broker for several freight carriers for transporting confiscated material from Saigon to Hanoi.

Additionally, Hung said he was a member of a resistance group known as the Inter-Denomination Resistance Movement.

Hung claimed to have first seen forty-nine American prisoners in June 1975 at the former USAID II building in Saigon. "At that time I heard voices speaking in English. I recognized what language it was although I did not know what was being said. I asked some of the guards to tell me who the people were who was speaking English and they said they were American POWs," he said. Allowed to enter the facility, he saw them for himself.

During the following two-year period he continued making deliveries at various locations and watched as the prisoners were moved from Saigon to Tay Ninh, Ban Me Thout, Nha Trang and Quang Ngai between June 1975 and April 1977.

When he told the resistance movement leadership about the American POWs, he was urged to document as many details as possible. He was provided such gifts as a radio, a watch and a small refrigerator with which to bribe the prison commander, Captain Huynh Van Tao, and gain his confidence. Consequently he was allowed to enter and move about each of the prison compounds where the Americans were held.

He said he could recall the specific features of only a few of the men with whom he'd exchanged casual remarks, limited to "Hello" and "How are you?" The prisoners, he said, wore shorts and flip-flop sandals but no shirts. Their health seemed generally good but during that twenty- two month period he learned that three died — one by suicide and two from natural causes. Another man had attempted suicide but survived.

When Hung made mention of a notebook in which the names, ranks, dates of birth, hometowns and other pertinent information was recorded, League members tensed with anticipation but their hopes were soon deflated.

Hung had been able to steal glances at the roster and secretly copy information into a notebook. "...I would then go to a bathroom or such place and make notes. Later I would report this information to Resistance Movement." The data was written in Vietnamese, which he understood, but the names were in English and he could only reproduce the letters.

In the spring of 1977, Hung said, he came under the suspicion of the Communist officers. Fearing arrest, he bought a fishing boat and moved his family to a remote area where they remained until escaping in February 1978 with thirty-one other refugees to Thailand. During the journey Hung's boat was disabled and knife-wielding sea pirates boarded, robbing all on board. Along with Hung's personal effects, his notebook was taken.

All that he could recall from memory of what was written in his notebook was that of the forty-nine men, twenty-six were Army personnel, twenty were Air Force, and three were civilians. None were Navy men or Marine Corps personnel. They included three lieutenant colonels, fourteen majors, seventeen captains, nine second lieutenants and three enlisted men.

When Hung finished speaking, he was deluged with questions. Families wanted to ask about missing relatives, and reporters wanted specific details on locations and dates he had seen the prisoners. He was shown photos of missing men and asked if he remembered seeing them. Almost no one got reassurances but it substantiated the League's growing belief that prisoners had been left behind.

Foley recalls that not everyone that day was interested in Hung's story. "Frank Sieverts did not even attempt to hide his anger," Foley said, describing Sieverts as flying into a rage.

"At first," said Foley, "he accused me of acting in bad faith and when I asked him to explain what he meant, he walked away. He then went over to Hung and several other refugees and, in front of literally hundreds of MIA/POW family members, berated them, scolded them and declared that they were telling a pack of lies. It was an obvious effort at harassment and intimidation. Fortunately, it didn't work."

Sieverts has since defended his reaction, explaining that Ngo Phi Hung's reference to forty-nine live Americans created psychological havoc among the families. "Put yourself in that position," said Sieverts. "You've lost a husband or a child...you get word he's missing, then you are told he's dead. And five years later a Vietnamese appears and says forty-nine are still alive. It just interrupts the entire acceptance and grief process. I think what concerned me was that this particular Vietnamese was not a credible source."

Moreover, Sieverts was irked over the unannounced public presentation of Hung. "There was a proper way to deal with Ngo Phi Hung and that was to let us debrief him. We could have done a job of debriefing him, correlated his information and checked it with others to see if there was something to it.

"That would have been the responsible way to do it. It would have maintained the possible credibility of the source and protected the source as well as the information.

"Suppose what he had said was true. What have you done? You may have just doomed forty-nine people in Vietnam who, up until now, the Vietnamese had protected very carefully year after year since it was information which might outrage the U.S. If the first thing you do is publicize it, what might happen to those men? There was a perfectly good procedure to follow and the families knew it."

Hung later testified before the House Subcommittee on Asian and Pacific Affairs and agreed to be interviewed by the DIA at the Pentagon in August 1978. Following DIA's four-day interview with Hung, the agency issued an eighty-five-page document analyzing his account and detailing alleged discrepancies.

The DIA investigation was thorough. They spoke with refugees who had been on the boat to Thailand with Hung. They talked with persons knowledgeable about areas where Hung said detention facilities were located. They checked Hung's information with American officials in Thailand and discussed it with government experts, as well as making comparisons with maps and photographs. The Socialist Republic of Vietnam also responded to Hung's charges, denying any truth to his allegations.

Agency analysts found errors in Hung's description of the overall shape of the USAID II building in Saigon. They said he was inconsistent when he said that at one point he could look out a third floor window to the street below, but at another point he claimed that the windows were covered. Later, during congressional testimony, he stated the windows were not covered.

They found variance in his descriptions of camps and the routes he took between them. In one situation, the DIA analysts said, he reported a road was dirt, then later said it was an improved all-weather road.

Hung was inconsistent in relating how he learned of the deaths of the three prisoners, according to the DIA report. One time he said he'd read of them in the roster and another time that the guards had told him. He gave conflicting dates for the deaths, the DIA noted.

The DIA stated that several refugees described Hung as a constant troublemaker and agitator in the refugee camp and accused him of thievery and of exploiting others for his personal gain. During the investigation Hung had refused to be polygraphed unless those who had criticized his character also submitted to such a test.

"Mr. Hung's recall ability for certain alleged details is seemingly uncanny," the DIA reported. "He remembers dates, exact times of day, the text of his travel pass, the text of a falsified letter of recommendation and the rank of each prisoner, to mention a few. He would not, however, even attempt to reconstruct some of the names which he so tediously extracted — sometimes by memory — and transcribed."

The DIA was also critical of the "brotherly" relationship between Hung and the prison commander, Captain Tao.

Analyzing Hung's details of the forty-nine prisoners, the DIA experts argued against there being no blacks, Navy or Marine Corps personnel and only a few enlisted men in such a large group of POWs. They concluded that a cross-section of Americans lost in North Vietnam and Laos would include virtually all white, Navy and Air Force officers while Americans lost in South Vietnam would be represented by mostly enlisted Army and Marine Corps personnel — both black and white. Hung's information did not fit either category or a random combination of both categories, they said.

Regarding Hung's account of seeing POWs in Saigon in June 1975, the DIA report stated, "For many months after April 1975, Saigon was the least secure of any location in all of Vietnam with respect to concealing American prisoners. Hundreds of Westerners, including Americans and journalists, who were sensitive to the question of American prisoners, remained in the city. Saigon was rife with rumors about Americans during this period but no Westerners or Vietnamese refugees have reported information paralleling Mr. Hung's claim. It is inconceivable that the Communists would place forty-nine Americans in a centrally located facility immediately adjacent to a building still occupied by French nationals...and near other heavily used public facilities and believe that the Americans' presence would go unnoticed...

"Based on the inconsistencies noted in Mr. Hung's story," the report concluded, "DIA is not able to accept all his information as reliable and is unable to attribute credence to his report of live sightings."

Despite the official discounting of Ngo Phi Hung's story, Foley and other League members did not doubt it. "Make no mistake about it, Hung was a character, a real operator," Foley conceded. "He always made out well, he took care of himself. He was no Boy Scout."

But Foley argued that some, if not all of Hung's information was accurate. "He came up with things that made a certain amount of sense. While there may have been some weak areas in his story, the government's basis for discrediting him was incredible. Some of the objections they had were phenomenal. In certain instances they relied on other Vietnamese who had personal gripes with him. The DIA later admitted they handled the case badly, but they never reopened it. Hung ended up taking off. I think he's still out west some place."

Ngo Phi Hung and other refugees who reported seeing live Americans after the U.S. withdrawal from Vietnam provided the League with the much-needed impetus to continue its work. Until then, "We were just hanging on by our fingernails," George Brooks pointed out. "We had done just about everything we could think of to focus attention on the issue, but it seemed new national crises were always popping up, overshadowing concern for MIA/POWs."

Press coverage was sporadic — requiring new information or a new angle to grab attention — and funding was difficult, according to Brooks, who said that large donations from defense contractors and corporations came to a screeching halt after 1973.

"All of this was emblematic of U.S. attitude after the Vietnam War," he said. "Everyone decided that Vietnam had given us all the men and remains we were going to get and our nation wanted to close the book. The refugee sighting program renewed interest in our cause. Frankly, I doubt if the League would have continued operating if it had not been for the refugee sightings. It turned the whole issue around."

Part of that turnaround spelled change in the way the U.S. Government responded to the POW controversy. Not only did the refugee sighting program invigorate the League's campaign, perhaps more importantly, the sighting reports and a series of subsequent events sparked a more active investigation by the DIA, State Department and other government agencies.

CHAPTER SIX
THE GOVERNMENT FOCUS ON REFUGEE SIGHTINGS

For almost eight years after U.S. troops were withdrawn from Vietnam, the government's efforts in tracking down information about MIA/POWs can best be described as sporadic and perfunctory. From time to time various government agencies raised the issue — usually on appropriate occasions such as holidays — but their outcries were as brief and fleeting as blips on a radar screen.

"The mechanism had always been in place for the government to pursue information about missing military men, but information was only passively collected and apathetically pursued in the early years following the war," said Ann Mills Griffiths, who became executive director of the League of Families in 1977. "There was a standing instruction to pursue MIA/POW information, but initially it was not given a high collection priority. This was a reflection of national weariness from the war and a desire to move on."

Beginning in the late 1970s, however, the government began accelerating its investigative efforts, spurred into action by a number of factors. Not the least of these were the refugee sighting reports pouring into the DIA as a result of the League of Families' efforts.

In addition, the publicity given the Tring Hung and Ngo Phi Hung reports had increased public awareness of the issue and in

1979 League members added further impetus when they discovered U.S. intelligence had been negligent in following up refugee sighting reports that had come in during the early and mid-1970s.

More than 15,000 documents relating to MIA/POW information had been obtained by the League under the Freedom of Information Act. Sifting through the stacks of documents, George and Gladys Brooks gleaned an additional 353 refugee reports. DIA commentaries indicated that very few of these had been investigated and outraged League members began goading their congressmen to push for action.

Also in 1979, Vietnam began expelling all ethnic Chinese from the country and these refugees added their accounts of seeing American POWs still being held in Southeast Asia.

And in that same year, the Iranian hostage crisis revived the spirit of nationalism among Americans. A public awareness of other Americans being held captive was reawakened, creating the optimum climate for more intensive effort on the part of the U.S. government.

"It was around this time that we got high level government participation," Ann Griffiths recalled. "It gave the issue real credibility when government officials started saying what the families had been saying for years."

Congressmen and concerned citizens added their voices to those of the League families, but most importantly, the issue gained the attention of the Reagan administration. "The administration's prioritization of the issue in 1980 resulted in more active perusal of intelligence information and greater ability to investigate," Griffiths said. "Consequently, the greatest number of sighting reports ever collected came after 1980."

At long last the appropriate government agencies began upgrading their investigative efforts. The DIA continued to handle refugee reports submitted by the League but it also increased its own access to refugees. The collection of intelligence was enhanced through a coordinated effort of the DIA and the Joint Casualty Resolution Center (JCRC) in Bangkok, Thailand.

A key figure in promoting these more intensive efforts was General Eugene Tighe who served as DIA director from 1975 until 1981. Tighe's interest was more than academic; he was a Vietnam veteran and had been director of intelligence for the Commander in Chief of U.S. Forces in the Pacific, serving under Admiral John McCain whose son, a naval aviator, was held captive seven years in Hanoi. As a veteran of World War Two and the Korean War, the general knew the anguish of having friends missing in action and the subsequent elation whenever any of the men returned safely. He brought to the DIA a heartfelt concern for the men reported as missing in Southeast Asia.

Under Tighe's direction the DIA increased its staff and expanded its investigative network.

"As the volume of the reports grew, so did our attention to it," said Tighe. "It was part of a more determined effort on the government's part. There were few reports coming in when I got to DIA in 1974, but with every boatload of refugees which came out of Vietnam came reports of live sightings. As these reports increased — many very believable — the small DIA staff gradually had more work than their few numbers could handle."

With an enlarged staff and a worldwide reporting network, and with the cooperation of foreign governments, incoming refugees could be questioned about live Americans they had seen and about grave sites and crash landings they knew about.

Under procedures initiated by General Tighe, whenever a credible sighting report came in from anywhere in the world, the DIA could dispatch a team of linguists, professional interrogators and polygraphers to investigate. Eventually refugees in camps in Thailand, Malaysia, Singapore and Indonesia were solicited for information by three JCRC interviewers. In refugee communities, both abroad and in the U.S., the State Department circulated leaflets and posters, seeking information.

To discourage refugees from fabricating accounts in the hope of rewards, all were told beforehand they would not be compensated and were forewarned that their cooperation would not in any way enhance their chances for resettlement in the U.S.

The refugee reports were then submitted to an analyst who extracted specific details such as descriptions of the men seen, pertinent facts relating to any vehicles involved, locations where captures were said to have taken place and what was known of the fate of the POWs seen. The information was then electronically stored to provide a data base for matching details given in any similar accounts.

One DIA procedure Tighe instituted called for placing the latest reports in distinctive blue folders and sending them to his desk daily. He wanted to know how many reports had been received, their contents and what had been done to correlate the reports with other intelligence.

"Let's say, for example, it's week one in a year of investigation and a report comes in from a refugee picked up in Hong Kong," Tighe began, referring to intelligence cross-checking. "If, in answer to our question, 'Did you see any Americans in the last couple of years in Vietnam?' he said, 'Yes,' then we began asking specific questions about the location of the sighting, the date of the sighting, descriptions of the prisoners' behavior and their clothing. Many times there would be a ring of truth to the report. Then, several weeks later, another refugee might come through a refugee camp in Indonesia, and when interrogated, give very similar responses to questions about live Americans. We would check to see if the refugees were connected or related in any way and often we found that they were not. They had never seen each other, came from different areas and were talking about different time frames."

Also, DIA analysts had access to maps and photographs of geographic locations and terrain, against which they could check the accuracy of refugee observations. If a refugee said he saw Americans near a forest or beside a stream in 1975, the analyst referred to old photographs to check whether the forest or stream existed at that time. "It's that kind of jigsaw puzzling and cross-checking that the DIA is regularly involved in," explained Tighe.

The continuing flow of data convinced Tighe that Americans were being detained in Southeast Asia. "Down through these years, until I retired in 1981, we dealt with a phenomenal flow of information on this subject. As soon as a report seemed to have substance and could be verified by other intelligence, we took extraordinary measures to resolve it. Of course, there were reports by cranks or ill-informed people but such reports could be disposed of easily. But from the mass of reports, we got down to the hard cases which proved to me there was substance to the reporting. By 1981, I became convinced but could not prove that groups of live American military personnel still remained in Southeast Asia long after all American forces had pulled out of Vietnam."

Tighe first expressed his beliefs publicly during a 1981 hearing conducted by the House Foreign Affairs Subcommittee on Asian and Pacific Affairs. He expressed his opinion even more forcefully when he again testified before the subcommittee on June 27, 1985, four years after his retirement.

"General Tighe," said Subcommittee Chairman Stephan Solarz, as he began the questioning, "you said in an ABC interview on May 7, that 'it was inevitable for me at least to draw the conclusions that there were still Americans in Vietnam.' What about the evidence made such a conclusion inevitable to you?"

"The intelligence business" Tighe responded, "is one of putting pieces together over a long period of time and getting a certain amount of confidence in one type of source. The human reporting that came out of Southeast Asia on live Americans held there against their will was among the most detailed human reporting I've ever seen. And, I've said before this subcommittee before that if we had that quality of human reporting on the Soviet Union, our knowledge of what's going on in the way of detailed planning and strategy in the Soviet Union would be rather immense. It is high quality intelligence...I cannot forget it. It's still a part of my data base." Tighe's response was articulate, convincing. Although the silver-haired retiree now appeared in civilian clothes, a dark suit and tie, instead of the uniform of a Pentagon general, his soft- spoken assurances carried weight.

Congressman Solarz leaned forward in his chair. "You indicated in the ABC interview that you believed there were fifty to sixty people still alive in captivity. How did you arrive at that particular calculation?"

"First of all," the general replied, "I want to say that I should have been the last one to ever be talking about numbers because I've tried to resist that over the years." Tighe was referring to the danger of underestimating the number of POWs and possibly impairing the release of an even greater number of captives being held elsewhere. "I based my suggestion that there may be somewhere that many, in a ball park number, on my memory of three rather more precise live sighting reports at three locations in Vietnam. The numbers added up at the time to somewhere between fifty and sixty."

Interest in Tighe's testimony deepened; New York Congressman Ben Gilman picked up the questioning. "...Those fifty or sixty American personnel still alive in Vietnam, is that based on any specific information...?"

"Those are based on live sighting reports which we had no way of resolving unless we go in and invade and or get a human source in whom we have great confidence specifically to check the area and the subject itself. It is my feeling that those were very factual reports and they were the basis for my testimony before and I have no reason to believe they are not still true."

"But what can we do about these unresolved sighting reports?" Gilman continued.

"My first suggestion is that we get a primary collector, right in the area, in each area concerned."

"What's a primary collector?" Gilman asked.

"A human being in whom we have the greatest confidence who is able to view for himself what is or isn't there," Tighe said, refraining from using such words as "agent" or "spy."

"So, if we get a primary collector and get some additional information, what then?"

"Then, I think there comes a time when you have to use whatever proof he comes back with to apprise the public of what you know and/or, having exhausted all your diplomatic efforts with Hanoi, make it public to the world and look for world judgment to help you out."

"General Tighe, while you were in the DIA, were you able to utilize any of those prime collectors?" Gilman asked.

"During my time, we never had a primary collector on any one of those live sightings."

"Is there a reason why?"

"This isn't an easy task," Tighe explained, "it takes a long time. It takes a lot of priorities which if you'll recall that for years our priorities on Southeast Asia after the war were very low. As you would expect, there wasn't a great deal of interest in Southeast Asia after the war."

"Is this prime collector idea something we're capable of doing?"

"Yes sir," Tighe said.

Tighe's comments piqued the interest of Arizona Congressman John McCain, who was himself a prisoner of war in Vietnam and the son of Navy Admiral John McCain with whom Tighe had close ties. "Isn't it very difficult to implace a primary collector in a country such as the northern part of Vietnam where most of the sightings come from since it's such a heavily controlled society where virtually everyone is watched and examined?"

"I think it's very difficult, but it's certainly not as difficult there as it is in many other parts of the world where we're successful."

Tighe's recommendations also called for the appointment of a presidential commission to investigate the POW controversy. A commission, he explained, "would resolve the issue on a permanent basis rather than going away or changing with each election...the same group would be doing the analysis and recommending action to the president." The commission would have access to all records, would be able to directly levy collection requirements on intelligence agencies and get direct responses from them.

Only minutes remained in the hearing before the congressmen would be called back to the floor of the House. Iowa Congressman Jim Leach directed the next question. "Do you think there's a greater probability that POWs are being held in Laos rather than Vietnam?"

"I don't distinguish," Tighe said succinctly. "I believe the North Vietnamese government has official control over the geography of Laos so when I talk about the area, I refer to Southeast Asia rather than Vietnam or Laos."

Leach persisted. "Do you have a belief that there is a greater or lesser likelihood of POWs in Laos?"

"I have no way of balancing numbers," said the general. "I do believe, however, that the Vietnamese would not be above stashing them anyplace they chose in Southeast Asia."

Although Tighe denied on every occasion that the government was guilty of a cover-up where the POWs were concerned, in retirement he was willing to admit to a certain laxness on the part of DIA investigators. He had been quoted in the *Wall Street Journal* as saying there was a tendency toward "a mindset to debunk" in the intelligence community.

Questioned about his comments by Solarz, Tighe answered, "I certainly don't want to indict anybody but I would suggest that

I've run into this mindset before. Some of the people with whom I worked and who, in my judgment, held that mindset are still around. It goes throughout the government; I don't necessarily want to criticize all of them because everyone has their own opinion...but if their job directly deals with trying to resolve the veracity and accuracy of these specific live sighting reports, then it bothers me a bit. I don't know that that mindset exists today, but I'd be very surprised, on the part of several people, if it didn't."

General Tighe's testimony once again added credibility and momentum to the POW issue. Although he freely admitted he lacked necessary proof to substantiate his opinion, his beliefs were respected as coming from a former intelligence officer who had spent thirty-seven years cultivating intelligence information that helped win wars.

After the fall of Saigon in 1975, when intelligence capabilities dropped dramatically, refugee reporting became the major source of information about American POWs. Since 1975, the U.S. Government has collected nearly 4,800 MIA/POW-related reports — ranging from those about live Americans to grave and crash site information. The reporting takes on a measle pattern, coming from all areas of Southeast Asia.

Further refinement shows that of all the reports received, approximately 800 of them, or twenty percent, are eyewitness accounts — reports from refugees who said they had seen live Americans. It is on these accounts that investigative efforts are focused.

Of these 800 reports, sixty-three percent have been resolved. In these cases, most of the Americans sighted have since returned from Southeast Asia, but still, the percentage of resolved cases speaks to the reliability of the refugee reports. Only twenty-two percent of the reports were judged to have been fabrications.

This leaves 122 sightings still under investigation. According to intelligence analysts, these reports cannot be substantiated without additional confirmation.

Of these 122 sightings, roughly half have come from refugees who said they saw Americans who were apparently not being held against their will. That is to say, they were not under guard. Some, in fact, were described as having assimilated into the Vietnamese culture. Intelligence experts argue that in some cases, refugees could have mistaken Caucasians for Americans when in reality, the Caucasians might have been Soviet advisors, Western diplomats or reporters.

"If we eliminate these reports," said one DIA official, "we're left with forty-three firsthand live sightings of Americans. These are the hard-core reports which appear to have merit...on which we focus our greatest efforts." The reported dates of these sightings range from 1972 to 1979.

By 1986, six of these forty-three refugees had been polygraphed. Of these tested, two claimed to have seen Americans who did not appear to be prisoners; the other four said the men they had seen were being held in detention. Polygraph results indicated that all six refugees were telling the truth.

Polygraphing refugees has, however, been a problem for the DIA. According the LTG James Williams, who headed the DIA from 1981-1985, it is a slow process.

"In some cases," said Williams, "hundreds of man-hours go into researching a source's information and background, planning relevant questions and bringing the participants together for the interview and polygraph exam. Generally the examination itself takes several days to administer. Inasmuch as this involves bringing together a polygraph team, linguists, interviewers and the source, often in a foreign country, the logistics are not simple."

There are added difficulties when a refugee cannot be located in a camp or when, at the last minute, a refugee declines to be tested.

Consequently, the DIA uses the polygraph as only one of a number of tools in the evaluation process. "It's unrealistic to assume that a single refugee report will justify follow-on action without additional verification," Williams explains. "One hope is that a report can be strengthened and supported through technical means, or that more than one report will be specific and similar as to time, place and circumstance."

However, Williams added, "The conviction that the many reports, the known perfidiousness of the Communist governments in Southeast Asia, [and] the logic that implies some of the many missing must have survived, all suggest that Americans may be alive in Communist-controlled Southeast Asia."

Because of the classified nature of the sighting report investigations, public knowledge of the contents is limited. Yet, the government's handling of investigations is not without its critics.

One of the most vocal of these is North Carolina Congressman Bill Hendon who has argued that what has already been learned through refugees' reports is sufficient to call for decisive government action, and that he is in a position to know.

During his first term in Congress, 1981-1982, Hendon served on the House MIA/POW Task Force and made six trips to Southeast Asia to discuss missing Americans. As a freshman congressman, Hendon, along with New York representative John LeBoutillier, had gained recognition with the "Hendon- LeBoutillier Initiative," a plan with which they had persuaded the U.S. Government to donate over $275,000 worth of medicine to Laos. Their intent was to soften relations with the embittered Lao, and hook them on U.S. medicine as a way of developing leverage for extracting information about POWs.

Although the initiative was showing signs of progress, the effort was stopped short in 1982 when Hendon stepped down from his Congressional seat. He was re-elected, however, in 1984. But during the two-year interim, Hendon spent six months as a researcher for MIA/POW affairs inside the Pentagon. There he had access to classified material, including refugee reports.

Hendon later recalled the afternoon he sat at his desk sifting through piles of refugee accounts when he came across one of the most illustrative cases. He found a cluster of nine individual reports, each one corroborating the next. All nine accounts referred to sightings of Americans in one small town in North Vietnam.

In fact, it was the name of the town that jumped off the page at Hendon as he came across the first two reports, each one listing the town's prison as a site where American prisoners were being held. The first report, he noted, was from a former Vietnamese guard who had fled North Vietnam; in his account to U.S. officials, the guard spoke of Americans who were being held in the town's prison in the late 1970s.

In the second report, the refugee, a former administrative clerk at the same prison, stated, "there are GIs in that prison." Hendon quickly leafed back through the pages, double-checking the spelling of the town's name, then pausing to compare notes on the personal backgrounds of the two refugees. According to the information before him, the two young men had left Vietnam at different times, on different boats, and apparently had no prior personal connections.

Continuing his careful study of additional reports, Hendon discovered that the accounts from the first two refugees were further substantiated by stories from three or four other Vietnamese who had been imprisoned but had escaped, eventually reaching freedom traveling by land through Cambodia. They too claimed the town's prison was a detention site for Americans. And, in yet two other reports, refugees described having seen Americans being taken to the prison.

Finally, the ninth story was from an elderly lady who, after fleeing Southeast Asia, reported catching a glimpse of Americans as she stood outside the prison, waiting to take food to her husband, who was being held. According to her report, a truck pulled up, the driver threw back a tarp and dumped several Americans out on the ground, their arms trussed up behind them. The guards banged on the prison door and yelled, "We've got the Americans, let us in." The door opened, her account continued, the guards pushed the Americans in and closed the door. They threw the tarp back over the truck and drove off.

Hendon pushed away from his desk, refilled his coffee cup and leaned over the desk top, reading again the nine reports, again comparing details. Perplexed by his discovery, the tall, lanky congressman spun around from his desk and strode down the wide Pentagon corridor to question his superiors. He walked into the office, still holding the stack of reports in his hand.

"Boys, what in the hell is going on? Why aren't you doing anything about these nine reports?"

"Congressman, you don't understand," came the reply, "we know about those reports but we're not going to do anything because we don't have a name of a prisoner."

Hendon's jaw dropped. "What do you mean you don't have a name?"

"If we had a name we could do something but we can't move without proof — such as the identity of a prisoner."

Hendon, irritated and confused, shuffled back to his office, still thumbing through the stack of papers. He plopped down in his chair. He was driven to learn all he could about the refugee reports.

Days later, Hendon came across another equally distressing report, this one from a Communist guard who defected in the late 1970s and gave U.S. authorities the name of an American whom he claimed to have been guarding. According to the transcript, the defector had been guarding "a bunch of American pilots." The guard talked about Americans escaping, getting out into the jungle, being captured, dragged back, escaping again and being recaptured. Hendon checked the casualty list containing names of the missing men. The name the guard offered appeared on the list. Now they had a name!

"Good God! What's going on here...why isn't something being done here?" Hendon inquired. The pitch of his voice accentuated his southern drawl. "Here's a man's name."

"Can't be," he was told. "That guy was killed in a plane crash...there's no need to pursue the story."

Hendon resigned his position at the Pentagon weeks later. Having already been politically active in the POW issue, he believed he could continue those pursuits, accomplishing more in the private sector.

He left his job, confounded by what he perceived as an attitude of indifference. "It's incredible the way the incoming information is discounted. If a refugee is told by another refugee that a guy was an American, that's not good enough; he has to have firsthand knowledge. But if he has firsthand knowledge that a guy was an American, then U.S. experts attack it, saying the refugee doesn't really have the credentials to know what an American is. It doesn't matter what the test is...it changes. It's 'this story is too old — we can't be talking about that.' Conversely, it's 'this story is too new — it's still under investigation.' Then, it's hands off until a point which serves the interest of those doing the classifying. They eventually say that the newest information has become too old so it's useless. It's a constant catch-22."

Having studied dozens of classified reports from refugees, Hendon concludes that the timing of the reports reflects a pattern which also support their validity. "Things happen and subsequent events begin to develop. The Chinese invasion in 1979, for instance...things correlate to that, corresponding almost to the minute of the invasion. A number of sighting reports start pouring in — American POWs being moved south, GIs walking south, being flown to camps south. Are these reports true or false? I don't know, but they make sense to a normal person.

"The toothpaste is out of the tube, and it can't be put back in," Hendon declared, insisting that the refugee reports alone — without technical substantiation — create a credible body of evidence. "I know some people in the intelligence community who believe that this thing will be cracked by hearsay evidence. The hearsay evidence is unbelievable. It's like knowing there's a prostitution operation going on across the street; we can't prove it but we see people coming and going and everyone in the neighborhood knows. There are numerous stories in which it was common knowledge that Americans are being held in caves nearby. Do you launch World War Three over that? No, but it seems to me you'd take a really close look at the caves."

CHAPTER SEVEN
THE MORTICIAN

Rear Admiral Jerry Tuttle stared disconsolately at the stack of letters on the desk in his Pentagon office. There were eighty-one of them. All from congressmen demanding to know what the DIA was doing to find the men still reported as missing in Southeast Asia. Each letter would have to be answered. But when? And how?

First of all, Tuttle didn't have the time to reply to eighty-one letters, and second of all, he didn't have enough information to supply the answers. He glanced at the digital calendar on his desk: "August 4, 1979." He had exactly thirteen days to prepare General Tighe's testimony before the House Subcommittee on Asian and Pacific Affairs . . . thirteen days to come up with more answers to a barrage of questions about the missing men.

For someone more familiar with the MIA/POW problem the pressures might have been less but Tuttle had just taken over the job of overseeing DIA's analyses — serving directly under General Tighe. He knew the flood of letters and the subcommittee hearing were the result of lawmakers having to explain to their constituents why the missing men weren't getting the attention they deserved, why they were being forgotten. Tuttle admitted that he himself hadn't given much thought to the POWs since Operation Homecoming in 1973. Until now. And now the thought of men still being held in captivity gnawed at his conscience. Maybe he didn't yet know the answers, but he'd damn sure try to get some.

Tuttle sensed the charged atmosphere the issue was creating on Capitol Hill. Congressmen were finding themselves on the hot seat. They were having to answer complaints from folks back home, complaints that the POW issue wasn't being pursued with sufficient vigor and that lackadaisical investigations were leading nowhere.

The pressure was due in part to George Brooks's inquiries. "George Brooks was doing a remarkable job of pouring over intelligence files that had been made available under the FOIA [Freedom of Information Act]," said Tuttle. "He had come out with what appeared to be insensitive comments and a lack of complete intelligence investigation on refugee sightings, so this was getting a lot of congressional attention."

Tuttle knew that to get answers he would have to cut against the grain of institutionalized attitudes adopted earlier. Not necessarily the policies, but the government's attitude had implied to the public that accounting for the war's missing was as complete as it ever would be. General Tighe wanted that impression erased and Jerry Tuttle was under orders to intensify intelligence efforts and bear down on the investigations.

Tuttle met the challenge by sending an advisory to U.S. Defense Attache Offices abroad to be on the alert for any Indochinese refugees claiming to have knowledge about American POWs, gravesites, or downed U.S. planes. All such information, he stipulated, was to be promptly routed directly to him.

Several weeks later he received a communication from the DAO in Hong Kong. A Marine Corps officer there had learned of a refugee who said he knew of the skeletal remains of over 400 Americans being stored in a Hanoi warehouse. The warehouse formerly had been a POW facility known to the Americans as "The Plantation."

If true, the information was mind-boggling. Few in the agency doubted the Communists were capable of such an atrocity, but that someone with firsthand knowledge of it had been forced out of the country was almost beyond belief.

Following up on the DAO report, Tuttle learned the refugee was among the people of Chinese ancestry forced to leave Vietnam, including those who had lived there for generations. A mortician by profession, this refugee had been a loyal employee of the Hanoi government and claimed that he had personally processed the remains of several hundred American servicemen. The hitch, Tuttle was told, was that the refugee was reluctant to talk with the DAO. He had not volunteered to be interviewed despite notices posted in the camp asking informants to come forward. The DAO had learned of him only from other refugees.

Tracking down the reluctant informant, the Hong Kong DAO was able to hear the mortician's account and to provide Tuttle with a valuable piece of substantiating evidence. In 1976, when the Vietnamese had released the remains of twelve U.S. pilots, the mortician had been photographed during the ceremonies at which the American delegation accepted the remains. He had been among the technicians.

In yet another startling revelation, the mortician said the American delegation had been deliberately deceived. They had been told the remains were recovered from shallow gravesites when, in truth, they had been removed from 426 skeletal remains stored in the Hanoi warehouse, he had told the DAO.

Media coverage of the 1976 repatriations had been extensive, Tuttle remembered. Contacting the Defense Department's public affairs office, he ordered copies of any file photos taken during the 1976 ceremonies at the Gia Lam Airport. To identify the mortician he would have to rely on a minimal but telling point of description — the man was uncharacteristically obese for an Oriental.

When the photos were brought to his office, Tuttle scanned them and singled out the mortician from a group standing on a ramp near the flag-draped coffins. It had to be him, Tuttle told himself with mounting excitement; there was only one fat man among the Vietnamese group pictured.

Wasting no time, Tuttle put in a call to the DAO in Hong Kong. "Get his ass on a plane and send him to us!" he ordered.

With the cooperation of the State Department and Immigration and Naturalization Service officials, all red tape was cut and the mortician, whose surname was "Lac," was cleared for entry into the United States.

"I'm not even sure if it was legal," Tuttle admitted, but legally or illegally, in November 1979 at Hong Kong's Kai-Tak Airport, Lac was put on board a plane bound for the U.S.A.

With typical DIA prudence, however, Tuttle was not relying solely on the mortician's statements, even on the basis of the supporting evidence supplied by the photo. Tuttle was taking no chances. He had arranged for a Vietnamese-speaking FBI agent to talk with Lac during a four-hour layover at the San Francisco airport. The agent was to identify Lac as being the man in the picture. Tuttle also wanted to make certain that if Lac was the right man, he didn't do a disappearing act the moment his feet hit American soil.

Late in the afternoon of the scheduled day of the mortician's arrival, the call came in from San Francisco. "We've got your man here, Admiral," the agent said. He assured Tuttle that Lac would be kept under surveillance until he was safely aboard the plane for Washington.

It was almost midnight as Tuttle, accompanied by an interpreter, waited at Washington's Dulles Airport for Lac's arrival. The flight was on time and Tuttle watched the stream of deplaning passengers. Finally he spotted Lac — a short but hefty man wearing lightweight trousers and a short-sleeve shirt, shivering in the chilly night air. Lac scanned the crowd, searching for a face that would recognize him. He appeared to be exhausted as he stared around him in bewilderment, nudged and jostled by the other passengers.

As Tuttle moved cautiously forward he reminded himself not to hope for too much. The man Lac might be a vital link in the chain of intelligence but he could also be an imposter whose claims wouldn't hold up under close examination. That had happened all too often in the past, Tuttle recalled as he approached the waiting man and introduced himself.

"Hello," said Lac with a quick nod of his head and a smile as he extended his hand to shake Tuttle's.

The interpreter interceded, conversing with Lac in a tone of mounting dismay while Tuttle looked on apprehensively. "What's wrong?" he demanded to know.

"He's hungry," the interpreter chuckled. "He hasn't eaten in the twenty-four hours since he left Hong Kong."

It had been Lac's first trip by airplane. Penniless, he had refused the meals served on the planes, not knowing they were included with the price of the fare.

Watching Lac tuck into a thick cheese omelette at a nearby restaurant, Tuttle sat quietly sipping on a cup of coffee, contemplating the investigation that lay ahead. It would take teams of intelligence analysts, skilled polygraphers and expert bilinguists to prove or disprove the man's claims. It took no skill, however, Tuttle thought to himself as he watched Lac clean his plate, to see that the famished refugee was grateful for his first American meal. Smiling, Tuttle glanced across the table at the interpreter. "I may not speak Vietnamese, but I know one hungry Chinaman when I see him."

It would have seemed likely not to begin the initial phase of investigation until the next day, but it was set to get under way soon after Lac reached the hotel that night. The DIA had stationed a Vietnamese man at the hotel, posing as another refugee awaiting interrogation by U.S. officials. The "plant" was to befriend Lac and learn from conversation whether the story he told a fellow refugee would be the same as he told the DIA.

The ruse only succeeded in confirming Lac's credibility; he had one story to tell. Lac's account to his "fellow refugee" dovetailed in all respects with the facts he gave the DIA, and in time, virtually every aspect of his account would stand up under examination.

"The next day we put him in a safehouse with an interpreter and an analyst," Tuttle recalled. "We didn't want someone putting him on a hit list."

The mortician's information was not confined only to his knowledge about skeletal remains; he also knew about the existence of missing men among the living. He had seen, he told DIA analysts, three Americans in Hanoi under loose guard.

Lac's claims satisfied General Tighe. "He spoke about the same people twice," the general pointed out. "I had little doubt he was talking about people who were alive in 1974 and in 1979. In both time frames he saw them on the streets of Hanoi."

From Lac's description of the men, an artist compiled composite sketches in an attempt to identify them, but the attempt failed. Positive identification was not possible.

Still, Lac's report became the basis of further investigation, the details of which were supplied by LTG James A. Williams, who succeeded Tighe as DIA director. Testifying at a later date before the House Subcommittee on Asian and Pacific Affairs, Williams said, "The mortician was told by Vietnamese personnel that they were Americans. According to his description they were closely supervised but they did not appear to be prisoners in the classic sense." However, the DIA was unable to learn anything more of the men last seen by Lac in 1979. "We have not been able to ascertain their location, identity, nor, in fact, have we been able to verify that they were indeed Americans," Williams told the subcommittee. "However," he said, "as I indicated, this source is considered credible."

During intensive and repeated polygraph examinations administered by the DIA, Lac's story remained unchanged. He stated that he had been a senior mortuary technician for the Hanoi Municipal Cemetery Management Committee. In 1971, he said, the People's Army of Vietnam undertook a program of collecting remains of American servicemen — in many cases disinterring them and storing them in Hanoi. He estimated that between 1971 and 1977 he alone processed the remains of about 300 Americans that had been recovered and brought to the Van Dien Cemetery in Hanoi. At least 100 additional remains had been processed by other technicians, he said. All were taken to be stored at 17 Ly Nam De Street in Hanoi, in the warehouse. He had processed the last of the remains in mid-1977, he stated.

To substantiate his words, Lac produced several documents — records he said he had pilfered from the files of the Cemetery Management Committee, and which appeared to be authentic to the DIA investigators.

What Lac could not provide, to everyone's disappointment, was any list identifying the remains. He was never given this kind of information, he said. He was responsible only for the processing and for sorting through any artifacts that came with them.

To confirm Lac's testimony beyond any reasonable doubt, several polygraphers tested him. "I believe the polygraph is only as good as the polygrapher," Tuttle explained. "Since most potential error lies with the operator, we used more than one operator, in a sterile room, under best conditions, with control questions — proper questions."

Lac stood up well under this repetitive interrogation, answering all questions without hesitation and with no signs of deception. In minute detail he described how the harbored remains, as well as those returned to the U.S., had been packed together with personal effects.

Even his knowledge of the mortuary profession was thoroughly explored. He was questioned by a senior U.S. Army mortuary specialist who was able to confirm that although Vietnamese practices differ from American, Lac was well-grounded in mortuary science.

Lac's claimed association with the French was also researched after he revealed that he had helped prepare remains for the repatriation of French casualties after that nation withdrew from its earlier conflict with the Vietnamese. Again his story checked out and a French military representative to the French-Vietnamese Joint Graves Commission corroborated Lac's assertions.

To make certain Lac was not an agent, primed and planted by the Communists, he was questioned in detail on a variety of other subjects. He proved knowledgeable about Hanoi and its politics. He was indisputably familiar with the city, even to knowing that the railroad ran close by the warehouse on Ly Nam De Street. And the explanation for his exodus from Vietnam was credible — he had been deported together with all other Chinese ethnics because they were suspected by Hanoi of having ties with Peking.

General Tighe, for one, was convinced of Lac's credibility. "We put him through every proof and cross-check that we could possibly run and there's no doubt in my mind that he was not only very truthful, but also what he reported was very accurate," said the former DIA director. Nor did Tighe doubt Hanoi of having the basest of intentions. "There's no doubt in my mind that when they choose, the Vietnamese can pick and choose from that collection of nearly 400 remains they're keeping."

Several months after the DIA investigation, Lac underwent equally rigorous questioning by a House Subcommittee, and at some risk to his personal safety.

From the time the DIA had brought Lac into the country, he had been provided with heavy security. When he was ordered out of Vietnam he had been forewarned by the Vietnamese government not to divulge what he knew about the remains of the U.S. servicemen stored in Hanoi. To ensure Lac's safety from any possible retaliation, his identity and whereabouts had been kept secret, and, from time to time, his hiding place changed.

"They had stashed him around the country so no one would know where he was, for his own protection," Tuttle explained.

Lac, frightened about making public disclosures, asked that his identity not be revealed during the Congressional hearing. To shield his face from view, he wore a motorcyclist's helmet with the visor lowered. New York Congressman Lester Wolff chaired the hearing before the Subcommittee on Asian and Pacific Affairs; Colonel Jean Sauvageot of the State Department's Bureau of East Asian and Pacific Affairs interpreted.

MR. WOLFF: Sir, what was your occupation in Vietnam, and how long did you practice it, and where have you worked?

MORTICIAN: I was head of a mortuary.

MR. WOLFF: Where did you work?

MORTICIAN: I worked right in Hanoi.

MR. WOLFF: How long did you work at this job?

MORTICIAN: I worked from 1951 to 1954, before the Communists liberated Hanoi.

MR. WOLFF: And can you describe the work that you did?

MORTICIAN: When a person would die in the Hanoi area, they would hire us, or me, to care for the remains.

MR. WOLFF: Did you work for the same organization all the time?

MORTICIAN: Up until 1954 I worked for a private — in private business — but after 1954, and Communists took over, I of course worked for the state.

MR. WOLFF: How long did you work for the state?

MORTICIAN: From 1958 until 1979 when I was kicked out of Vietnam.

MR. WOLFF: Did you work with French officers on the French remains?

MORTICIAN: Yes, three French officers.

MR. WOLFF: Do you remember their names?

MORTICIAN: The French Government knows me very well in that business, and they know my name very well.

Processing U.S. Remains

MR. WOLFF: I think the Vietnamese know you pretty well, too.

MORTICIAN: I need a clarification.

MR. WOLFF: When did you process American remains in Hanoi?

MORTICIAN: From 1969 till 1975, sir, in the Graves Office of Hanoi. And now that is understood, the Military Law Division of the Department of Defense. This is not something that the diplomatic corps in Hanoi is concerned with; it's under the Military Law Division.

MR. WOLFF: Were any American remains reprocessed?

MORTICIAN: Yes, there were times when I had to reprocess some of them, because after a certain period of time some of them would begin to deteriorate.

MR. WOLFF: How does the gentleman know that he processed American remains?

MORTICIAN: Because I am a specialist in this kind of work and have worked for Hanoi since 1958 in these affairs and, therefore, they entrusted me with this mission.

MR. WOLFF: But how could he identify them as Americans as distinct from other Caucasians or other Europeans?

MORTICIAN: Because the Military Law Division of the Ministry of Defense let me know what I was working with, and they said that, "After all, these remains are a vestige of the war and we rely on you to process them."

MR. WOLFF: How does he know that more than 400 caskets were stored in the building? Did he physically see these? Did he have anything to do with them?

MORTICIAN: It's very clear because I know that I processed some 400, some 452 of these remains, that 26 were turned over to the United States; that leaves about 400-plus. I have seen them.

MR. WOLFF: Do you think you know that precise room in which these remains were stored?

MORTICIAN: Yes, 100 percent.

MR. WOLFF: This building which we have identified, is this the building that he was talking about?

MORTICIAN: Yes, I have identified it many times previously to the Department of Defense.

MR. WOLFF: Have you identified this photograph before?

MORTICIAN: Yes. That house and that picture and — wait — and also some Americans who were prisoners there and have returned to the United States also know very well that building.

MR. WOLFF: But they do not know that the remains were stored there; am I correct in that?

MORTICIAN: Yes, just that they know the building but not the remains.

MR. WOLFF: How would they know the building and not know that there were remains stored there?

MORTICIAN: I have to ask for a chance to clarify the question.

They entered that house but it was after that, some time after that, that they started to harbor remains. In other words, the prisoners probably went in there, had occasion to go in there and be familiar with it, before Hanoi started bringing remains in there. That is the reason they are familiar with the building but would not associate it with the remains.

Guarding the Building

MR. WOLFF: How did the Vietnamese guard the fact that these remains were in the building; in other words, if there were remains in the building and other people came into the building, how did they hide the fact that these remains were being stored there? Or did they hide it?

MORTICIAN: They had it well guarded. It is a military area under the Military Law Division, and it is guarded and they don't let people just go in and out.

MR. WOLFF: Do you know if U.S. remains are located in any other site either in Hanoi or elsewhere in the country?

MORTICIAN: They constituted all of them, stored all of them at the citadel.

"Tool of Peking"

MR. WOLFF: Now, the Government of Vietnam, in their white paper they prepared, said that you are a tool of Peking and said this is a hoax. How would you respond to that?

MORTICIAN: I don't have any real reaction to that. Obviously they wanted to say that; they wanted to accuse me of that; they, after all, kicked me out of Vietnam.

MR. WOLFF: Have you had any connection, before or since you have left Vietnam, with the Chinese?

MORTICIAN: You said the Chinese Government, sir?

MR. WOLFF: Yes.

MORTICIAN: I have no relationship with the Government of Peking or the PRC.

MR. WOLFF: When you were —

MORTICIAN: I went straight to Hong Kong.

Kicked Out of Vietnam

MR. WOLFF: When you were, as you say, kicked out, number one, why were you kicked out, and did you receive any information or threats or any instructions from the Government of Vietnam, when you left there?

MORTICIAN: They kicked me out because I am ethnic Chinese. Now I will get to the other question.

All they did was just tell me where I had to go to get — to get ready to get out, and they have threatened me not to divulge information to the United States.

MR. WOLFF: Why, if you were so valuable and were entrusted with this highly sensitive job, why would they move you out of the country?

MORTICIAN: Well, they kicked me out because I am ethnic Chinese and also because they accused me of being a lackey of Peking.

MR. WOLFF: So they did make this charge, though, before you were let out. Did they have any evidence of this other, than your ethnic background?

MORTICIAN: Yes, they did threaten me before I left Vietnam, or they did accuse me, they did accuse me of being a lackey of Peking before I left Vietnam, and that was just based on my being ethnic Chinese, and they concentrated a number of ethnic Chinese together for deportation.

MR. WOLFF: Were you born in Vietnam?

MORTICIAN: Yes, In Hanoi.

MR. WOLFF: I have no further questions. Mr. Guyer?

Reasons for Keeping Remains

MR. TENNYSON GUYER: Thank you. I am going to go very rapidly because we have panel members who have some questions. There is one pervasive question in my mind and many others.

Does he know what their reasons were for keeping these remains? Were they to be sold to us, held as ransom, or for bargaining purposes, diplomatic reasons? Does he happen to know why they were holding these remains?

MORTICIAN: I think it's very much like they did in the past, with the French, where they used these with the French.

MR. GUYER: Does he have knowledge of the fact that we have knowledge — does he have knowledge that they were selling French remains one at a time, even up until now?

MORTICIAN: I know about that. They did a lot of that.

Restoring Remains

MR. GUYER: About two more questions. He personally restored these remains? In other words, did he put dog tags and pictures into the smaller boxes, as he made the transfer?

COLONEL SAUVAGEOT: I broke your question down in two parts. You will see the reason in a minute. I asked first if he personally processed the remains. He said yes. Now I am going to ask the part about the ID's.

MORTICIAN: I know that they did take photographs and established records that were lined with the remains that I processed. However, that was the authority and the privilege only of the Military Law Division that handled this. I did not see the photographs and the ID cards and things like that.

MR. GUYER: Our impression is they knew exactly what they were doing so they knew which one was which, because they made their own records for future reference.

MORTICIAN: Yes, because they followed this, their specialists followed this procedure from the time that an airplane was shot down; they arrived on site, and began to follow the whole procedure from that time.

MR. GUYER: So this whole charade we have been listening to for years has been wrong from the beginning. They knew every time there was a crash site, or a death site, or a pickup, they knew exactly how they were talking about all these things they have told us, according to his testimony, is absolutely false; they knew every one.

MORTICIAN: Yes, that is correct.

MR. GUYER: Two fast questions. Did he ever have any formal training as a mortician, since he is known as a mortician? Did he ever work from a funeral home or have the art of embalming or does he know anything about that?

MORTICIAN: Yes, I did study that.

MR. GUYER: Two questions. Is his family out of the country safely, here now?

MORTICIAN: My children are out safely and in the United States. I do not know about my mother and father and three sisters yet.

MR. GUYER: One last question. Does he believe, knowing their habits and customs and operations, that since we now have challenged them openly, that maybe they have moved these remains from that site since then?

MORTICIAN: I think they certainly could, because if we review what happened, they refused a request by the delegation to go to the site. [The mortician referred to an earlier request by the subcommittee to visit the warehouse; subcommittee members had made the request after first learning about the body cache during an informal, private meeting with Lac a month before the public hearing.] Now, what I think they may do is, say, reconsider and say surely you can go there, but when you get there, there will not be anything to see, and it reminds him of some of the charades they played with the French.

MR. GUYER: Thank you very much.

MR. WOLFF: Would you yield?

MR. GUYER: Yes.

Files on Remains

MR. BEN GILMAN: As part of your duties in collecting the remains, did you also have an opportunity to examine the files on these remains?

MORTICIAN: Never had permission. That is secret. That was the Military Law Division that had access to these files.

MR. GILMAN: When the remains were delivered to him at the Plantation or citadel, whatever we call this building, were there also personal belongings or identification markers, such as dog tags or bracelets, things of that nature, with the remains?

MORTICIAN: Every remains had its file.

MR. GILMAN: And was the file with the remains when he received it?

MORTICIAN: No.

MR. GILMAN: Did he ever see any?

MORTICIAN: They only just gave a numerical sequence, but the Military Law Division had the —

MR. GILMAN: Files?

MORTICIAN: Files.

MR. GILMAN: Did he ever see any identification material, bracelets, dog tags, any type of identification markers along with the remains?

MORTICIAN: No, sir, but I heard them talking about them.

MR. GILMAN: What were these conversations?

MORTICIAN: They would say well, they had the serial number, they had maybe the flight jacket, or different personal effects.

MR. GILMAN: They were stored by the military division; is that correct?

MORTICIAN: Yes, they stored everything.

MR. GILMAN: And in each box of remains they had only a serial number, is that correct, a number to identify the box?

MORTICIAN: Not the serial number, just the numerical sequence number.

MR. GILMAN: For filing purposes?

MORTICIAN: Yes, sir.

MR. GILMAN: Did he know what the origin of the remains were when they were delivered to the citadel or Plantation?

MORTICIAN: You mean from which site it came, sir?

MR. GILMAN: Yes.

MORTICIAN: Only that they came from North Vietnam.

MR. GILMAN: Were any remains delivered from Laos?

MORTICIAN: No, sir.

MR. GILMAN: Were any remains delivered from Cambodia?

Work in Cambodia

MORTICIAN: They did not bring the remains from Cambodia into the citadel. In 1974 I thought I was going to have an opportunity to go to Cambodia to work, but that did not materialize because of the anti-Chinese campaign that started up in 1975.

MR. GILMAN: Did they tell him that there were remains in Cambodia that he had to look at?

MORTICIAN: Yes, they did; they said 16 remains.

MR. GILMAN: Sixteen American remains?

MORTICIAN: Yes, Americans.

MR. GILMAN: Was he told by the Vietnamese military that all of the remains in this warehouse were American remains?

MORTICIAN: Yes, the Military Law Division said that, because it was a matter of priority for them to have these processed because they looked at these as being necessary for the implementation of the Paris agreement because they wanted to force the American Government into war reparations.

Process of Identification

MR. WOLFF: One question that remains is, how could he identify from his professional experience other than hearsay, these were bodies or these were remains of Americans? Although we have gotten this information from previous meetings, I should like for the record to ask how he, professionally, as a mortician can identify the fact that these were Americans and not other Europeans.

MORTICIAN: Actually I can deduce that from the nature of my mission from 1969, when I was put, assigned as part of a delegation to this four-party joint military commission with the purpose of working on these Americans.

MR. WOLFF: Well, now, I talk now on a professional basis. Is he able to identify remains as to their ethnic origin, in other words, other than the idea that this was just a deduction? Can you positively identify from your experience as a mortician, the fact that these were American remains?

MORTICIAN: I just wanted to be so sure of this answer; I apologize for asking several times. I said can I have permission, will it be reflecting your idea if I say to the chairman that there is no scientific methodology to tell for sure whether it is the remains, the set of remains is an American or European, or some other ethnic group, a black or a white, and put that way, he said yes, I could respond that way. The reason I did that is that he reiterated the inductive process by which he could conclude that they are Americans but —

MR. WOLFF: Are there physical characteristics or anything like that that would in some fashion or anything like that that would in some fashion lend credibility to his deduction?

MORTICIAN: In some cases. For example, the Oriental, the remains of an Oriental can be distinguished from the remains of non-Orientals by the bridge of the nose, which is differently configured lower than the nose of a non-Oriental.

MR. WOLFF: Are there other characteristics? What we are trying to do here, as I would ask you to communicate, please, is to find some method of positive identification rather than the idea of conjecture, because I think this is so serious a matter that we have to be sure, and not permit conjecture to take over.

COLONEL SAUVAGEOT: He said he understands and emphathizes with the reasons that you are asking these questions; that is all right.

MR. WOLFF: Are there other physical characteristics? I know the Joint Resolution Center uses the length of the bones of the individuals, things of that sort, physical characteristics.

MORTICIAN: For instance, the hip bones, the shoulder bones, and femur also can be clues. Some ethnic groups have larger bone structures.

American Prisoners

MR. GILMAN: Did the witness at any time observe any live American prisoners?

MORTICIAN: I saw three Americans who came into the military law jurisdictional area.

MR. GILMAN: What date was that, please?

MORTICIAN. The Military Law Division took very special care of these people.

MR. GILMAN: What date was it that he observed these three American prisoners in the military compound?

MORTICIAN: Once in 1969 and many times during 1970.*
One blond and two with dark hair.

---

*The dates appearing in the Subcommittee hearing transcripts are apparently in error. According to DIA officials, the mortician observed the three Americans in 1974 and in 1979.

MR. GILMAN: Subsequent to 1970, did he observe any American prisoners?

MORTICIAN: Yes, up until 1974, sir.

MR. GILMAN: Did he know the identity of those prisoners?

MORTICIAN: Not clearly know their identity. I do not know their identity clearly but they were coming in and out. Up on the second floor they had a place for soft drinks and ping-pong and they were moving around and I do not know very clearly.

MR. GILMAN: That was in Hanoi?

MORTICIAN: At No. 3 Thang Street.

MR. GILMAN: Is that the plantation or citadel that we are referring to?

MORTICIAN: It is near the place that we have been talking about, but it is a different place. When we talk about the citadel, in English, from that report, in Vietnamese we are calling it No. 17 Ly Nam De Street. Before we came here, I asked what the Vietnamese called this place when it was still a prisoner-of-war camp and he said they just simply call it by the street and number. I will let you know that.

MR. GILMAN: And this is No. 17 Ly Nam De Street?

MORTICIAN: Where the 400-plus bodies were located, where you have been calling the citadel, that is 17 Ly Nam De Street.

MR. GILMAN: Is 17 Ly Nam De Street on the route between the Foreign Office and the guest house where American congressional delegations are normally housed and on the road to the airport?

MORTICIAN: Yes, sir; it is very near.

MR. GILMAN: Is it near the bridge?

MORTICIAN: Yes, sir.

MR. GILMAN: The date that you observed the American prisoners —

MORTICIAN: About 200 meters' distance, 200 meters' distance from the road to the airport and the citadel —

MR. GILMAN: It can be observed from the roadway; is that correct?

MORTICIAN: The Ly Nam De Street is very small and it comes close and you can observe it.

MR. GILMAN: From the roadway on the way to the airport.

MORTICIAN: From the roadway to the airport.

MR. GILMAN: The witness said before that he had been connected with some military units in a civilian capacity; is that correct? Was he ever connected with the 776th Division?

MORTICIAN: No, sir.

MR. GILMAN: What divisions was he connected with?

MORTICIAN: Just the military — I remember the 887th Military Law Unit and that gets its number from the area in which they had political jurisdiction.

MR. GILMAN: Had he ever been associated with any military division that had to do with prisoners?

MORTICIAN: No, sir.

MR. GILMAN: No further questions.

Lac appeared before the House subcommittee in June 1980. Several months afterward, a congressional delegation headed by Representative Wolff traveled to Hanoi to discuss the MIA/POW situation with Vietnamese officials. The trip was prompted by Lac's testimony as well as by an increasing number of sighting reports by other refugees.

Wolff intended to confront the Vietnamese with the facts supplied by Lac and to request an unscheduled tour of the warehouse at 17 Ly Nam De Street. His request was not denied, but it was cagily side-stepped.

"They told us there was not sufficient time to go to the place because it was too far away from where we were staying," Wolff reported. "What happened, however, was that on the way to the airport, our official entourage passed right in front of this place. In fact, Congressman John Meyers took a picture of it. But again we were told there was insufficient time to go inside. It seems to me there should have been time. We didn't have a plane schedule to meet; we had our own plane."

Wolff did not let the matter rest there. After returning to the States, he wrote the same Vietnamese officials, telling them the delegation was willing to return at a moment's notice in order to inspect 17 Ly Nam De Street.

His offer met with more evasion. "It was not convenient at this time to receive us. Those were their exact words," said Wolff.

Since that time it has been reported that the 400 sets of American remains have been moved from the warehouse, but U.S. authorities do not know where.

For Wolff, the outcome was bitterly disappointing. "The mortician's story was a real breakthrough in terms of having facts to use in pushing the Vietnamese for an accounting. We had in our hands a very good and vital piece of information," he said.

The case was subsequently submitted to the United Nations by the U.S., but Wolff charged that the U.N. "treated it in a cavalier fashion. If they had been responsive to our appeals and focused some world attention on the issue, results might have been forthcoming," Wolff maintained.

It was his opinion that "If the U.N. would turn a sympathetic ear to the MIA families, like it does to terrorists, we might have had a resolution and this kind of activity could be avoided in the future."

The congressman had no doubts about the truth of Lac's testimony. "I think the one thing that impressed me with the mortician was the fear that I saw in his reactions to certain questions we asked him. It showed that what he was telling us was really hard fact."

Meanwhile, the Vietnamese government steadfastly denied the mortician's claims, declaring that his story had been concocted by U.S. leaders for political purposes. The fictitious account, they said, was intended to confuse American public opinion during an election year.

As for Lac, the mortician, he and his family were settled at an undisclosed location within the United States.

CHAPTER EIGHT
THE NHOM MARROT MISSION

From the day in early spring of 1981 that the aerial photographs arrived on Admiral Tuttle's desk at the Pentagon, they generated hope — a hope that would culminate months later in a CIA-trained team of mercenaries stalking the Loatian jungle to search for American POWs.

The black and white photos had been taken by a surveillance satellite as it passed over Southeast Asia. Received first by NIMIC, the National Imagery Interpretation Center in Washington, D.C., the aerial views were forwarded next to Tuttle, and then to CINCPAC command headquarters in Honolulu, there to be scrutinized by military experts in photo reconnaisance.

The satellite cameras pictured an isolated clearing in the jungle east of central Laos near the Thai border. The actual location was pinpointed as being in Savannakhet Province, at some distance from Nhom Marrot. But what had drawn the attention of photo interpreters was one particularly alarming image.

Faintly visible in several photos was the number 52. The figures had been formed by flattening the tall grass in a field. Measuring some three feet wide and fifteen feet high, the numerals evidently could not be seen from the guard towers because of the trees.

The question uppermost in everyone's mind was, could the camp be a holding facility for American prisoners of war? Before any such speculation was warranted, more photographs would be needed — the efforts of the spy-in-the-sky were intensified and satellite photos of the facility began to arrive daily.

The pictures showed that the clearing, hacked out of the dense vegetation, was enclosed by high wire fencing topped with concertina coils of barb-studded wire. Inside the clearing were wooden buildings with corrugated tin roofs. The shapes and sizes of the buildings and their layout left no doubt in the minds of the military that this was a prison camp.

In all respects, the camp site was awesome. Not only was it situated in a forbidding and remote area, it appeared to have no contact with the outside world. No radio tower could be seen in the photos and most certainly, no signs of power lines. Too, there was evidence that the isolated prison camp was self-sustaining; crops were planted in adjacent fields and a nearby river was judged to be the camp's source of water. Detached from civilization, it was as though the camp were lost in time.

Although the photos clearly showed the activities taking place at the camp, close-up views of the prisoners' faces were impossible by long-range photography. Nothing about their features was distinguishable. The telephoto shots showed some men harvesting crops in the adjacent fields and others clearing out a wooded area as if a lumbering operation might be getting underway. Intelligence analysts were reminded of refugees' reports of seeing Americans being used for slave labor — clearing forests and building roads.

The importance of discovering the numbers was immeasurable, but there remained the perplexing question: What did they signify?

"The '52' was unmistakable," Admiral Tuttle recalled. "Anyone who looks at the photograph and can't see a 52 needs a cane and spectacles," he told colleagues at the time.

Analysts agreed the numbers were unmistakably there, but labored over their possible meaning. If it was a signal from American POWs, what message were they sending? One interpretation was that the numbers referred to a B-52, signifying the prisoners were pilots and/or crew members of downed bombing planes. In brainstorming sessions, it was pointed out that the figures five and two corresponded to the letter W in the prisoners' tap code grid — the code used to communicate messages between adjoining cells. Beyond that the analysts were baffled, unable to interpret what the letter W might mean.

Some theorized the 52 referred to the fifty-two American hostages in Iran who had been released about a year earlier. It was reasonable to believe, they asserted, that prisoners would be given such news by their guards, who would delight in telling POWs that Americans had been kidnapped from their own embassy.

Neither could Southeast Asian refugees solve the mystery. "The number 52 had no significance among the Vietnamese or Lao culture," said Tuttle. "I sought out every Asian I could find to see if the number had any meaning."

Regardless of the fact they could not decipher the number's meaning, the analysts generally accepted the theory that the number was a call for help from Americans being held at the remote and almost inaccessible prison camp. This assumption was further bolstered by knowing that with the rainy season at an end, captive Americans would correctly assume the satellite cameras again were focused on Southeast Asia.

The mounting evidence propelled Tuttle into action. He promptly appointed a task force to concentrate all its energy on the Nhom Marrot camp. Analysts and photo interpreters worked long hours, scrutinizing every inch of the photographs and describing their findings in detailed intelligence reports.

To enhance details in the satellite pictures, a stereoscope was employed. Like the old-fashioned stereoptical slides, the aerial views were enlarged and juxtapositioned, adding the third dimension of depth; hills, planes and depressions became visible.

As the number of photos grew, intelligence findings increased and files soon bulged with information about the camp, its inhabitants and their activities.

The enlarged pictures disclosed that the camp consisted of an inner compound ringed by an outer one. Separating them was a twelve-foot high stockade with pointed posts and guard towers at each corner. Buildings identified as administrative offices, a mess hall and several long barracks occupied the outer perimeter. Inside the inner compound were two barracks believed to house the prisoners. The stockade's resemblance to a Hollywood movie set of a frontier outpost prompted analysts to dub it, "Fort Apache."

For a prisoner to escape, he would have to pass through the stockade barrier within view of the guards, then make it through the fence topped by the coils of barbed wire. Once outside the camp, the escapee would find himself surrounded by jungle with no way of knowing in which direction freedom lay.

The intensified efforts also supplied at least two significant findings. Some of the men in the camp were tall — towering over other men believed to be Asians. The convicing factor was the length their shadows cast on the ground. Measurement of the shadows when the men stood in ranks or when two men stood together, proved the point. Linked to this was the observation that the tall men, when at ease, sat with ankles crossed "Indian" style; the shorter men crouched in the customary Asian squatting position.

After two months of intensive analysis, the documented observations led to the conclusions the prisoners were Caucasian. What was lacking, however, was the necessary proof. Without proof, Tuttle knew, no search and rescue mission would be attempted.

But, the satellite photos were not the sole source for Tuttle's belief that Americans were being held at the isolated encampment.

"I had more than one source of the corroborative intelligence that convinced me and others that the situation warranted the risk of sending in a team to get that confirmation. In fact, the photos were not the convincing thing to me; it was an all-source issue," said Tuttle.

Part of what Tuttle had in the way of corroborating evidence was an abundance of refugee reports coming out of that region. One former Royal Lao Air Force pilot had reported knowing of forty or fifty Americans, most of them pilots, who were shot down over Laos, being held in the area. And while intelligence experts had no precise fix on the number of men inside the prison, they did have reasonable estimates.

All this convinced Tuttle to seek authorization for sending in a reconnaisance team. He was convinced Americans were being held there and his certainty, supported by the information gathered, convinced others. It was not an easy accomplishment but he succeeded in getting authorization for the mission.

"There was no question in my mind that at the time there were Americans there," Tuttle explained. "I wouldn't have gone through that type of damned thing if I didn't think so," he emphasized.

What Tuttle requested was a limited mission — a team to approach the camp and confirm that Americans were being held captive there. The risks were high but nothing to compare with the dangers of a rescue mission if suspicions proved valid. It should be noted that the U.S. track record for rescuing American servicemen from Southeast Asian prisons was dismal; during the long history of war in Indochina not a single combat rescue of captives succeeded. In 119 rescue attempts, not one prisoner was retrieved.

A most painful reminder was the U.S. raid on the Son Tay camp outside Hanoi in November 1970, conducted by intra-service specialists, volunteers who trained for the mission at Eglin Air Force Base in Florida. The presence of American POWs at Son Tay had been confirmed in May of 1970 but by the time the rescue attempt was made, the prisoners had been moved. The would-be rescue team launched its attack on an abandoned camp. This failed mission underscored the highly perishable nature of intelligence information required for strategic preparations.

But despite the history of past failures, Tuttle succeeded in mid-spring in getting authorization for the Nhom Marrot mission. It was to be the first such government-sponsored foray since the war's end and it was to be limited to photo reconnaisance. The outcome would determine whether a rescue attempt would follow.

Training began in Thailand just before Easter. The team consisted of some thirty Laotians recruited by the CIA. The volunteers were to be handsomely paid for undertaking the risky venture. Although the Pentagon refused to confirm reports, the team was said to be made up of Hmong tribesmen — Lao hill men who had fought on the U.S. side during the war. Many of these men had prior CIA training in covert operations and were veterans of the interdiction campaign against the Viet Cong and North Vietnamese forces.

The instructions were simple in view of the hazards involved. The men were to travel on foot, slip across the Lao border, then cut their way through the jungle to the prison camp. Their success obviously depended on their ability to avoid capture. Issued high-powered cameras equipped with telephoto lenses, the men were not told that they were looking for Americans, but were told only that they were to return with photos of the camp and its inhabitants. The region they would travel through was termed "porous" by intelligence experts, meaning that any suspicion of their mission would be leaked like water through a sieve; the risk of any team member compromising the mission had to be minimized.

From the outset, the clandestine operation ran into trouble. Rugged terrain slowed their movement and encounters with enemy troops forced them to find alternative routes. At the border several of the men were discovered and wounded by patrol guards firing at them. From then on they moved in fear that prison authorities might have been forewarned of their approach. Nevertheless, the band of mercenaries pressed on for Nhom Marrot.

Even as the CIA-backed team moved toward its target, military strategists were planning the anticipated assault on the prison. An assault by the Delta Force was to take place immediately if the photographs disclosed the captives were Caucasian. The strike had to be swift, allowing no time for the prisoners to be moved, repeating the tragedy of Son Tay. Yet another inescapable fact was that an armed incursion into a foreign country was a veritable act of war. All told, there was no margin for error.

Another possibility faced by Tuttle's task force was that even though the prisoners might be Caucasians, they might not be Americans. Canadians and Frenchmen, arrested for drug smuggling along the Mekong River, could have been prisoners at Nhom Marrot. According to intelligence reports, however, this seemed unlikely and so planning for the rescue mission moved ahead.

The plan called for the professional strike force to drop onto the prison by helicopter and, holding the guards at bay, load all Caucasians aboard. Questions could be asked later. The command given by one senior officer was, "Anyone who's not white does not get on board the chopper" — another way of saying no guards or prison personnel were to be taken alive. The POWs were to be flown out of the country to receiving facilities which stood ready.

The rescue operation involved a mass of details. Air routes to and from the prison camp had to be determined, taking into account the location of enemy airfields and radar installations. The rescue choppers could be totally destroyed by a Soviet MiG attack.

The strength and composition of Lao forces in the area was another logistical consideration. How many troops were there and how were they armed? What were their communication capabilities and how quickly could they move in? Should the rescue force be prepared to engage in defensive skirmishes to accomplish its mission, or shouldn't it?

These determinations were made in an atmosphere of mounting tension as the return of the CIA-trained team was awaited. Finally, after weeks of delay, the reconnaisance team arrived back in Thailand on May 13. The rolls of exposed film were rushed to the dark room to be developed. Hour after hour the film processing went on and the still-wet prints were rushed to the analysts to pour over them, searching for significant clues. At best these would include recognizable Caucasian faces, at the very least, images of tall, wide-shouldered, light-skinned men. But as picture after picture was cast aside as useless, discouragement increased. When the last photo had been examined, all hope was gone.

"It looks like the assault is off," one analyst grimly commented. "No shit," was the sarcastic reply of another.

Not one Caucasian or a reasonable facsimile appeared in any photo. The proof they had sought so painstakingly had eluded them. Yet, analysts were quick to see a problem — the evidence was inconclusive. The team had photographed only the outer compound. They had no way of penetrating the inner compound to get pictures of the prisoners inside. The stack of photos did not tell the whole story.

After first describing the mission as "a farce," one intelligence expert amended his assessment to say, "I think the real word is 'travesty.' But it's part of the problem in dealing with mercenaries," he explained. "They were paid to go in and do a job. They reached the target, snapped the photos, and headed back."

The lack of proof, however, did nothing to shake Tuttle's conviction that the camp was a POW facility. "Most likely the Americans would have been kept in the inner compound, especially if word leaked out about the mission. The photos we got certainly did not eliminate the possibility that Americans were being held there. The Americans could have been kept inside, out of sight," he surmised.

What the reconnaisance mission did provide was more details about the camp layout and the startling remoteness of the prison's location. What had appeared as trees in the satellite films showed up as a triple canopy jungle in the ground views. And the only prisoners shown were Laotians — pictured walking through the camp to "re-education classes."

Consequently, the assault plans were shelved, and any possibility of the Lao team returning for more photos was wiped out, in part, by a leak to the media. News editors had honored the Pentagon's request to hold the story until the mission was completed, but on May 21, 1981, the *Washington Post* and other major dailies ran an account of the failed reconnaisance mission.

The futile effort was particularly crushing to Tuttle; it was to be his last direct involvement with the POW/MIA project. He had been promoted and transferred — he was shipped out even as the mission wound down. He had worked hard for its success, investing not only long hours of duty but all his faith and confidence.

"I am convinced in my own mind...that there were live American prisoners in Laos in 1981," he says to this day. "I also believe there were live prisoners in Vietnam as late as December 1978. I would bet my life on it, I'm so damned sure of it," he said.

Unfortunately, Tuttle's views were overshadowed by accounts explaining that a U.S. mission had produced no evidence of captive Americans in a Laotian prison camp. The prevailing perception — that there were no prisoners in Laos — perpetuated the public mindset created a few years earlier by the U.S. Government's two official probes into the POW controversy.

CHAPTER NINE
U.S. GOVERNMENT STUDIES ON THE POW QUESTION

The Select Committee on Missing Persons in Southeast Asia

December 6, 1976. It was 8:30 a.m. and the members of the House Select Committee on Missing Persons in Southeast Asia were meeting in the Rayburn Building with Mississippi Congressman Sonny Montgomery, the committee chairman. The purpose of the early morning session in the chairman's office was to approve the final proofs of the committee report before publication. The report, which was to fill five volumes, concluded a fifteen-month investigation of POWs allegedly being held in Indochina.

The congressmen meeting with Montgomery to give their final approval to the stacks of accumulated documentation included: Henry Gonzalez of Texas, John Moakley of Massachusetts, Patricia Schroeder of Colorado, Dick Ottinger of New York, Tom Harkin of Iowa, Jim Lloyd of California, and Paul McCloskey, Jr., of California. Two members were absent: Ben Gilman of New York was attending a memorial service for his daughter, and Tennyson Guyer of Ohio was detained by a heavy snowstorm in his home state. Ironically, Congressmen Gilman and Guyer had been the most frequent dissenters during the long investigation — the government's first major inquiry into whether any Americans remained involuntarily in Southeast Asia.

The committee's task, mandated by the House, had been arduous. During the course of the investigation the committee had conducted twenty-four open hearings and seventeen closed sessions. They had listened to the testimony of fifty-one witnesses and had interviewed more than 150 others.

The members had traveled extensively, meeting with top-level Indochinese government officials in New York, Paris, Hanoi and Vientiane, and conferring with both American and foreign diplomats in Peking, Bangkok, Vientiane, Paris, and Geneva.

Additionally, they had examined the debriefings of returned POWs, studied the files of those men reported missing or killed in action, and met with dozens of concerned citizens, including members of the League of Families and VIVA representatives.

They had been severely handicapped, however, by the lack of crucial records. Most of the information they needed was in the hands of hostile governments and inaccessible to them. They were not allowed to visit the areas of conflict; for the first time in the nation's history, U.S. representatives were not permitted to see for themselves where American servicemen died, were wounded, or captured. They were denied access to Vietnam's records of Americans reported missing, possibly captured. Instead, the committee was forced to rely on statements — including opinions — of people who had served in Southeast Asia, such as military personnel and civilians assigned there.

Talks with the Indochinese in the early stages of the investigation had progressively worsened, producing reactions ranging from frustration to outrage. The North Vietnamese had released seventy Americans trapped when Saigon fell but denied any knowledge of other Americans known to be there at the time. Appeals on humanitarian grounds fell on deaf ears.

Having released the remains of several Americans, the Vietnamese volunteered information about pilots they claimed had been killed, but a full accounting, they said, would not be made until the United States government kept its pledge of monies "to heal the wounds of war."

This demand came as a startling revelation to the Select Committee during its initial visit to Vietnam in December 1975. During one of their first meetings, Vietnamese Deputy Foreign Minister Phan Hien referred to a "secret promise" made by President Richard Nixon to Premier Pham Van Dong.

Hanoi's statement left the congressmen speechless. In effect, the Vietnamese were demanding ransom in the form of reconstruction aid. But equally appalling was the fact that Congress was unaware of any promises of financial assistance made to the North Vietnamese government.

What secret promise, the committeemen demanded to know. Phan Hien replied that in a letter dated February 1, 1973, Nixon had pledged to assist the Vietnamese in rebuilding their war-torn country — promising aid totaling more than $3 billion. The committee demanded to see the letter but Phan Hien declined to produce it. Instead, he presented an extensive list of materiel the reconstruction program was to provide.

Once back in the U.S., the congressmen attempted to contact the former President and his Secretary of State, Henry Kissinger, about the so-called secret promise. For several months the two men evaded the committee's questions, then Kissinger agreed to a meeting. At that time he denied the offer of reparations was an agreement, as such, insisting it had been a tentative proposal, subject to compliance with the Paris Peace Accords and subject to approval by Congress.

When, in 1977, the Nixon correspondence was at last made public, the terms were incontrovertible. The text read: "The government of the United States will contribute to postwar reconstruc-

tion of North Vietnam without any political considerations..." As to
the amount of funding, that also was clearly stipulated.
"...[P]ostwar reconstruction will fall in the range of $3.25 billion of
grant aid over five years." Phan Hien had told the truth.

It was not until long after the House Select Committee completed its investigation that Nixon retreated from his position of
"executive privilege" to reveal what had actually transpired between
himself and Premier Phan Van Dong. In 1978, threatened by a sub-
poena, Nixon agreed to a telephone conference with the House Subcommittee on Asian and Pacific Affairs, chaired by Lester Wolff, to
relate his side of the reparations agreement.

The telephone conference lasted about an hour and Wolff
later disclosed what had been said.

"Nixon did agree that he had promised aid to heal the
wounds of war," Wolff said. "His letter even spelled out the
methods to be used in providing reparations. However, after talking
with Nixon and learning the full extent of it, our committee agreed
that the Vietnamese had breached the agreement by attacking South
Vietnam in 1975 and that the letter was no longer applicable. However, the promise set a precedent for the Vietnamese. They don't
agree for one moment that they breached an agreement. There's no
question that this 'broken promise' is still at the crux of the accounting problem today."

This subsequent disclosure, however, was of no help to the
congressional committee meeting with Phan Hien in 1975.

At that time the delegation was seeking specific information
on the fate of two Americans known to have been captured during
the fall of Saigon — Arlo Gay and Tucker Gouggleman.

Gay was a civilian captured in the Delta of South Vietnam in
April 1975 and subsequently imprisoned at Cantho before being
moved to Hanoi. Gouggleman was a retired CIA employee taken
prisoner when he returned to Vietnam that same month to bring out
his adopted children.

The Vietnamese denied knowledge of either man, but a sequence of events would reveal that Gay was being held at Son Tay prison outside Hanoi at the very time the Montgomery delegation was asking for information about him. This came to light when Gay was released in September 1976 and returned to the U.S. with his wife and child. Gouggleman's fate would remain unknown until long afterward.

Gay's eventual release threw the lie into the face of the Vietnamese who had denied knowing his whereabouts. But this kind of doubledealing did not surprise those familiar with the thinking of Asian Communists. It had existed throughout the war, they pointed out.

During testimony before the Select Committee, Lt. Gen. Vernon Walters, Deputy Director of the CIA, traced the development of POW intelligence efforts during the war, stating that from the beginning of the conflict few American commanders had any clear idea of the Communist policy concerning the capture, exploitation or release of POWs.

Walter's presentation on intelligence — one of the most crucial aspects of the POW question — had a twofold effect. First it demonstrated the importance of an elaborate intelligence gathering network and that even with extensive collection, information was highly perishable. Secondly, although the intelligence community did not believe prisoners were being held at the time, Walter's portrayal of the sharp, postwar decline in collection capabilities emphasized the difficulty in confirming the existence of any live American captives in Southeast Asia.

"There is no easy way to recount the intelligence effort of the past several years," Walters told the committee in his opening remarks. "The war in Indochina was immensely complex, and the problem of missing persons reflected that complexity. Americans...were lost in combat with four related but distinct enemy organizations: the North Vietnamese nation state, the National Liberation Front of South Vietnam, the Pathet Lao faction, and the Khmer Rouge guerrillas. This confusion of factors complicated the intelligence problem to an inordinate degree."

During the early phases of American involvement, he said, few Americans were taken prisoner but when the U.S. stepped up the bombing of North Vietnam in 1966, increasing numbers of Navy, Marine, and Air Force crewmen were shot down and captured. North Vietnam's threat to try the prisoners as war criminals prompted Washington to upgrade the priority on POW intelligence gathering.

With the buildup of U.S. forces in 1965 the intelligence capabilities had been expanded so that POW information flowed through many channels...the CIA, DIA, NSA and the State Department. The DIA, which had been established in 1961, oversaw the analysis effort.

"In addition to the military and diplomatic installations of the United States reporting from many parts of the world, there were friendly official, commercial, media and private persons providing information through whatever contacts they might have," Walters stated, being careful not to disclose specifics about sources.

"The CIA and the military services cooperated in directing intelligence agents against key requirements such as the location of prison camps, information on the movement of prisoners, and the identification of prisoners. The large network of debriefing and interrogation centers developed in liaison with local government intelligence agencies...produced a most useful product," Walters explained, referring to the thousands of indigenous prisoners of war, refugees and ralliers who were debriefed. The best sources were interrogated in depth, often yielding valid information on prison systems or locations, and occasionally identification of prisoners.

"Photo reconnaisance," Walters continued, "produced quantities of imagery, an expensive but effective tool when used in conjunction with interrogation reports."

The photography was essential in evaluating information coming from areas no longer accessible, but aerial photography was not effective as a means of locating prison camps; the camps were seldom visible from the air. As a result, massive efforts were launched worldwide to collect overt and unclassified media coverage, particularly photographs of POWs and the prisons where they were held.

"...[A] huge volume of captured documents flowed regularly into a joint document analysis center," Walters explained. "Hundreds of documents were found that helped explain the Communist prison system, plans for exploitation or movement of prisoners and prison locations."

Communications intelligence was used to confirm shootdowns and to follow truck movements; indigenous reconnaisance teams operating in hostile territory were interrogated to confirm these reports.

Communist radio broadcasts were also monitored for information about POWs. "Alleged confessions by the PWs, a favorite device with the North Vietnamese Communists...were carefully examined for general information on the condition of PWs," said Walters.

But despite the intense focus on POWs, the Vietnamese refusal to provide information in accordance with the Geneva Convention, made the reliability of incoming intelligence data questionable. Of particular concern was the delay between the time data was collected and the time information was reported.

The committee gained new insights from Walters on the problems of intelligence gathering efforts from 1961 to 1973. Considering him a foremost authority, members bombarded the CIA expert with questions.

"You said, General, that you felt for good reason that Hanoi has more records than they are giving us. Do you know where these records are kept?" asked Congressman Moakley.

"I do not have any hard intelligence information. I would presume they were kept probably in the Ministry of Defense in Hanoi," Walters replied. Earlier in his testimony he had said, "There is no question that the North Vietnamese have knowledge concerning the fate of some unaccounted for U.S. personnel. A wealth of information on specific aircraft downings was published in the North Vietnamese press throughout the Vietnamese war...at times the fate of the pilot was mentioned. A locality or unit was oftentimes commended for capturing a U.S. pilot. Based on...the known Communist proclivity for detailed reporting, it is believed that the DRV/PRG hold significant amounts of accurate information...they did keep good records."

California's Jim Lloyd, recapping the committee's purpose, asked the general if he thought the issue could be resolved within the committee's given time frame.

"All I can say, Congressman," said Walters, "is that we do not have hard evidence of the existence of any live missing in action. Now, I can't tell you there isn't any, all I can tell you is there is no evidence to us at this time.

"On the time factor, to give you my own personal opinion, the only view that I can see is if these governments were willing to provide additional information. I think insofar as we have lost access to the sites, to the indigenous team, to the local reporting, this is a very difficult job to do."

"How would you approach the [Vietnamese] government? What is the best way based on all the intelligence you have gathered about that country?" asked Moakley.

"I think no matter how tough they are, we should hold their feet to the humanitarian fire and point out the human suffering that is caused by this insensitivity and this stubborness...I think the inhumanity of this thing being exposed might have more influence with them than even diplomatic moves. These are very tough people, Congressman, they don't give out. They regard prisoners of war as a card to be played in a game."

With that Walters stepped down from the witness stand and the hearing rapidly drew to a close.

The same problems Walters had presented to the congressmen in 1975 were to plague the POW issue for years to come. How could the existence of POWs be confirmed with no access to the area or the records?

The Select Committee hearings continued with dozens of witnesses appearing — returned POWs from North Vietnam, South Vietnam, Laos and Cambodia, MIA wives and parents, military generals and commanders, newsmen — including CBS's Walter Cronkite who headed an international committee on missing journalists. A host of experts testified on subjects ranging from the French POW experience in Indochina to escape-and-evasion techniques in enemy territory.

Some witnesses made impassioned pleas that the government not give up on finding any men left behind, but others, equally emphatic, insisted that all POWs had come home in 1973. A few, like Roger Shields of the Defense Department, were undecided.

Reflecting later on the committee investigation he said, "I know men were alive the last time we knew anything about them, but I don't know if they survived. I can put up a convincing story in my own mind but the most I can say is, I don't know.

"I think the committee did a very extensive job; had I not been in the position I was, I would have thought it was absolutely exhaustive. But, I knew things they still probably don't know. There's no way someone who's not connected with this could ask all the right questions...it's absolutely impossible."

After extending its investigation by three months, the Select Committee published its final report in late December 1976. The conclusions offered cold comfort. "The results of the investigation and information gathered during its fifteen-month tenure have led this committee to the belief that no Americans are still being held as prisoners in Indochina, or elsewhere as a result of the war in Indochina."

A few blocks from the Capitol, in a second floor office on K Street, the National League of Families expressed its discontent with the committee's conclusion in the form of a twenty-five-page rebuttal. The League argued that the committee carried out virtually no independent investigation of raw or primary sources. In the League's view, Montgomery had allowed Defense and State department representatives to influence the committee. The rebuttal, submitted by League Director Carol Bates, stated, "Consequently, the committee staff relied primarily upon DoD and State liaison personnel to do the 'investigation.'" Moreover, the conclusions in the final report were not based on a majority ruling, League members insisted. Their individual pollings showed there had been a five-to-five split among the committee's ten members, they said.

League leaders also questioned why the U.S. government had painted itself into a corner. How could the Communists ever come forward with prisoners whose own government had claimed they didn't exist, they asked. The U.S. was sending a signal that it was closing the books rather than striving for the fullest accounting, the League charged.

Closing the books, they argued, also diffused public concern and eroded support. Americans would be convinced more than ever that all the prisoners were home.

The League rebuttal also criticized individual members of the committee, including committeeman Paul McCloskey who was quoted in the rebuttal as saying publicly in the first week he was appointed that no Americans were alive in Vietnam. The committee's staff director, said the League, was quoted in the *Washington Post* as saying that some of the families were becoming "professional MIA celebrities," and were more interested in financial matters than in gaining an accounting.

The committee also came in for criticism from some of its own members. Ben Gilman and Tennyson Guyer attached their opposing views to the final report, stating, "We believe the committee should not consider that all POW/MIAs are dead until the United States has received as full and exhaustive an accounting as is possible. Until the Government has taken every reasonable step...there is no justification for erecting a POW/MIA tombstone."

John Moakley admonished the committee for recommending that the military resume status changes, declaring all missing men dead. The committee had no authorization to offer such a recommendation, he proclaimed. Moakley took his criticism a step further by sending President Carter a letter in which the final paragraph stated, "Above all, I would urge you to reach no decision until you have discussed these issues personally with the real experts. Our committee worked for fifteen months on the MIA issue but the families have lived with the issue, in some cases, for more than a decade and I sincerely hope that they can be given the same opportunity afforded our committee."

On the other hand, the committee's work did not go unpraised. A *Washington Post* editorial called the study, "A Textbook on MIAs...so exceptionally well done...so comprehensive, incisive and compassionate a study that it ought to be treated as a textbook of sorts for further consideration of this excruciating issue left over from the Indochina war."

Other members of the committee have expressed their satisfaction with the investigation, among them Iowa's Tom Harkin. "I think the report was judicious. We really dug into it. I believe we came to an accurate conclusion and tried to settle the issue once and for all even though there are those who keep wanting to bring it up all the time."

The man who spearheaded the effort, Sonny Montgomery, has stood firmly behind his committee's conclusions. "I thought people wanted to know the truth. That's the problem around here, nobody will bite the bullet. Some guy writes a tough report, tells the truth and then gets battered over the head with it. If you're not on the side of the League of Families, they'll eat you alive."

The Woodcock Commission

A few minutes before ten o'clock on an early February morning in 1977, League members Sarah Frances Shay, an MIA mother; Betty Foley, whose husband was missing; Carol Bates and Earl Hopper, were ushered into the plush Cabinet Room of the White House. An aide seated them at the long, oval conference table and served coffee.

The League members waited somewhat nervously. They were to meet with President Jimmy Carter who had been in office only thirteen days. During his election campaign, Carter had declared that one of the most "embarrassing failures" of the Ford administration was its inability to obtain an accounting of the missing men in Vietnam. If elected, he'd pledged to send a delegation to Hanoi to push for the fullest accounting possible.

League spirits were buoyed in anticipation the new Chief Executive would lend an empathetic ear to their concerns. A favorite uncle of Carter's had been a prisoner during World War Two and declared dead two years after he was reported missing. He had later turned up alive in Japan as an isolated prisoner forced to work as a train crewman.

Joining the League members at the table were DoD representative Roger Shields, Frank Sieverts of the State Department, and several White House staff members.

Moments later, all stood as President Carter entered the room. He shook hands with his guests and, inviting them to be seated, took a seat between Earl Hopper and Carol Bates. How could he help, he asked.

Earl Hopper was the first to answer — after apologizing for his hoarseness as a result of flu. "You may recall, Mr. President," he said, "that last September when you were campaigning in Phoenix we spoke to you about our concern for our POWs. We want these men back, and we still strongly oppose any aid, trade or recognition of Vietnam until they've given us an accounting for these men." Hopper was voicing League fears that talk in Washington about normalizing relations with Vietnam might become policy and subsequently relieve the pressure on Hanoi to make a full accounting.

"I recall that conversation," said the President, jotting notes on a thick white pad.

The second request was put forward by Carol Bates. "Mr. President, we are asking that there be no more status changes." The League's plea to halt status changes was intended to prohibit the military from continuing to declare the missing men as presumed dead.

In addition, the League was asking that the U.S. vote against the admission of Vietnam to the United Nations and that a Presidential Commission be named to investigate the POW issue.

"I'm willing to set up a commission," Carter agreed, "however, I'll ask that you not say anything to the press right now." He explained that he wanted to have his new administration in order before making the announcement.

The League members agreed to the President's request and when questioned by the media as they exited the White House they refrained from mentioning the subject of the commission.

Two weeks later, on February 26, 1977, the State Department made the official announcement; President Carter was sending a high-level commission to Hanoi and Laos to discuss the resolution of the MIA issue. Arrangements had been completed between Secretary of State Cyrus Vance and the Vietnamese Minister of Foreign Affairs, Nguyen Duy Trinh.

A State Department spokesman announced that "In seeking an accounting we will make clear that we are concerned about all Americans lost in Southeast Asia, our servicemen and civilians." A parallel objective, he said, was to discuss matters affecting long-range U.S. goals for establishing normal relations.

The delegation was to be headed by Leonard Woodcock, president of the United Auto Workers. Three of the members were former Senator Mike Mansfield, former ambassador Charles W. Yost, and Marian Wright Edelman, director of the Children's Defense Fund. Much to the chagrin of the League, the fourth member was to be Mississippi Congressman Sonny Montgomery — who had announced months earlier than no live prisoners were being held in Vietnam. Exasperated League members feared Montgomery's opinion would influence the commission.

The Woodcock Commission was not to be a diplomatic mission, in the usual sense, it was explained, since the commission was not empowered to negotiate any matters involving relations between the U.S. and the two countries to be visited. The commission was, however, given authority to negotiate any agreement related to an accounting of the missing American servicemen. The Woodcock Commission was to make its report directly to the President upon its return.

The three days of talks with the Vietnamese were preceded by a stopover in Honolulu where the delegation was briefed by DoD, State Department, Joint Casualty Resolution Center and Central Identification Lab personnel.

During the DoD briefing, Lt. Colonel Carlos Mathews told the commission, "We know they have information about some of our missing people but, for reasons of their own, have withheld it from us." He emphasized that in certain cases the Vietnamese could, if they chose, readily provide information. Mathews had prepared slides which listed the categories of missing men. He turned off the lights and switched on a slide projector.

"We have established categories to determine which men the Communists should know about," he said. "After the cease fire, the Vietnamese gave us information about some men we did not expect them to know about. On the other hand, they denied knowing about some Americans who were known to have been in their custody, some of whom had even been exploited by the enemy for propaganda purposes."

Pointing to the projection screen, Mathews said, "Category One, Confirmed Knowledge, includes personnel who were identified by the enemy by name or who were identified by reliable information received from releases, escapees or other forms of intelligence." Category Two, he went on, included servicemen who were involved in the same incidents as individuals reported in Category One and who were lost in areas where the enemy might reasonably be expected to know of them. Category Three, "Doubtful Knowledge," referred to those lost over water or in remote areas, where the enemy likely did not have knowledge of the incidents. Category Four included individuals whose time and place of loss were unknown, and Category Five, persons whose remains were determined to be nonrecoverable.

Mathews cautioned that the categorizing was at best an inexact science, based on DoD estimates. The commission was mildly shocked to hear him say, "If we must give a number, we would say that it would be reasonable to expect an accounting for those men in categories one and two — a total of 1,339. Mind you, I said 'an accounting,' not bodies." Mathews defended the estimate with a reminder that before Operation Homecoming, the DIA had been ninety-one percent accurate in predicting which POWs were alive and expected to return.

"These data represent our best knowledge of some of the nation's finest young men," said Mathews. "We have an obligation to them, their families and to the nation as a whole not to allow them to be used as pawns in a brutal game of diplomacy."

At the close of the briefing, DoD representatives gave the delegates more than seventy individual folders, outlining cases of missing servicemen in the first and second categories. The folder program had been started in 1973. Each folder contained a photograph, personal data, a map showing the man's last known location, physical description, and unclassified details about the incident that indicated the Vietnamese should have knowledge about the individual's status. The information was printed in English and in Vietnamese.

Delegates were encouraged to give the folders to the Vietnamese representatives to elicit their comments. Rumors had come to DoD officials that the Vietnamese might release the remains of several Americans during the commission's visit. DoD reps wanted the delegation well briefed and unwilling to settle for only a few remains.

Woodcock and his delegation next boarded their private plane for the Philippines to be briefed by the U.S. Ambassador William H. Sullivan, who had years of negotiating experience with the Vietnamese. Sullivan had negotiated the protocol on prisoners of war in Vietnam prior to the signing of the Paris Peace Accords in 1973 and had also served as ambassador to Laos from 1964 to 1969.

The presidential jet, carrying the Woodcock Commission on the last leg of its 12,000 mile journey landed in Hanoi late in the afternoon of Wednesday, March 16, 1977. As the delegates emerged from the plane, they loosened neckties and mopped their brows in the sweltering tropical heat.

The commission and its entourage of eleven aides and five American reporters literally had the red carpet rolled out for them. They walked along it to be greeted by the Vice Foreign Minister, Phan Hien. He was accompanied by protocol officials and a dozen or so Vietnamese journalists.

It was a quiet welcoming ceremony after which, to the delegates' surprise, they were taken to meet with Foreign Minister Nguyen Duy Trinh.

"I am prepared to listen to you," he told the Americans.

"We are pleased your government is receiving us and we look forward to fruitful discussions," Woodcock replied. "I hope by the end of our visit we have laid a basis for a closer relationship."

Woodcock spoke confidently but in truth he was worried. In all his years of union negotiating he had never gone in with so little leverage. If this were a union negotiation, he thought, I'd say we were at an impasse for another six weeks. He had told reporters before leaving for Hanoi that unless the Vietnamese were forthright, the mission was doomed to failure.

Following the brief welcoming by the Foreign Minister, the delegation was taken to their living quarters — a new five-story government guest house. They were to receive VIP treatment all the way, with formal dinners, cultural performances and even beer and bottled Soviet spring water on their bedside tables. The Vietnamese hospitality was sending a political message — the Vietnamese were willing to talk. But the Americans would soon learn that the talks would be on Vietnamese terms.

The next day's agenda featured an important meeting — one with the country's top leader, Premier Pham Van Dong.

Again the red-carpet treatment was accorded the Americans as the Premier approached them, saying, "I am indeed very pleased to meet you today because you come to us with good will and, as I understand, President Carter's wish to solve our problems in a new spirit. And if so, I see no obstacle to resolving our problems."

Woodcock replied, "Too long have tragic events kept our countries apart."

The white-haired Pham Van Dong, wearing a Vietnamese Army uniform, looked into Woodcock's eyes and smiled.

Although the Premier's words and manner appeared soothing, in reality they masked the hard line the Vietnamese were again to take.

It was during a tea break that Deputy Foreign Minister Ngo Dien reminded the delegation of the U.S. promise of financial aid. "This is not just a question of money but of national responsibility and honor," he said. He explained that his people viewed the pledge not as a commitment made by Nixon but by the United States.

Throughout the talks, the Vietnamese were to focus on what they considered the three key areas of discussion: the MIAs, normalization, and aid. None of the key areas was a precondition to any other, they insisted; however, they subtly noted that the three were "interrelated."

Roger Shields, as the DoD representative, recognized the approach as being of "the carrot on the stick" variety. "At that time I, along with Frank Sieverts from State, had more institutional memory and experience than any other member of the team," he said later. "I quickly realized that we were being given the same kind of treatment that we'd gotten so often in Paris. Like so many others before, we were being fed a line."

Nor were the conversational nuances lost on Shields.

"Are there any Americans still in Vietnam, either voluntarily or involuntarily?" asked one delegate.

"No, there aren't," was the smiling reply. "All Americans who registered and wanted to leave have been allowed to leave."

This prompted another to ask, "Were there any who registered and didn't want to leave?"

"No. All who registered wanted to leave."

"Were there any who didn't register?" asked another.

A slight shrug and an amused smile. "We asked them to register and if they didn't, then how would we know?"

Shields whispered a suggested question to Woodcock who nodded and asked, "Are there any Americans being detained or living in Vietnam under any circumstances whatsoever?"

"No." The answer was curt.

To Shields it was an evasive answer. "It was a fabrication, there's no question about it. Robert Garwood was there and they knew it. However, at the time we could not have put our finger on Garwood."

It was on the Friday, the day before the delegation was to leave for Laos, that the Vietnamese, as expected, announced they were turning over the remains of twelve U.S. pilots. Also, they said, they were releasing the remains of another American who had died in a Saigon prison in June 1976. His name was Tucker Gouggleman. Gouggleman was one of the two Americans they had denied having any knowledge of to the Congressional Select Committee, fifteen months before.

The White House emissaries were then driven to Van Dien Cemetery in Ha Dong Province, about twenty kilometers from Hanoi, where the pilots' remains were stored. Upon arriving, Rep. Montgomery asked for a moment of silence for the twelve fallen soldiers.

Shields, however, did not want silence; he wanted answers. He wanted to know about a B-52 crewman known to have been buried at Van Dien. The Vietnamese had said the flyer was killed when his plane crashed, and DoD officials believed the man might have been Air Force Captain Craig Paul. The Vietnamese had reported Paul's death and had taken a letter to his parents from his body and broadcast it over Radio Hanoi.

The Vietnamese had previously returned twenty-three bodies interred at the Hanoi cemetery but had not included the B-52 crewman's, claiming that because he was killed in action and did not die in captivity with the others, he was not eligible for repatriation.

But when Shields asked about the B-52 crewman, the answer was, "We know nothing about it." The Vietnamese official, visibly flustered, said he would make inquiries. Shields sensed his blunt question had also embarrassed Woodcock.

On leaving Hanoi, Shields was further chagrined to learn the individual case folders the DoD had prepared were not left with the Vietnamese after all. He concluded the delegation members might have considered the information in the files too embarrassing and too damaging to the Vietnamese.

"It's that kind of politeness that is so typical of high-ranking American diplomacy," Shields complained. "We choose not to ruffle feathers. We were given all these shallow responses by the Vietnamese and we accepted them and thanked them graciously for their cooperation. It's part of the drawback with American diplomacy. And on top of that, we change our tunes with administrations; we lose a lot of expertise."

Early Saturday, the delegation flew on to Vientiane where several meetings were scheduled during the brief, twenty-four-hour stopover. Behind a warm welcome, the Lao denied they held any live Americans or any remains. While referring to the MIA issue as a humanitarian one, they made it clear that the solution to the problem depended on U.S. assistance "to heal the wounds of war" and rebuild their country. They expressed the view that the two problems should be resolved together since both resulted from the war.

A week from the day the Woodcock Commission arrived in Hanoi, it was back at the White House reporting the findings to President Carter. Their report concluded, "There is no evidence to indicate that any American prisoners of war from the Indochina conflict remain alive." Parroting the Vietnamese line, they submitted that "Americans who stayed in Vietnam after April 30, 1975, who registered with the Foreign Ministry and who wished to leave, have probably all been allowed to depart the country."

As photographers snapped photos of Woodcock handing the report to Carter, he was telling the President that the commission was satisfied there were no living Americans in either Vietnam or Laos.

Praise abounded for the commission's work. Meeting with reporters, the President said, "Every hope that we had for the mission has been realized." He added that the Vietnamese had not linked "economic allocations of American funds with the MIA questions. We believe they have acted in good faith," he said.

Sonny Montgomery lauded the delegation's effort. "The commission was very thorough in its work. There were some very important Americans on that committee. The Vietnamese and Lao tell us they are not holding POWs. I'm taking their word for it, based on my extensive travels to Southeast Asia and conversations with their top officials. All this just creates false hopes for families. It's not easy to hide Americans in Southeast Asia...where would they be keeping them?"

Shields walked away from the commission believing the members had been hoodwinked. He was embarrassed, having been a DoD representative who supported the commission. He felt the Carter administration had used the commission's report to bury the MIA issue by assuring the public no Americans remained in Indochina and to pave the way for eventual normalization of relations.

Said Shields, "I'm sure the Woodcock Commission left Vietnam, giving the Vietnamese the impression that we were satisfied with what we had been given — that we would accept their performance. But in reality, we missed a golden opportunity. The commission seemed to be acting on the belief that the world is a decent place and if you're nice you'll get what you want. It's hardly the approach to take with the Communists."

CHAPTER TEN
A REVIEW OF COMMUNIST TRENDS ON POWs

Had the Presidential Commission members or other government committees before them been more familiar with the history of Communist treatment of prisoners of war, perhaps the approach to resolving the POW problem would have been different. Those who know the ways of the Asian Communists have come to realize the futility of expecting humane treatment. However, the Communists' disregard for the welfare of prisoners and their propensity for withholding prisoners is not restricted to the Vietnamese; it has been a Communist pattern in other wars, down through generations.

In point of fact — the American POW experience in Korea. At the close of the Korean Conflict, 5,866 men were listed as missing in action, although as many as 4,735 of those were believed to have died. Still, the accounting was incomplete, and the U.S. Government was persistent in its efforts to obtain an accounting for the several hundred men who were known to have been alive in North Korean and Chinese hands at one time. These were men who had sent letters home or who had been used for propaganda purposes during the course of their captivity.

But, from the time truce negotiations began to the time a peace settlement was signed in 1953, the Communists continually failed to provide the accounting they had pledged. During this two year period, U.S. representatives attended some seventy meetings with the Chinese in Geneva to discuss prisoner exchanges and the accounting issue. The talks produced no results.

Later, debriefings of returned prisoners and other intelligence reports would show that the North Koreans and the Chinese violated virtually every provision of the Geneva Convention governing the treatment of prisoners of war. Thousands of Americans died or were executed in POW camps. One U.S. investigation established that the Communists were guilty of such war crimes as murder, assaults, torture, starvation, isolation and coerced indoctrination.

The North Koreans and the Chinese were also quick to extract as much propaganda value as possible from the POWs. Operation Little Switch, a prisoner exchange in the spring of 1953, was a prime example.

The Communists had agreed to first return those American prisoners who were sick and wounded; however, this promise was not upheld. Realizing that the first releases of prisoners would have a significant emotional impact on the United States, the North Koreans and Chinese returned men who had only minor health problems — they wanted to create the impression that prisoner treatment had been good. Those who were seriously ill were not repatriated until later. Further, the Asians carefully selected for return any prisoners whom they felt had been influenced by Communist indoctrination, in hopes that these men would become troublemakers once back in the States. These prisoners were selected on a geographical basis, with their hometowns located near industrial centers. The intent was to perpetuate psychological warfare long after the fighting on the battlegrounds had stopped.

Wringing still more propaganda value from the prisoner exchange, the Communist prisoners, released by the U.N. Command, were instructed to feign illness and injury upon release. They tore or threw away new clothing and discarded soap and tooth brushes to make it look like they had been mistreated. Others limped or fell to the ground during the exchange in effort to convince the world they had been treated harshly.

Even though a total of 12,000 U.N. and South Korean captives were released, there's reason to believe that POWs, including Americans, were withheld in Korea. The man who served as Commander-in-Chief of the U.N. Forces in Korea, General Mark Clark, expressed this view in his book, *From the Danube to the Yalu.* "Through Big Switch we learned that the Chinese and the North Koreans, like the Communists in Russia, had refused to return all the prisoners they captured. Why the Reds refused to return all our captured personnel we could only guess. I think one reason was that they wanted to hold the prisoners as hostages for future bargaining with us, possibly for some concession such as a seat for Red China in the United Nations.

"As I have said, we had solid evidence after all the returns were in from Big Switch that the Communists still held 3,404 men prisoner, including 944 Americans." (This estimate was later reduced to 389 by U.S. Graves Registration officials working in Korea.) These 389 men were known to have been alive in Communists hands but were never accounted for.

Numerous case studies support Clark's position. Army Private Roger Dumas is but one example; he was a prisoner of war in Korea, yet never made it home. His brother, Robert, spent nearly three decades trying to prove that his brother was known to be alive in North Korean prison camps between 1950 and 1953. He finally succeeded in 1984, in U.S. District Court in Hartford, Connecticut.

Based on his research, Robert Dumas claimed that the government knew more about POWs who didn't return in 1953 than they were telling. He cited summary sheets written about each missing man, based on classified reports from repatriated POWs, intelligence reports, military command reports, letters from POWs, International Red Cross reports and enemy propaganda.

However, Dumas built much of his court case on the testimony of a former prisoner in Korea, Lloyd Pate, who had first seen Roger Dumas at Camp No. 5, in Pyuckthong, North Korea, in April 1951. Dumas had been captured in the fall of 1950; Pate was captured on New Year's Day, 1951. Both were in the Army's 19th Regiment, 24th Division.

"The first time I laid eyes on Roger Dumas he was near death," Pate recalled. "He had been wounded during his capture and had a bad wound between the bottom of his rib cage and his hip bone. He was rotting from that wound...everybody had given him up. So I took a handful of maggots and packed 'em in there and put a dirty rag over it to hold them in there just in case he turned over."

Pate did not see Dumas again until the summer of 1951. "Then, I saw him down at the river. He came over and introduced himself to me and said he remembered me treating his wound. We talked and that's when we discovered we were from the same outfit." Pate saw Dumas several times during that summer on the river bank where the prisoners were allowed to mingle occasionally and to bathe and wash clothes.

In October of 1951, Pate was sent to Camp No. 3 and did not see Dumas again. "I didn't see him after I was transferred, but hell, the last time I saw him he was walking around and except for a bad scar on his side, he was in as good a shape as the rest of us."

Based on the evidence presented during the three-day hearing in U.S. District Court, the Army Board for the Correction of Military Records changed Roger Dumas' status from "Missing in Action" to "Prisoner of War." The board ruling, however, did not change the earlier presumptive finding of death status.

Whether Roger Dumas was dead or alive during Operation Big Switch, the final prisoner release in 1953, the North Koreans and Chinese could have accounted for him. The cases of Dumas and others who never returned are legally closed, but questions about the fates of these men have gone unanswered.

The case of John Downey and Richard Fecteau further demonstrates the Communist proclivity for withholding prisoners. Downey and Fecteau were civilians, CIA employees, shot down over Northeast China, November 29, 1952, as they were attempting to pick up two Chinese agents who had been airdropped into the country earlier. Both Downey and Fecteau were captured within five minutes of their crash landing and were subsequently held for the next twenty years. Downey was released March 9, 1973; Fecteau was released about a year-and-a-half earlier, in the fall of 1971.

"We were not treated as POWs but as war criminals and after two years were tried and sentenced. That was in the fall of 1954 and at that time I was sentenced to life in prison," Downey said. Their sentences were later reduced, however, once relations between the U.S. and China improved in the early 1970s. The Chinese government granted President Nixon's request that both men be released.

The Downey and Fecteau cases differ from those of other men captured in Korea for whom there has never been an accounting. The Chinese did eventually admit that both men were in captivity; both were permitted to receive mail and were also allowed visits from relatives several times during their two decades in prison.

The history of the French experience in Indochina from 1946 until 1954, including its efforts to repatriate captured survivors or the remains of its war dead, serves as a backdrop to the U.S. involvement in Vietnam.

In 1946, France attempted to regain its sovereignty in Indochina which had been challenged by the Viet Minh. The guerilla-style fighting continued until July 1954 when the French agreed to withdraw. More than 20,000 French Union soldiers are yet to be accounted for. Although many of the missing were presumed dead and several thousand prisoners were released, the French contended that the Vietnamese were still holding 9,537 prisoners of war. (Roughly 3,000 of these were Frenchmen; the others were Europeans and Africans who fought with the French ground forces.) The Vietnamese insisted that all prisoners had been released, in accordance with the terms of the Geneva Agreement. However, after repeated announcements in 1954 that all POWs had been freed, during the next two years, the Vietnamese released several hundred prisoners. Between 1954 and 1956, the North Vietnamese released a total of 380 men whom they said were "ralliers" or defectors. Moreover, they released another 450 members of the French Foreign Legion during the period between 1955 and 1956. And, reliable Western observers in Vietnam during the time reported that hundreds of other legionnaires were released through China without notice to the French Government or the International Control Commission (ICC). This unannounced, unmonitored release was, therefore, unverifiable and was another violation of the Geneva Agreement.

All of these late releasees, the Vietnamese asserted, were "ralliers." However, some experts doubt the Vietnamese claim. Among those experts is Anita Lauve who served as a consultant for three weeks to the 1976 Select Committee. With two decades of experience in Vietnamese foreign affairs, Lauve had served as a Foreign Service Officer in Vietnam from 1954-56, and conducted private research on the French MIA/POW experience in Indochina for the Rand Corporation during the 1960s and early '70s.

"I should point out that a "rallier" was a term used by the North Vietnamese to describe a defector from the other side, who had allegedly rallied to their side," Lauve told the committee. "They drew a marked distinction between POWs and ralliers...whether these men had remained in North Vietnam voluntarily is not known, but in some instances there were indications to the contrary," she explained, referring to the members of the French forces who were released late.

Members of the Select Committee were eager to understand the parallel between the French and the American POW experience in Vietnam. Congressman Ben Gilman asked, "You mentioned in your testimony that there were ralliers and deserters who were returned some ten years after the war ended. Did the Vietnamese acknowledge that they were holding these ralliers or deserters after the war?"

"I don't believe they specifically said that they were holding these particular men. They did admit to holding many whom they called 'ralliers,'...they were usually... Foreign Legionnaires, Central Europeans, Spaniards and Italians. They also belatedly released many Africans whom the French had listed as missing."

"You seem to imply the possibility that some of these ralliers or deserters actually were not ralliers or deserters. Is there a basis for that?" Gilman continued.

"Yes," Lauve replied. "I think it more than possible that some of those repatriated to Communist countries in Eastern Europe were neither ralliers or deserters. There were a great many Germans in the Foreign Legion, and Poles and Hungarians, and Czechs. Many had fled their country when the Nazis were gaining control. Some later fled when the Communists took over. The Communists' governments asked the return of these men who had been captured."

"Where were these people held following the end of the war?"

"In camps in North Vietnam — in prison camps," she replied. "Some of them escaped. Some of them were able to get in touch with the International Control Commission."

"What was the longest period of time that these people were detained following the cessation of the Vietnamese and French hostilities?" the congressman asked.

"I think the longest held that I have heard about were African prisoners. About 212 were released sometime between 1965 and 1968. Some of them were from French territories in black Africa and some from North Africa."

"That is fourteen years after the war was over; is that correct?"

"Yes," Lauve said.

Lauve's research also showed that some of the French POWs who were released in 1955 reported that they had not known the war had ended until they were released. A number of prisoners were kept in the South...not in large prisons, but in remote villages where they were forced to raise their own food. Their captors depended on the thick jungle to discourage escape.

Committeeman Tom Harkin of Iowa was interested in a prescription for resolving the American MIA/POW problem. "As a final question...how can we reduce the amount of time involved in really getting an accounting of the MIAs. How can we shorten that period of time?"

"I think by not seeming to be too eager," Lauve responded.

"How is that going to work?"

"Well, they have something that we want, and we have something they want. And it depends upon bargaining, I think."

"What do we have that they want?" Harkin asked.

"Money. Money, very definitely. I think what has happened to the French is incredible — the things they have had to put up with to recover the remains of men they themselves buried."

As Lauve pointed out, the Hanoi government has been brutal in its demand for money in exchange for the remains of fallen French soldiers. In 1955, the French and Vietnamese Governments signed an agreement, stating that necessary measures would be taken to repatriate remains of servicemen who died on both sides of the conflict. But, of the 22,000 Frenchmen already buried on

French soil, only 1,500 remains were repatriated during the next two decades.

Hanoi has since demanded millions of dollars from the French Government for the exhumation and return of remains. In addition, the French continue to pay thousands of dollars annually for the upkeep of French cemeteries on Vietnamese soil.

The Communists' harsh treatment of prisoners of war did not begin with the French experience in Indochina; it was a Soviet pattern with millions of Polish, German, Japanese and other prisoners taken by Russian forces in World War Two. According to a historical study of Communist treatment of prisoners of war, prepared for the U.S. Senate Internal Security Subcommittee in 1972, nearly one-and-a-half million World War Two POWs taken by the Soviets were never accounted for. Estimates of the numbers of men withheld range into the hundreds of thousands. Many men were reported to be working as forced laborers, building a northern link of the trans-Siberian railroad. Certain German officers and skilled specialists were also reported to have been screened and detained by the Soviets.

Eight years after the war had ended, the Russians did release hundreds of German troops who had been held in Siberia, and the Chinese released Japanese soldiers eight years after Japan had surrendered. But, countless others were believed to have been still in captivity.

U.S. Senator James O. Eastland chaired the Senate Subcommittee which called for the 1972 historical study. In the report's opening paragraphs Eastland stated, "What emerges from this study is that there is nothing essentially new about Hanoi's treatment, or maltreatment, of Americans and Allied POWs and about the numerous violations of the Geneva Convention which have characterized its treatment of prisoners. If anything, the records of the Soviet treatment of POWs in World War Two and the Chinese-North Korean treatment of POWs during the Korean War are even more grisly than the dismal record established by the Vietnamese Communists."

"In the eyes of the Communists," the senator continued, "POWs are not human beings but political pawns to be broken psychologically so that they can be used against their own country and to be exploited, without pity of any kind, as instruments of political warfare directed, in the first instance, against their own families."

The testimony of returned American POWs in Vietnam bears this out. They are the men who served...and who know.

CHAPTER ELEVEN
RETURNED POWs REMEMBER...

It was late January of 1973 when the prisoners shuffled out of the cell blocks of Hoa Lo Prison, sensing that they were being assembled for some out-of-the-ordinary purpose but trying to give way to neither hope nor despair. It was better to believe they'd been called out for the guards to search the cells — for what, only God and the Vietnamese knew.

In the prison courtyard the anxious Americans formed a gray semi-circle. Their prison garb that had been issued as black "pajamas" was faded and sun-bleached. All wore the pallor of those confined to dark, humid cells. Their features were grim, their jaws set — the faces of proud men abused and humiliated but not humbled.

Among them was Commander Jerry Coffee who, within weeks, would mark his seventh year as a POW. A Navy pilot, he'd been shot down February 3, 1966.

There was no denying that something was in the air, thought Coffee. The signs were subtle but unmistakable. In the last few days the men had been given mail from home. They'd been allowed more time in the prison yard. And the food had improved from their daily diet of cabbage or pumpkin soup and hard rolls.

Into the center of the waiting men strode the prison commander — "The Dog," as he was known to the prisoners. He was accompanied by his senior staff officers and an interpreter. In his hand was a sheet of paper.

Raising the paper to eye level, he read aloud from it in the peculiar sing-song cadence of Vietnamese, then, without lifting his gaze, paused for the interpreter to translate the words into English.

The mind has its own method for receiving startling news — be it good or bad. The brain accepts the words heard by the ears then suspends the meaning of the message as if to give the consciousness time to absorb the impact. The message conveyed to Coffee's ears by the translation would need much time to register. The Paris Peace Accords had been signed. The POWs were going home. He was going home.

Preparations got underway immediately with the reassignment of cells. The prisoners were reassigned to cell blocks according to the chronological order they'd been shot down. They were to be released in groups every two weeks — the sick and wounded to be among the first repatriated, as the POWs themselves had insisted.

New uniforms were issued. Dark trousers, light blue shirts with long sleeves and gray lightweight jackets replaced the shabby pajamas. High-topped black leather boots were distributed to replace worn or nonexistent rubber sandals. They were given small black duffle bags for their "belongings" and a command that they were to take nothing with them from the prison.

What Coffee prized the most — his freedom — still lay ahead, but on the night before his scheduled departure another treasured possession was returned to him. "My wedding ring... It had been confiscated when I was captured and I had never expected to see it again."

When the morning of Coffee's release came he was still in a state of shock. He dared not believe. "I couldn't believe it was going to happen...that I was going home." None of those told they were leaving dared to believe it. "We all knew how inconsistent the

Vietnamese were and that the whole damn plan could fall apart at the drop of a hat," he recalled.

But on the morning set for the release of the first contingent, the departing POWs breakfasted on hot fresh bread and hot tea with sugar, then were told to line up in columns of two, again in order of their shootdown.

The air was tense with apprehension and Coffee had added cause for concern — the duffle bag he carried was not empty. In it were letters from home, his prison spoon and cup — a chipped, greenish porcelain cup with Korean printing on it, together with a stack of empty cigarette wrappers. On the inside of the flattened packets was written the prison poetry. The poetry had survived many a cell search, but Coffee's chances of smuggling it past the guards were slim. Not much of that kind of thing made it out of the prison, he knew.

Beyond the prison wall waited the buses that were to take the first group of POWs to the Gia Lam Airport outside Hanoi. The departing men should have been filled with happiness beyond measure. "But we could see all our buddies standing on tip toes, looking out their cell windows, watching us leave the prison...It was hard," Coffee said. The fear was that those left behind might be detained longer than a few weeks. "You just had to take a big gulp and hope the entire release would come off the way it was supposed to." With mixed emotions the first group boarded the buses for the airport where three Air Force C-141s were waiting to fly them home.

Coffee's memories of that morning are vivid. Near the ramp area at the airport a big canopy had been raised and under it were two tables. A Vietnamese official sat at one, an American official at the other. One by one the POWs' names were called out through a megaphone and one by one the men stepped forward, crossing the line, taking the first step to freedom.

Still carrying his duffle bag, Jerry Coffee heard his name called and he walked toward the canopy. The bag had not been searched; his keepsakes — inanimate objects which were almost like companions — were not discovered.

"The American was an Air Force colonel, Dick Abel," recalled Coffee. "He was wearing his Air Force blue uniform, and honest to God, he looked like Steve Canyon! I shook hands with him, then an Army Special Forces major put his arm around my shoulders and said, 'Come on, I'll take you out to the airplane.' "

Each man was escorted to the plane and welcomed on board by Air Force nurses who greeted each returnee with a hug. Doughnuts and coffee were served the men while they waited for the loading to be completed. Then the tail ramp was slammed shut and secured; the engines thundered to life, and the plane was airborne.

As it gained speed and altitude, the landing gear thumped into place and the pilot announced, "Gentlemen, we just left North Vietnam."

"That's when I believed it," Coffee explained. "Until then I couldn't grasp the reality of what was happening. I remember standing by one of the porthole windows of the C-141, looking out at the South China Sea as we headed for the Philippines, thinking about the last seven years and overcome by the realization that it was really over."

At the Clark Air Force Base hospital, Coffee and the others were given medical check-ups and assigned rooms — with bathrooms and hot water. "God, that first shower with hot water was unreal! I spent about forty-five minutes in the shower," he remembered.

Ahead lay innumerable debriefings, first at Clark then in the U.S., where intelligence officers focused on the returnees' knowledge of men they knew to have been in captivity or whom they'd last seen on the ground. They were asked about men still classified as missing and were asked to recite any prisoners' names they had memorized. They were shown photos of MIAs and asked if they knew anything about them.

"When I first came home I was among those who felt very certain that every prisoner the Vietnamese held had been released," Coffee admitted. "But over the years, the volume of circumstantial evidence indicates that men probably are still being held."

Although not all returnees agree, Jerry Coffee is not alone in his opinion. And those who believe as he does, draw from years of experience in Communist prisons to back up their convincing arguments that not only could men have been withheld but also that they could have survived.

Jim Warner was a Marine Corps pilot when he was shot down over the DMZ — the demilitarized zone — on October 13, 1967. It was his belief during his five years in captivity that the Communist Vietnamese would hold back some prisoners.

"For one thing, they told us all along that they were going to," he said. "They lied about everything else but they never lied about how they were going to treat us. If they said they were going to do something to us, they did it. They told us from the first day that they were going to keep some guys, so I have no reason to doubt them. They even told us why they would do it; it never made any sense to me but they said they were going to do it for the good of humanity. I just thought it meant they would do it to have some kind of bargaining chip after the war."

Warner described the Communists as people without morals. "They have absolutely no reservations about doing such things to human beings. One of the things one has to do to get into the party is show that you're not burdened by bourgeois sentimentality — meaning the normal human emotions.

"It's impossible to explain their logic for holding men. They don't think logically like we do. Understand that these people have lived all their lives as cogs in a Marxian wheel and logical thinking is not necessarily encouraged in Marxian society. It does not lead to good citizenship. So God knows what was in their minds. Maybe somebody came up with a scatterbrained idea to withhold some men. Once the rationale behind the idea became discredited, they didn't know what to do. So they were stuck. They just kept on doing what they were doing."

Air Force General John Flynn, the senior ranking returnee, captured two weeks after Warner, on October 27, 1967, echoes Warner's assessment of the Communist mentality. "Once you live with them for awhile, the one thing you figure out is that you can't figure them out. They're crooks. Their ethical orientation is much different from ours. They think it's a very honorable thing to cheat a non-Communist. That's what they're supposed to do and they do it continually. They tell us Americans lies...then we forget about it...then they lie again. One of the biggest problems with this whole issue is that we Americans ascribe to the Vietnamese the same motives and rationales we have... but they live in a completely different world. Their entire value system is different; their sense of time is so much different."

One of the most common challenges to the belief that men were withheld is the question of survival — could the prisoners have survived these many years since the 1973 POW release? A number of returnees answer by arguing that their will to survive coupled with a physical ability to overcome extreme illness and injury, kept them alive year after year.

John Flynn is a case in point. Flynn was forced to bail out of his F-105 over the outskirts of Hanoi. Traveling faster than the speed of sound, his aircraft began rolling after it was hit by a surface-to-air missile. As he pulled the ejection trigger, there was a loud bang and he was knocked unconscious.

"When I came to I looked down and the Red River was below me; I thought I was going to land in the river. I reached down to deploy my dinghy but passed out again. When I awoke, I had landed in a rice paddy. I thought I was hearing a dog barking, but it was a chattering Vietnamese peasant squatting beside me.

"A crowd gathered and pulled me out of the mud. I was drifting in and out of consciousness and the pain in my right leg was excruciating. When I emerged from the mud I saw a funny-looking stick poking out of my thigh. It was my femur! The Vietnamese fertilize their rice fields with human excrement so I figured I was in for a serious case of infection." At that point the crowd turned ugly and beat Flynn until he was unconscious. The last he remembered of being in the rice paddy was a Ho Chi Minh sandal stomping his face.

"I ended up in the torture room of Hoa Lo, stripped naked and my hands tied behind me with wire. I underwent a torture session before ever being given medical treatment. Subsequently, I was given penicillin and my bone was set."

Navy Lt. Commander Eugene "Red" McDaniel never received medical treatment for vertebrae crushed when he fell from a tree after parachuting from his aircraft. And worse was to come. Later during his captivity, after being accused of knowing about an escape attempt by fellow prisoners, John Dramesi and Edwin Atterberry, McDaniel was given a "torture flogging," said to be the worst suffered by any American prisoner. During a two-week period in the torture chamber, he was lashed some 700 times with a rubber whip.

As John Hubbell, in his book, *P.O.W.*, wrote, "One inexperienced torturer tied him [McDaniel] into ropes with such force that the bone in his upper right arm snapped, loudly, and a jagged end ripped through the flesh. Heedless, the torturers continued with the roping and left him tied in the unspeakable agony for three hours. His back, buttocks and legs swelled hugely. His wounds, raw, purplish red, oozing blood, became infected. He developed a high fever. He vomited blood."

There were three phases of captivity treatment in North Vietnam, according to the Center for Prisoner of War Studies, Naval Health Research Center, which operated in San Diego from 1972 until 1977. During the mid '60s, the Center learned, those captured experienced little physical punishment. However, between 1966 and 1969, prisoners suffered brutal torture sessions and demands for propaganda tapes, press interviews and letters to their fellow pilots and congressmen. Then, in the third phase, starting with the fall of 1969, treatment improved; torture was virtually eliminated and the diet was improved.

Still, most returnees insist that the key to survival was the psychological will to live. "If you want to survive, you can do so for a very long time on very little," explained Laird Guttersen. "I think what keeps a man alive is the belief that someone will rescue him or that he'll be released. As far as treatment...look at men who were chained to an oar and forced to work as galley slaves for twenty years...they survived."

Returnee Terry Uyeyama, an Air Force captain held for five years, is also convinced men can survive long-term captivity. "I could have gone on for another fifteen or twenty years if I had needed to," he said. "Every year in captivity becomes easier. The thing that torments you most of all is your family — the guilt, the knowledge that you have kids who are growing up. But as the years go by, your family and former lifestyle, your country and everything becomes remote. Your life and every minute of your day revolves around what happens within the cell walls. It becomes your life. Hope becomes a salve to your intellect so that you can survive. The human spirit never dies."

Ralph Gaither, the forty-second American to be captured, was a Navy ensign when he was shot down north of Hanoi October 17, 1965, on his seventy-third mission. Gaither was twenty-three when he was captured and he was released just prior to his thirty-first birthday. "You might say I sort of matured over there," he said of his time in captivity. "It became a way of life...you don't wait until you get back to the states to go on living."

Based on his seven years as a POW and his subsequent twelve-year association with the Code of Conduct and Survival Training with the Navy SERE (Survival, Escape, Resistance and Evasion) School, he's made several observations about the psychological adaptation to life as a prisoner of war.

According to Gaither, a POW moves through three stages. "The first stage is shock. It may last only forty-eight hours, but it's quite a shock. One minute you're flying faster than the speed of sound...a few minutes later you're a prisoner in the hands of Communists. You go from freedom to captivity very quickly...your whole world is shattered. You don't know if they are going to kill you or feed you. Your mind is wracked with questions about what they'll do to you.

"After several days you get your feet on the ground...you get some sleep, realize they aren't going to kill you; you get some food. You make contact with the other prisoners and you begin to adjust.

"Then you move into the second or transition phase. This lasts for six to eight months. During this time, you review your entire past. You feel sorry for yourself...mope...cling to memories more than the reality of what's going on. This is a hard time because you're fighting the fact that you are there...you haven't been able to escape.

"After six or seven months you begin to tire of feeling sorry for yourself. You begin to focus on the fact that you're alive and that you have a life to live...to make the best out of a bad deal. Here, you move into the third phase...which is acceptance of long-term captivity. Anyone who's been a prisoner over a year is into this phase. When you reach it, it becomes a way of life. You develop routines."

Gaither equates a POW's attitude to that of a rich man who suddenly loses everything. "He's left standing on the same corner he passed every day in his black limousine. He never realized that there were people on that corner and that there was a world around him. He learns to make a life out of that corner; it becomes a way of life. He can even find happiness."

John Parsels, an Army captain held for three years, confirms Gaither's views. "The first year was the hardest; I just couldn't accept the fact that I was there. I kept asking, 'Why me?' I was very depressed. If they had caught me in some of those depressed points, I probably would have done anything they told me — denounce anybody or whatever. I don't quite understand the psychological process, but after the first year, I got into a routine...I just started living day to day, learning ways to pass time, and sleeping a lot. I guess it's like being in any prison; you adjust to a routine."

By the time Parsels was captured in 1970, treatment of prisoners was much improved. "We didn't just sit around with long faces all day, we played cards and told jokes and stories. We even joked around with the guards. We had one very young, naive guard. We called him "Repercussion" because he was always saying 'there will be repercussions if you don't be quiet in there.' But we got to be friendly with some of our guards; we'd tell them about our wives, our houses and colored televisions. To them, a bicycle was a luxury."

It's all a matter of adjusting, said Parsels. "Once you learn to do that I don't see any problem doing it for nine years or nineteen years."

Returned POW Everett Alvarez was put to the test of surviving nine years as a POW. Captured August 5, 1964, and released February 12, 1973, Alvarez was one of those held longest in Vietnam. (Jim Thompson was the American held longest. He was captured March 26, 1964, some four months before Alvarez.)

"I think the real key to my hanging on was the unity of the group of POWs I was with," said Alvarez. "We spent virtually all our time communicating with each other and keeping each other going...providing information to one another and maintaining a cohesive unit. This unity gave all the individual members strength...knowing that we were not alone, that we were organized and still fighting."

Because most prison camps forbid prisoners to communicate, the POWs developed ingenious methods to outwit their guards. They tapped messages on their cell walls and, if a guard's presence prevented this, they would cough, sniff or spit in code. A man sweeping his cell might even whisk the broom across the floor in code, or drag his sandals in code.

"Faith and the belief that I would someday go home was important too," Alvarez explained. "You can never given up hope. That's why our communication was so important; if you weakened one day you had the others to prop you up. The unity gave us inner strength.

"After we were there for five or six years, we had adapted to it. Even though conditions were harsh, we had grown accustomed to the mode of living. It was our life and our world. As long as we got food and medicine we could have gone on forever."

The System

"The System" consisted of eleven prisons in North Vietnam. Four were located in Hanoi: the Plantation, the Zoo, Alcatraz and the Hanoi Hilton — as they were named by the POWs. The Hilton, officially named Hoa Lo, was the main penitentiary and was virtually escape proof.

Six other prison camps were within a fifty-mile radius of Hanoi. They were known as Briarpatch, Son Tay, Faith, Skidrow, D-1, and the Rockpile. A camp known as Dog Patch was located in the mountains in the northernmost part of North Vietnam — five miles from the Chinese border.

Returned prisoners who had been in The System believe that anyone in it either died or came home. Assumptions, based on the debriefings, were that the releases had been complete. But some prisoners claim their methods for keeping track of other men was not flawless and that some POWs could have been kept elsewhere.

By the time of their release most returnees had committed to memory the names of all men in their particular prison. With no writing materials, the POWs had to rely on their memories and they resorted to these "name banks" during the debriefings after Operation Homecoming.

"Our System for keeping track of men inside the prison was a good one," explained Guttersen, "but it didn't go far enough. When we returnees refer to 'The System,' we're talking about the POW camps that we knew about." Also, he points out, "The Vietnamese controlled, for the most part, how much we knew about others. The only way we got information about men in other camps was when someone from another camp was moved into our camp. I had the feeling while I was in prison that we didn't know about everybody who was there."

To illustrate, Guttersen said, "Some guys were brought into New Guy village for torture and we would never see them again. They either died or were taken elsewhere. Several who became mental cases were removed from the prison. Guards told us they had been taken away and that they died, but you can't believe that since some of those they said had died, showed up later in the System. Other prisoners might have been isolated for other, unknown reasons."

Such was the case of Bobby Joe Kieze who was held for years unknown to other prisoners until found by Guttersen.

During Guttersen's last week of captivity at the Hanoi Hilton, the Vietnamese allowed the POWs to walk in the prison yard during the day. One day Guttersen saw a guard carrying food to an isolated section of the prison. With his release nearing, Guttersen sensed he wouldn't be punished if he were caught off-limits, although it was not anything he would have dared attempt several years earlier. Waiting for the guard in the watch tower to turn his back, Guttersen ducked behind a bamboo fence and crept up on the isolated cell where he'd seen the guard take the food. To his astonishment, he saw a Caucasian, thin and pale, huddled in a back corner of the cell.

"Who are you? Are you an American?" Guttersen asked.

The man winced and drew back, too frightened to answer. "Tell me your name...are you an American?" coaxed Guttersen.

The man nodded shakily. "Yes," he whispered, darting glances around him. "I'm an American...a civilian... My name is Bobby Joe Kieze."

"How long have you been here?" Guttersen asked.

"Many months," muttered Kieze. "I've been in prison for five years."

Guttersen was the first American Kieze had seen during his imprisonment. He told Guttersen he had been captured with a group of civilians in Hue, then moved to Hoa Lo. He had tried to escape and was recaptured. The Vietnamese had pulled out his toe nails.

Looking down at the solitary prisoner's feet, Guttersen saw that he had no toenails. "My God, man don't you know we're going to be released in about a week?" he asked.

Kieze said he knew nothing about it. "Don't worry," Guttersen assured him, "we'll make sure the Vietnamese don't keep you behind. We'll let them know we know you're here."

Guttersen went back to his cell block and reported his finding to Colonel John Flynn, the ranking POW, and together they went to the prison administrators and raised an uproar, demanding that Kieze be permitted to associate with the other prisoners.

Kieze was subsequently united with the others and was released during Operation Homecoming.

"The point is," said Guttersen, "there was no 'System.' That's one of the big problems in understanding this whole thing. Americans want to think of things in terms of the way they would do them. In America, if we were keeping prisoners, someone would draw up regulations and all the prisoners would be processed in a similar fashion, but it's not done that way in Communist countries. There is no systematic way of doing things; the people in charge locally can do whatever the hell they feel like doing on the basis of what's best for them."

Gaither added yet another example of the System's weakness. "The Vietnamese were quite successful in segregating us from prisoners in other camps. We had a group of guys brought up from the South who we later learned were being held in a camp which we thereafter called Camp Huey. We named it after a pilot, Ken Huey, who was put in that camp by mistake for a couple of days and then moved over to the prison with us. He told us about a group of fifty to sixty POWs in Camp Huey. It was the first we knew of it, despite our system of keeping track of everyone. These people at Camp Huey were totally isolated and it proved to me, in retrospect, that the Vietnamese could segregate us if they wanted to.

"I also remember an incident in which an Army major, Benjamin Purcell, escaped. We never heard from him again. We figured his escape was unsuccessful and that he had died. But at the end of the war he was released. The Vietnamese had held him in some little prison up in Laos. It just illustrates that our system was not foolproof."

Robert Garwood

Many returned POWs grant the possibility of Americans yet being held, but one returnee attests to having seen captive Americans in Southeast Asia long after Operation Homecoming in 1973.

The case of Robert Garwood is unusual. Captured on September 28, 1965, PFC. Garwood made national headlines when he returned to the U.S. in 1979, fourteen years later. Detained in North Vietnam after other Americans had been released, Garwood eventually became a handyman, and was allowed to travel the region around Hanoi doing odd jobs for the Vietnamese, but always under guard. Eventually, he was able to smuggle a message out and was released.

Upon his return, the Marine Corps charged Garwood with desertion and collaboration. During his 1981 court martial he was found innocent of desertion, but guilty of collaboration. He lost rank and all accrued back pay.

From the first day of his return, pending litigation precluded any debriefing by the DIA or State Department and for five years after his return he made no public statements about seeing other Americans in Vietnam. However, he broke his silence in an exclusive interview with a *Wall Street Journal* reporter, Bill Paul. In a front page article, on December 4, 1984, Paul detailed Garwood's account of having seen dozens of captive Americans still in captivity when he left Vietnam in 1979.

Paul and Garwood first met in September 1984 at Garwood's house in northern Virginia. Paul was a seasoned journalist with eighteen years as a *Journal* reporter. He had done his homework on the Garwood case and suspected the former Marine could have reliable information about Americans still being held by Vietnam. But Paul kept in mind the fact he was dealing with a convicted collaborator and retained a healthy skepticism.

It was an informal interview. Garwood offered Paul a cold beer, then stretched out on the couch. Paul sat in an armchair facing him. The reporter tempered his approach, letting Garwood make the first move. He wanted to judge the former POW's credibility, not only by what he said, but by how he said it. After all, it was Paul's credibility that would be on the line when the story was published.

Garwood seemed tentative. He said he was having second thoughts about being interviewed; he was hesitant to put himself back in the spotlight. Also he was afraid, he admitted, not for himself but for the men still in captivity. He couldn't know how the Communists would react to his disclosures.

Yet Garwood wanted to talk. Paul could see the confusion in Garwood's eyes and hear the sadness in his voice. The man had a festering psychological wound that needed cleansing, thought Paul, and he listened patiently as Garwood recounted the details of his capture, his years in Vietnam, and his delayed return.

"I thought I would be going home in 1973," Garwood said. "I heard the broadcasts of the names of the men who would be released. I kept listening for mine. It was only after it was announced that the release had been completed that I found out I wasn't going home. The Vietnamese just kept stringing me along. They tried to tell me that when the U.S. troops left Vietnam I would return to my family. According to the peace agreements, they said it would be soon. But it never happened. Then by 1975 they were saying, 'Upon normalization of relations between the U.S. government and Vietnam, you will return to your family,' It was just one excuse after another.

"They said whether I lived or died was totally up to me. Basically, they told me that if I failed to do what they said it would be no problem for them because the blood and bones of many foreigners had already enriched Vietnam. But, they said, there was no doubt in their minds that certainly one day normalization between the U.S. and Vietnam would take place and then there would be negotiations for the return of prisoners."

Paul asked why Garwood thought he'd been let go finally. "I guess it's because I made my presence known...that I was alive," Garwood answered. "They could not deny that I was there. The person I gave the note to was the one who took the note out. If he had destroyed it and just told someone he ran into a guy named Garwood, I doubt if anyone would have believed it."

Garwood had been released by the Vietnamese after he slipped a note, saying he was being held, to a Caucasian — a Finnish diplomat. The diplomat, whom Garwood saw in a hotel bar during an errand for the Vietnamese, passed the note on to the State Department.

During his last two years in Vietnam, Garwood had fixed trucks and done repair work for his captors. "I chose to work because my aim was to get out of Vietnam," he said. "That's what put me in that hotel that night. If I had refused to work I would still be sitting in a cell somewhere in Vietnam and no one would be the wiser."

Paul wanted to know why Garwood had decided to finally come forward.

Garwood explained that even though the Vietnamese had threatened him, he now felt compelled to talk. "I was under no uncertain terms threatened...if I said anything about anyone I saw while I was in Vietnam that I would have their blood on my conscience. But, I thought from the time I got out of Vietnam up until about a year ago that there was some kind of private negotiations going on with the Vietnamese... between the U.S. government and the Communists for the release of these people. In the meantime, the only thing I've seen leave Vietnam is bodies and bones...and I really got upset about it."

Paul had brought along a map of Southeast Asia; he spread it out on the coffee table and asked Garwood how many Americans he had seen and where he saw them. Garwood sat up, lit a cigarette, and paused a moment before answering.

"There were at least seventy Americans that I knew of in the late 1970s..." He pointed out four locations on the map indicating the prison camps at Bat Bat in Son Tay province, thirty-five miles northwest of Hanoi; Yen Bay, eighty miles northwest of Hanoi; a warehouse in Gia Lam, a suburb east of Hanoi; and a military complex he said was on Ly Nam De Street in Hanoi.

"Actually, I saw these Americans rarely... But between 1973 and 1975 I saw them more often than I did between 1975 and 1978. The times I did see them it was usually a shock to see other Americans, so the picture sort of stuck in my mind," Garwood explained.

Paul wanted to know if some of the prisoners could have been deserters captured after the fall of Saigon rather than legitimate POWs. Garwood said there was no doubt the men he'd seen before 1975 were POWs and he could only judge from the condition of those he'd seen after that, that they were captured before 1975.

"I'm going by condition," he told Paul. "I have no other way of knowing for sure."

Asked when he'd first seen the Americans, Garwood said it was in the fall of 1973 at Bat Bat. "I saw twenty or so Americans..." He was kept in a hut separately, he explained, and saw the Americans being escorted through the prison complex. "I would lay on my bamboo bed and hear the guards talking. They were always complaining about how much trouble the American POWs were. Claimed they were dirty."

"There were other times I saw Americans when I would hear guards talking; some guards bragged about holding the Americans. I also heard Americans speaking and recognized their accents."

The reporter said he had heard that prisoners were moved around a lot and asked Garwood's opinion. It was true, Garwood said, but there was no set pattern and was probably done for security.

"I remember one occasion in particular," he told Paul. It was a hot summer night in 1977 and he had been sent to fix a truck in the Yen Bay vicinity. At a railroad crossing, a train had stopped and unloaded a group of prisoners — some of them Americans who were being transported in boxcars.

"They had them so packed full of people that several of the Vietnamese prisoners had died of suffocation inside the boxcars. The other prisoners were taking the bodies off the boxcars and laying them ten to fifteen feet from the railroad tracks...just laying them on the ground. Someone gave the order down the line to open all the boxcars. I guess just to let them breathe. And that's when I saw the Americans."

There were between thirty and forty of them, Garwood said. All were speaking English and cursing about the heat. He described them as being clean-shaven and dressed in khaki work clothes. One man, he said, had only one leg; he was on crutches and was helped down by the others.

Some of the guards were young and apparently had never seen Americans before, Garwood said, because they were calling out, "Hey! Look at the Americans!"

In March 1978 Garwood was sent to Yen Bay to repair a generator at an island fortress that was part of the prison, he told Paul. During the day-and-a-half he was there, he said he'd seen about sixty prisoners, some of whom could have been in the boxcars months before. He wasn't allowed to speak to them. "They looked exhausted," he said, "but they didn't look starving. I didn't see any of them working. They were just walking around, wearing blue pajamas."

Garwood said he had also been sent to make repairs at the military complex on Ly Nam De Street in Hanoi and had seen Americans there. The building also served as headquarters for the People's Army and on the second floor were the offices of Colonel Phan Van Thai, vice commander of the military, and a recreational room.

The colonel directed Garwood to stay off the second floor, saying there were prisoners there, but didn't elaborate, and Garwood was determined to find out the prisoners' nationality.

"As I approached the second floor, one guard yelled at me, almost like he was in a panic," Garwood remembered. "As I stood there telling the guard that I just wanted to use the rec room, a head stuck out. It had a bearded face, deep sunken eyes and thinning hair. It definitely looked to be American."

Asked how how he could be certain the man was American, Garwood replied, "I told my guard and driver about the guards being so touchy and they did just what I wanted them to — they went to check it out. They found out that they were Americans — about seven of them. They had just been brought in from Cao Bang, near the Chinese border." Garwood theorized the Americans had been moved because of border skirmishes between the Chinese and Vietnamese.

The interview continued late into the night as Garwood went on with his disclosures. He recalled seeing prisoners in a warehouse at Gia Lam. The warehouse was on the Red River, one of a string of buildings. Five or six prisoners were there, he said, stacking, loading and unloading goods. It was from here that food, medicine, bedding and other supplies were distributed throughout the Vietnamese prison system. "These Americans were handpicked, what the Communists called model prisoners, less likely to get in trouble."

The model prisoners were shuffled in and out of Gia Lam every two weeks on a rotating basis, Garwood claimed. And this went on from 1973 until Garwood left in 1979, he said, adding that many times he heard the men speaking English and heard guards talking about the Americans.

Prisoners were divided into three categories, Garwood said. There were those who could work, those who couldn't, and the stubborn or incorrigible ones who wouldn't work.

Paul had listened carefully and he was prepared to believe Garwood, but not without double checking his stories. As if seeking clarification, Paul went over details of two of the sightings Garwood had described. He purposely interjected wrong details into the stories and each time Garwood caught the mistakes. Paul tried it again, repeating another story, but adding some inaccuracies. Again Garwood corrected him. Garwood's stories did not change. This man's uncanny memory is almost spooky, Paul thought.

The interview was beginning to wind down. Paul wanted to hear why Garwood felt these men had been withheld.

"For bargaining purposes," he answered, stretching out once more on the couch and blowing smoke toward the ceiling. "Like their ace in the hole. They were supposedly promised money for postwar reconstruction and they didn't get it."

But there might have been other reasons, Garwood said, which he explained by relating another incident. In the fall of 1977, he said, he spent several days in a Hanoi hospital being treated for a stomach ailment. During his stay he spoke with several Cubans and Palestinians who were on the same ward. They had become ill during a guerilla training program.

During three separate conversations the guerillas had described how Americans were used in their training. First, they said, they watched training films depicting Americans being captured. They were shown the Americans in the flesh and listened to them being interrogated or taking part in a mock press conference.

After his release from the hospital, Garwood said he had queried a Lt. Khoet, a propaganda officer, about the use of Americans in the guerilla training. "The way he put it to me is that the United States tried to build the image that the Americans are indestructible. They [the Vietnamese] are using the American POWs as guinea pigs for terrorists' groups...to show that Americans are only human, that we do suffer duress and strain. I guess the Vietnamese message was, 'We did it — so can you.' "

Asked if he thought the Communists — as he had known them after fourteen years — would ever admit they were holding Americans, Garwood said he couldn't be sure.

"This is what scares me," Garwood said softly. "There are still French prisoners of war in Vietnam. I've seen them working on a dairy farm on Mount Bavi."

Garwood had the full names, first and last, of two Americans he said were being held. He could also cite details of one of the men's shoot down, his capture, the extent of his injuries and the location of his detention. Garwood could offer only a smattering of other American prisoners' names he'd heard guards use. Some could have been first or last names.

Paul checked them against the roster of missing men. The men whose full names Garwood had mentioned were on the list. There were other possible match-ups.

Smith-McIntire Case

Like the Garwood story, the account by returned POW Mark Smith, a retired Army major, is unique. However, Smith's convictions about the existence of live American prisoners in Southeast Asia are substantiated by more recent information. Based on intelligence data he collected in Thailand and Korea between 1981 and 1984, Smith brought a lawsuit against the President of the United States and his cabinet members, charging that the U.S. Government has been negligent in effecting the release of Americans who are still captives of the Vietnamese.

Joining Smith in the class action suit was Army Sergeant Melvin C. McIntire who had served with Smith in the Special Forces Detachment Korea in Seoul.

Smith, captured and held in Cambodia in 1972, believed upon his release in 1973, that no American prisoners had been withheld by the Vietnamese. He first considered the possibility when he was introduced to intelligence information in 1981, while he was serving as his detachment's commander for an intelligence gathering operation in Korea. A Thai military officer, who claimed to have knowledge about American POWs, had approached him and inquired about the activities of Lt. Col. Bo Gritz who was in Thailand at the time, undertaking a private rescue mission for POWs. The Thai officer had assumed, incorrectly, that Smith's detachment was supplying support personnel to the Gritz operation.

Smith, eager to hear more, was briefed by the officer's staff and senior intelligence officer on known and suspected locations of U.S. prisoners of war. According to Thai reconnaissance teams, the POWs were being held in Laos.

Once skeptical, Smith was becoming more convinced with each report. After passing the information along to the DIA, Smith was instructed to seek additional information. From 1981 to 1984, Smith traveled to Thailand every two to three months to establish an agent net to gather intelligence data on the location and identification of Americans in Southeast Asia.

"This information was developed by talking with agents in the Thai military, the Lao resistance, the Pathet Lao, the free Vietnamese, gun smugglers, drug smugglers and anyone who could provide information," Smith explained. "By the early part of 1982, I and others were convinced that there were American prisoners of war who were being held against their will. I came to this conclusion by cross-checking the reports of approximately fifty different agents, the majority of whom had no knowledge of each other."

In January 1984, after three-and-a-half years of intelligence collection, Smith received a coded message from a Thai officer, instructing that three prisoners could be rescued from Laos in May of 1984. Again, Smith passed along the word to his senior officers. But much to his disappointment and confusion, the intelligence information was summarily dismissed, and the extraction never occurred. "When this information was passed on to a certain Army major and to the 501st Military Intelligence Group and to CIA stationed in Seoul, all Special Forces Detachment Korea operations to Thailand or to Southeast Asia were declared unauthorized and terminated," Smith said. "I was told that if I wanted to be a lieutenant colonel in the Army, I should forget about the POW/MIA information which had been reported to intelligence channels for the past three years. I was told in no uncertain terms that I should forget the matter." It was too controversial, too damning, their responses seemed to say.

Subsequently, in September 1984, Smith was reassigned to the 5th Special Forces Group, Fort Bragg, North Carolina, and three weeks later, he received mandatory retirement orders, effective February 1, 1985.

Sergeant McIntire, who had also been ordered back to the U.S. before his tour was to end, corroborated Smith's account. McIntire had had access to the same intelligence sources. "These sources had agents of their own in the field who were reporting on the general grid coordinates or locations where American POWs were being held. I learned of approximately 200 living Americans in Laos who were prisoners of war. I was being provided information in detail sufficient to identify the number of American prisoners of war being held in the general vicinity. I was also being told of the conditions under which they were being held." Those conditions, McIntire explained, included limited freedom — an offer some Americans had accepted to have a spouse and a chance to farm less than an acre of rice. Smith and McIntire also said they had the names of approximately forty of the prisoners.

Angry that the U.S. Government and military agencies explained away or discredited their intelligence data, Smith and McIntire filed a federal lawsuit under provisions of Title 22, United States Code, Section 1732, which requires that the President of the United States demand the release of any American citizens wrongfully imprisoned by a foreign government. The suit was filed in the United States District Court, Eastern District of North Carolina, on September 4, 1985.

Soon after the initial hearings began February 18, 1986, government attorneys moved to have the case dismissed, arguing that the U.S. Government had the exclusive power to determine whether American POWs were being held in Southeast Asia. Attorneys for Smith and McIntire countered that such a claim was excessive. Essentially, the court agreed. Presiding judge Terrence Boyle refused to dismiss the case.

But again, as the second round of hearings got underway on November 5, 1986, government lawyers asked that the judge reconsider his earlier order and dismiss the case. On June 24, 1987 Judge Boyle rejected the second motion to dismiss, allowing the lawsuit to proceed.

Air Force Col. Robert Standerwick parachuted from his F-4D over Laos on February 3, 1971. Standerwick is among the nearly 600 men lost over Laos for whom there has never been an accounting.

Navy Commander Harley Hall's F-4J was shot down over South Vietnam on January 27, 1973, just hours before the peace agreements were signed. Hall was last seen disengaging his parachute and running on the ground.

Army Sgt. Don Sparks, initially believed killed in action June 17,1969...until his parents received a letter from him written ten months later from a POW camp.

Civilian Charles Dean was captured in Laos in early September 1974. Intelligence sources reported him and his companion Neil Sharman to be alive in February 1975. The Pathet Lao takeover in August 1975, eliminated any further intelligence collection in the Dean and Sharman case.

Eugene DeBruin, left, is one of only two Americans photographed in captivity in Laos. DeBruin is pictured here in an enemy camp at Tha Pa Chon Village in 1964, along with (left to right) Pisidhi Indradat, Prasit Promsuwam, Prasit Thanee and To Yick Chiu.

The "Mortician," his face partially hidden to conceal his identity, testifies before the House Subcommittee on Asian and Pacific Affairs in Washington, June 27, 1980. Left, his interpreter, Col. Jean Sauvageot, State Department. The group behind includes family members of missing servicemen.

AP/Wide World Photos

Col. Earl Hopper (right) with Lao Ministry of Security officials at the crash site of an Air Force C-130 near Pakse, Laos. September 1982.
National League of Families Photo

The Gritz Team, just after court appearance in Nakhon Phanom, Thailand, March 11, 1983. Charged with illegal possession of a radio transmitter, all were fined $130 and given one-year suspended jail sentences. Left to right: Lance Trimmer, Gary Goldman, Scott Weekly, Lt. Col. (Ret.) "Bo" Gritz and Lynn Standerwick.

MIA/POW FAMILIES

On January 28, 1974, a year and a day after the Paris Peace Accords were signed, the Senate Foreign Relations Committee convened in a hearing room filled to overflowing. Seated at the raised concave platform, like a panel of judges, the senators leafed through three-inch-thick stacks of prepared statements and background data on the MIA/POW issue.

The audience spilled into the aisles and lined the walls of the hearing chamber. The influential committee was to discuss the issue of the missing men for the first time since the war's end. Many, if not most in the crowd, were families of missing servicemen. It was the families who had urged the senators to meet. The government, they charged, was prematurely abandoning its effort to account for those men still reported missing in Southeast Asia.

As the hearing was about to begin, one senator's chair remained unoccupied. Senator Claiborne Pell, noting the empty chair next to him, motioned to Earl Hopper, who stood near the side of the platform. "Mr. Hopper, move on up here and have a seat."

Hopper gratefully accepted the invitation and remained on the dais throughout the morning-long session. When the last witness had been heard and the session was adjourned, the briefing material intended for the absent senator still lay on the table in front of Hopper. He innocently scooped the papers into his briefcase and filed out with the crowd into the corridor.

Days later, at his home in Phoenix, Hopper sorted through the papers he had accumulated in Washington. Among the papers in his briefcase, usurped from the absent senator, was a document which would become known as "The Moose Memo." Written by a Senate staff member, Dick Moose, the memorandum briefed the senators on the background of the issue and recapped policy considerations. On the cover was the notation: "For Committee Use Only — Not for Publication."

Hopper scanned the memo and when he reached the concluding paragraph, he bristled with rage. It read:

"The North Vietnamese clearly have not fulfilled their obligations under Article 8(b) [of the Paris Peace Accords] and have violated other provisions of the agreements as well. But there have been violations on both sides. At this point U.S. policy seems to be to live with the imperfections of the agreement, rather than to seek a full implementation. This is where the MIA families are caught. No one wants to say to the families that we have done as much as is politically feasible or that the possibility of obtaining additional information must be weighed against other policy considerations. Many family members already know this, of course, but in the absence of unusual candor the cycle of hope, entreaty, assurance and frustration seems likely to go on forever."

For the families of missing men, that paragraph confirmed their worst fears...the government was abandoning their sons, husbands, brothers and fathers out of "policy considerations."

A year after the war's end the government was prepared to "live with the imperfections of the agreement" with the Vietnamese. The families were not, and their years of determination has since made them the focal point of the MIA/POW issue.

Having inherited the Vietnam conflict's most painful legacy, these families have struggled, in a constant race against time, to win a lonely, sometimes futile battle for truth about what happened to the men who never returned from Southeast Asia.

In the pages that follow, thirteen MIA/POW family members, armed with the belief that not all the prisoners came home after the Vietnam War, describe what life has been like on the front lines of the last lonely battle of Vietnam.

CHAPTER TWELVE
EARL HOPPER, SR.

My son, Earl, Jr., was one of the last MIAs to be declared dead; the Air Force changed his status from missing to killed in action on July 14, 1982. My wife and I had fought this change of status for over a decade because we were convinced that Earl had been alive on the ground after ejecting from his burning plane and had likely been taken prisoner.

Earl was lost in 1968 while flying an F-4 on a mission over North Vietnam. His flight was one of two which were protecting F-105s on a mission near the Hoa Lac MiG base northwest of Hanoi. After one of the F-105s hit the target, the F-4s butterflied out — Earl's aircraft circling to the left, waiting for the F-105 to come up and be escorted out of the danger area. The Vietnamese fired three surface-to-air missiles. Two went through the flight formation and exploded in mid-air, doing no harm. The third exploded about 100 feet below and to the right of Earl's plane, extensively damaging the fuel and hydraulic system. Earl and the craft's pilot, Captain Keith Hall, were able to climb to about 18,000 feet when both the right and left engines began flaming out. The aft end of the aircraft was catching on fire, going out, then catching on fire again.

The flight formation leader, Major Kenneth Lee, was in radio voice contact with Hall and ordered that both men bail out.

Hall later told me that Earl was having trouble with his ejection system and that Earl urged him to jump. Hall ejected at 18,000 feet; he established voice contact with the crew overhead and they picked up his beeper signal — the beeper is a small emergency radio which has two modes, automatic and manual. It can beep automatically, sending out a radio signal or it can be used to send and receive voice messages. At any rate, Hall was captured within twenty minutes after landing on the ground. Earl stayed with the aircraft for seven or eight minutes but was losing altitude. Just as the aircraft was going into cloud cover about 5,000 feet above ground, pilots of the other three aircrafts in the flight saw two objects leave the plane. One, we believe, was the canopy of the F-4; the other was Earl.

According to Hall, Earl was not injured by the initial explosion. Soon after the pilots saw the two objects leaving the plane, they picked up a second beeper which we believe was Earl's. They were never able to establish voice contact with him but picked up the beeper signals, which would have been sent manually since Earl's beeper was not automatic. Overhead planes continued to monitor the beeper for three consecutive days after the shootdown. On the second day, a pilot radioed, "Is that you, Lt. Hopper? If that's you . . . come back at fifteen second intervals." The pilot picked up the signal, being sent manually, every fifteen seconds.

All this leads us to believe that Earl had succeeded in ejecting from the aircraft and that he was alive on the ground. He was conscious enough to operate his beeper although we don't know if he was injured. We've never heard any more of him or from him except for something that happened in August of 1971. At that time, Captain Hall was taken from his cell and led to an interrogation room where the Vietnamese questioned him about Earl for nearly thirty minutes. They wanted personal information about him — marital status, his hometown and family background. We've never been able to determine the significance of that questioning which came two-and-one-half years after the shootdown.

In the early days, at least prior to the return of prisoners during Operation Homecoming in 1973, U.S. government officials told us families to be quiet about the missing men, to "not rock the boat." We were told not to tell anyone but our immediate family members that our relatives were missing. The government's position was that public information might endanger a captive's life or jeopardize the prisoners' eventual return. The military was not releasing the number of men lost, but as some of us began talking with other families, we became overwhelmed at how many MIA families existed. We were equally concerned about reports that known POWs were suffering, being tortured. We began meeting and once organized, we grew rapidly in strength and numbers. We incorporated the National League of Families in 1970.

Initially, I was the League's state coordinator for Arizona and in 1973 was elected to the League's board of directors. I served on the board until 1984. You'll find that the League has, for the most part, strongly opposed the government's policy and way of handling the effort to gain an accounting for the missing men. I think some of our statements over the years about POWs have been discounted because we were relatives, perceived as moms, dads and wives, who could not accept reality. Of course, for the families it has been an emotional issue, but, ten or fifteen years later, we're not operating out of emotion; we've traveled, researched, lobbied and in many ways become experts on Southeast Asia.

One of the biggest problems in resolving this issue, is the lack of U.S. intelligence efforts. My own background enables me to talk about intelligence work with some degree of authority. I'm a retired, thirty-year Army Colonel and worked in intelligence during the Korean War. I was an intelligence instructor in the U.S. intelligence school in Tokyo and have had Special Forces training. Early in the Vietnam conflict, I served as an advisor to the South Vietnamese Army. Prior to my retirement, my last assignment was serving as an intelligence advisor to the South Korean Army. I have long questioned why U.S. military intelligence or the CIA has not been able to prove or disprove that Americans are still being held captive. Ever since the refugees started coming out in 1978, saying they had seen live Americans, our intelligence community has not been able to totally confirm or deny these reports. This indicates a weakness. The bulk of the refugee sightings are quite accurate, with only a small percentage of fabrication. For example, a number of refugee reports were correlated to Bobby Garwood, the marine who was captured and then released fourteen years later. In other words, refugees were saying they had seen a man matching Garwood's description, and later, Garwood came out.

The Defense Intelligence Agency received reports about some sixty Americans trapped in the fall of Saigon. Refugee reports were correlated to these people. Other reports exist which have not been correlated to men returned. It suggests that some of those reports relate to Americans who could still be there now. The fact that these reports have not been thoroughly investigated signifies a weakness in the intelligence system.

Another example of weak intelligence efforts was evident when I traveled to Southeast Asia in June, 1981. The DIA asked me to look up the former driver for a South Vietnamese colonel and ask him ten questions to corroborate a story they'd received earlier. As a bit of background... in December of 1979, the League had gotten a letter from Colonel Trieu, a former South Vietnamese Army officer who had settled in France. He wrote that earlier in 1979, he had seen the same group of twenty-eight American prisoners on two separate days up near Tay Ninh, northwest of Saigon. In January of 1980, the DIA sent a team to France to debrief the colonel. He told his story but refused to be polygraphed, saying that polygraphs were for criminals and that as an Army officer he wouldn't submit to a lie detector test. However, to prove his story, he offered the name and address of his driver who had also seen the American prisoners. The driver was the man I was to locate in Saigon and question.

Here it was, eighteen months after the initial report from the colonel, and the DIA was asking me, a civilian father, to go interview a man whom our own intelligence people could have reached months earlier. In the end, we couldn't locate the driver. He had moved to another address.

All this caused me great concern. I scheduled a meeting with my state's U.S. Senator, Barry Goldwater, who was Chairman of the Senate Intelligence Committee. We met at Goldwater's home in Phoenix. When I expressed my concern about the weakness of our intelligence activity in Vietnam and Laos and our seeming inability to confirm or deny the existence of American prisoners, he said, "Earl, there are some countries in this world where our intelligence is not capable of operating. Unfortunately, Vietnam and Laos are two of those countries." I wasn't a believer of what Goldwater said. I knew we left some intelligence nets over there, people who simply needed to be activated. I've always wondered if our questions about American servicemen in Vietnam and Laos went unanswered because of a lack of capability or a lack of desire.

When I was visiting Washington in July of 1983, I met with two high-ranking intelligence officers. I mentioned to them my conversation with Senator Goldwater. One of them confirmed Goldwater's story. "I'm sorry, Earl," one of them told me, "the intelligence people we had over there were swept up. When the Communists came through, they located the intelligence agents and either killed them or put them in prison. Today we still have no covert capability over there." I asked several questions about why new intelligence nets weren't developed and why we can't even locate the 400 bodies the mortician talked about in 1980. Someone in Hanoi knows where they are. Someone had to transport them, move them and store them. I was angry, frustrated and disgusted. It was one of the most disappointing moments of my life. I lost more confidence in my government and I didn't have too much to start with.

A month later, in August of 1983, I had a private meeting with a State Department official. He was basically noncommital but implied the same thing, no capabilities. I still don't understand it. The president has said this issue is of highest national priority yet we have no intelligence capabilities? Something is not right. We need live, human agents in there on the ground to locate any POWs left behind, to give the president the proof he says he needs. Covert activities are the only reliable method of getting this proof. We can put a mole into the government of virtually any country in the world. We can penetrate the Kremlin, Peking, Great Britain or France . . . but I'm told we can't get into Vietnam or Laos. I don't believe it. I don't think the high priority expressed by the president has worked its way down the bureaucracy to the point where policy is implemented.

Because of this perceived lack of intelligence activity by the government, some of us families have set up our own intelligence networks. For example, in June of 1981, I went to Southeast Asia as a consultant to a humanitarian aid organization. During the visit, I went into Laos and Cambodia and met with members of the Khmer Rouge National Liberation Front, the anti-Communist resistance group under Son Sann in Cambodia.

We made arrangements for two teams to penetrate two areas in South Vietnam where we believed prisoners might be held. Each team consisted of four former South Vietnamese officers. The resistance leaders trained them; I helped organize and map out the plan. The effort cost $5,000. We instructed the teams to go to two locations. Both locations had been mentioned to me quietly by a member of the U.S. intelligence community. The teams were well trained and posed as civilians. They did not carry rifles or wear camouflage fatigues; we wanted them to blend with the local population.

We gave them cameras, making it clear that they had to come out with pictures of prisoners — that was the only proof we would accept. Unfortunately, they made the mistake of putting the cameras in their rice sacks. Rice collects moisture; the film was ruined. Although they could not furnish photos, we know the teams reached their target. They did find a highly secure area near one of the targets, but because local police were starting to get suspicious, they didn't want to risk penetrating the area.

The mission was important because it proved the capability of conducting covert missions in Vietnam. I offered the capability to the DIA but they couldn't act on it. I understand that because they are strictly an intelligence agency. Their charter does not call for covert operations overseas. DIA has to ask CIA to conduct covert missions. So, I tried for six months to meet with the CIA people. Finally, a DIA representative who had talked to CIA officials told me that a CIA figure had said to him, "If we met with Col. Hopper, he would probably be more frustrated than he is now."

Without greater intelligence capabilities we have no way of verifying various reports which have surfaced over the years. For example, I received a report in the fall of 1983 from a Vietnamese man who travels regularly to Paris, where he often meets with Communist government officials who travel between Hanoi and Paris. He is not a Communist but is friendly with some Communist leaders. He told me that in the summer of 1983, one of the Communist officials reported the movement of some American prisoners westward, from Hanoi toward the border of Laos. About a month later, another Hanoi official reported the same thing. I cannot verify these reports but it's this kind of continued flow of information that makes me believe there's a basis of truth in these accounts.

The continued movement of prisoners by the Vietnamese presents the biggest obstacle to locating them. Even the returned prisoners will tell you they were moved around. I have two thoughts on where the Vietnamese may be keeping men. One place is off the southern tip of Vietnam on Con Son Island; men could be kept in the old underground "tiger cages" where the South Vietnamese used to keep prisoners. The island is secure, no refugees are coming and going. By being placed underground, prisoners couldn't be photographed by satellites.

My second theory is that the Vietnamese may have moved prisoners into Laos where they're held under Vietnamese control. Consequently, the Lao can say that its government is not holding prisoners and the Vietnamese can say they are holding no prisoners in Vietnam. Neither side addresses the fact that Americans could be held in Laos by the Vietnamese. Therefore, technically, each side is telling the truth, but only a half-truth.

I don't know if the MIA/POW issue will ever be resolved in my lifetime. In theory, it should be resolved through government to government negotiations but both sides' policies are so set in concrete I doubt that either country will budge. Both the U.S. and Vietnamese governments rhetorically tell us that this is a humanitarian issue and should not be connected to politics. They refer to it as a unilateral issue; however, both sides tie geopolitics to it. The Vietnamese do not trust the U.S. Government any more than we trust the government in Hanoi.

When you look at the Vietnamese viewpoint, you'll see they have some valid points. President Nixon and Henry Kissinger secretly promised the Vietnamese 3.25 billion dollars in reconstruction aid, knowing at the time the promise would never be fulfilled. The Nixon promise was an act of deceit which, I'm sure, served to harden the position of the Vietnamese. The Vietnamese probably kept some of the POWs as insurance that they would eventually get some form of aid from the U.S. I doubt they'll hand over any of our men out of kindness.

We have to try to look at it through the eyes of Asians, although I don't think we'll ever understand the Oriental mind. Impose the Communist ideology on the Vietnamese and they don't even understand each other. The Vietnamese continually tell us they don't like our government, but they respect the American people and are concerned about public opinion. They are offended by public criticism and feel we've slandered them regularly. So, if any prisoners are brought out, it may have to be through some private means. I don't see it happening through the governments. The

U.S. won't take the first step nor will the Vietnamese. The League has asked that we send a negotiator to Vietnam and Laos to negotiate for these men. We're told the atmosphere is not conducive for negotiations. Well, damn it, it hasn't been conducive for the past ten years. Why can't we sit down with these people and talk? Why don't we make the effort? What price do we put on human life? Aren't these men valuable enough that we can swallow some pride? We got beat in Vietnam, not militarily, but politically.

My government tells me my son's life is not worth $250,000. In past years several family members have asked the government to offer $250,000 cash for every American returned alive, with no questions asked and with no U.S. condemnation of Vietnam or Laos. Our government has refused, explaining it's against U.S. principles to pay for men. I wonder how these government officials can explain those principles to the prisoners who eventually return. The country spends over a quarter of a million dollars to train a man, why not pay to get him back? I didn't agree with the government policy on the reward money, so when I was in Vietnam in September of 1982, I told officials in Hanoi I would guarantee them $250,000 for every American returned. I got no response except a surprised look and a statement that they held no Americans. Still, there's a chance some Communist will defect, bring a prisoner out and ask for a reward. I hope so. They're easily corrupted. They'll do anything for the dollar. Even if ten or twenty prisoners were brought out, I can get the money. No problem on the money. In the meantime, what's happening? The men who are left over there are dying off. How many died last week? How many will die next month?

Capt. George D. MacDonald
U.S. Air Force
Lost: December 21, 1972
Laos

CHAPTER THIRTEEN
JEAN MacDONALD

Varying reports describe how my son George was lost. I'm not too concerned over which account of the shootdown is most accurate. What's important is that I know my son was captured. I saw a picture of him. It's a bizarre story.

George was one of sixteen men on board an AC-130, known as the Spector 17. One Air Force report indicates the plane took a direct hit from ground fire and exploded in mid-air. Another Air Force report says the plane, after being hit near the right wing, came in on a slow slide, landing in an area between Pakse and Saravan, Laos. Two crew members were rescued, but after a one-mile radio search of the crash site, no other crewmen were found.

The report also mentioned open parachutes were found at the site and beeper signals were picked up in the vicinity. I put stock in the latter report since I later had contact with an airman who had been stationed with my son at Ubon Air Force Base in Thailand. This officer was in the first chopper to arrive at the crash site. He told me it was a bright, moonlit night and that the ground was covered with open parachutes and strobe lights. The airwaves were so full of beeper signals he couldn't count them all. His crew took photos of the site and continued on their mission.

Nearly two years after my son's plane crashed, in September of 1974, Reverend Paul Lindstrom of Chicago called me and said he had been contacted by two Asians who said they had information about my son. They explained that if I wanted the information, which they said included a photo, fingerprints and a letter, I would have to meet them in Mexico City. I was sixty-three then, still having complications from open heart surgery and really in no shape to be traveling, but a team of horses could not have stopped me from making the trip. People from my church paid my expenses and Reverend Lindstrom accompanied me.

Lindstrom was active in the MIA/POW issue. He had earlier gained international attention with his efforts to get the North Koreans to free the men aboard the American spy ship Pueblo. Through these efforts, Lindstrom developed numerous contacts, some he says, from Communist and Third World countries. He got the information about my son from one of his contacts at the Chinese embassy in Algeria in early 1974. His sources showed him a list of POWs who they said were being held in China. Because Lindstrom was from my area and knew me, he inquired about George. The source said he had proof of George's captivity and that Lindstrom would be contacted. It was September of 1974 before he got the call for me to go to Mexico City. Both Lindstrom and I were skeptical. We didn't know the identities of the two Asians we were supposed to meet nor did we know if they would show up. We also felt if they did appear they would demand a large sum of money for any news about my son. But it was worth a try.

Lindstrom and I proceeded on to Mexico City and met with the two Asians. I think they were probably Pathet Lao. They looked like twins, both dressed in black suits and white ties. They spoke good English and sounded well educated. They did, indeed, produce a picture of my son George. When I saw it, I started shaking, my whole body was trembling. In the photo, George was being held up by two other Caucasians whom we could not identify; he was in the middle with his arms around their necks. George and the other men looked awful. George looked malnourished, thin and pale. He was losing his hair before he was captured, but in this picture he had only a little fuzz on his head. He had a long, stringy beard. Two Orientals were standing off to the side of George. The dark background behind the men suggested they may have been standing in the mouth of a cave. The photo was a 5 x 7, in black and white and was torn off at the bottom.

The two Asians allowed me to look at the picture for only about five minutes and then said if I wanted to keep it I would have to pay them $25,000. I wanted that photograph so badly. I said, "Can I please have a copy of it? If you know where my son is, my government can meet with you and give you whatever your demands are but you must deal with them since there's no way I can give you that kind of money." They told me the photo was "one step on the way to recovering your son" and said they would contact me later. They also mentioned the picture had been taken three months before I saw it. If that was true, it would have been taken about twenty-one months after George was captured.

Even though I was terribly shaken at seeing my son in that condition, so miserable looking, I tried to study the photo carefully. I had learned a lot about photography from my dad, who was a journalist. I knew things could be staged. I tried to look for props or other clues in the picture. The bottom of the photo had been crudely torn off. I wondered if George had lost a foot or if the photo had been set up, taken from above with the men lying down. If they were on their backs, the bottom of the photo could have been torn off so their feet wouldn't show.

My other horrible thought was that the photo could have been taken after George died. He could have been dead in the picture although his eyes were open, and he appeared to be alive. It was a frightening experience. While in Mexico, I talked to an Associated Press reporter. He took a statement from me and the story hit AP wires across the United States.

When I returned from Mexico, Frank Sieverts, a Special Assistant to the Deputy Secretary of State, called me and was infuriated over the publicity about my experience and the photo of

George. I've never been so intimidated in all my life. He said, "I told you before you were too ill to be traveling around. That's our job. How dare you go to Mexico City." I tried to explain that I had to go to see if these Asians could actually produce a photo of my son and possibly other information. He continued to criticize me. I finally replied, "I'll be damned. You're my servant, not my master. You're ordering me about as though I'm in a slave state." Anyway, I tried to get the government to investigate and try to track the two Asians in Mexico City. To my disappointment, the government refused to question me or investigate the episode.

The only other strange incident that may be related had to do with a phone call I got several months later. A man with a foreign accent called, saying he had a letter for me from my son. He said, "We have a letter in our possession from your son to you and in it he speaks of the good times with Beer Rabbit." I can only guess he meant Brer Rabbit. I did tell my son Brer Rabbit stories when he was little, but that didn't prove there was actually a letter from George. Nothing else ever came from that phone call. If the man had a letter from George, he would have demanded money for it. I don't know if the call was from one of the men who had the photo of my son.

Assessing what has happened, we need to realize how our missing servicemen have been neglected so those serving their country in the future don't experience this betrayal. I'm patriotic; I love my country and am steeped in its traditions. One of my ancestors signed the Declaration of Independence. I'm proud of that. But it's a stain in our history if our government doesn't make every possible effort to recover its fighting men, alive or dead. I remember the Korean War and reports of Americans being left behind then. I can't believe it happened again, in Vietnam. The Reagan administration has made some progress.

We families and concerned citizens have worked for years staging rallies and launching public awareness campaigns, but our progress has been slow. Just look at the years that have passed since these men were captured. Some were lost in the 1960s. It's a tremendous emotional strain on families. There's no other tension like it. I try to put my complete trust in God. As a human, it's too much for me to handle by myself. I have awakened in the night screaming, having nightmares — visions of my son being held in a bamboo cage, being tortured. That's too much for me to cope with. I've told other family members, "We can't become hostile about this, we can't let our emotions get in the way. We just have to keep our faith." I may look calm but inside I'm not. I've had two heart surgeries, seven by-passes, and am due for more surgery. I imagine there's a relationship between the stress and my physical condition.

I hope my work on this issue will help protect families of the future. I've chronicled my research and hope someday to publish it, to get the story out so this kind of thing won't happen again. I've always believed that somewhere under this dark mess there's that great light of truth. I just hope to God that time is not far away when we'll get the answers. I try to work to purify things, to make it better for coming generations. Otherwise, what's the value? You can't be selfish about it . . . but I'd love to find out what happened to my son.

Eugene H. DeBruin
Civilian
Lost: September 5, 1963
Laos

CHAPTER FOURTEEN
JERRY DeBRUIN

I have worked for over twenty years to learn the fate of my brother Gene who was captured in Laos in 1963. He was known to be a prisoner for years and could very well be alive today.

Gene was a civilian, and had been in Laos for only one month when his plane went down. He was an air freight specialist on board an Air America C-46 and was on a typical rice-dropping mission, dropping sacks of rice and buffalo meat to refugees below, when the plane strayed over Pathet Lao territory and was shot down near Tchepone. The two pilots were supposedly killed but Gene and four other navigators managed to parachute safely. However, once on the ground, they were captured. Good friends of mine were on the attempted rescue mission. They were able to land briefly at the crash site and observed the rice sacks and blood-strewn buffalo meat about the wreckage but Gene and the others had already been led away. The rescue team could stay at the site only a few minutes; it was hostile territory and they were forced to take off. It was weeks before the Pathet Lao acknowledged the shootdown and identified the captives as Gene, three Thais — Pisidhi Indradat, Prasit Promsuwam, Prasit Thanee — and To Yick Chiu, a Chinese.

Two years later, two other Americans were captured and imprisoned with Gene and his crew. They were Air Force Lt. Duane Martin, captured in December of 1965, and Navy Lt. Dieter

Dengler, captured in January of 1966. Eventually, Dengler and one
of the Thais escaped and returned home. They have since provided
me with much information about my brother and his years in captivity.

My brother is one of only two American prisoners ever
photographed in captivity in Laos. The other is Air Force Col.
David Hrdlicka, also still missing, whose picture appeared in the
Moscow newspaper *Pravda*. The picture of Gene and his four
crewmen was taken in 1964 in Tha Pa Chon village, near one of
seven prisons that I know to be in that area.

I'm not sure why the photo was ever taken, but one theory
suggests it was taken as a precursor to eventual release, to show the
prisoners and acknowledge that they were being treated well. You'll
notice in the picture, the men appear healthy, their clothes are clean,
although military analysts I've talked to don't understand why Chiu
was wearing different clothes; the others were dressed alike. Analysts have looked at the photo for hand signals and feet positions to
see if anyone was trying to send a coded message, although I can't
say that we've interpreted any particular message. An American
intelligence team found the photo in a cache of supplies in Xieng
Khoung village in northern Laos. It had been published in a Pathet
Lao underground propaganda leaflet, "La Lutte Du Peuple Lao,
Contre L'Agression Des Imperialists Americans," in February of
1965.

Gene and his four crewmen were taken from village to village during the first three years of their captivity. Later, when Martin and Dengler joined them, all seven continued to be shuffled from
one prison to another. As I've talked to the two guys who returned,
I've been fascinated by stories of things they did for self and group
preservation and how they developed survival techniques. For
example, they would use vines as dental floss and store extra food,
such as rice, in bamboo tubes, little things to help them get along.

Gene also did some extraordinary things to improve his eye-
sight. He wore glasses but had lost them so for eight hours a day he

would stare at the outlines of tree leaves to strengthen the ciliary muscles in his eyes. Some medical evidence supports the claim that it is possible to strengthen those muscles in the eye. According to Indradat, Gene lost four front teeth, biting into buffalo hide, trying to get nutrients from the inside flesh. Dengler told me Gene was thin, didn't keep his weight up during the years he was in captivity. Food was scarce. Gene and the others suffered from dysentery and attacks of malaria.

Gene received one package during his captivity. It was from Air America and contained anti-dysentery medicine and other drugs. He received one letter from home, out of hundreds that were sent. It was a postcard which he reportedly carried in his back pocket throughout his imprisonment. It was like his one link to home.

Gene was known as the peacekeeper in the group; he was even-tempered, taking one day at a time. Although the seven were close, they had their spats. Lying on their backs, with their arms and legs tied down in irons for hours at a time was frustrating, if not torturous. Dengler told me Gene didn't get too uptight about things; he was able to cope. Dengler, on the other hand, was high strung. His first thought was always escape at any cost.

I've heard many stories about their escape attempts which were always planned in intricate detail. Prior to an attempt, they would save all their urine and later pour it at the base of the support posts in their cells. With enough moisture, Gene and Prasit Promsuwam could loosen the posts in preparation for escape.

The first attempted escape was in 1964, shortly after their capture. They pulled off the escape but made the mistake of escaping during the dry season and were soon recaptured. The Pathet Lao simply surrounded every water hole and waited for the thirsty escapees. They were free for about three days. An intelligence source later told me an elderly farmer had betrayed the five and tipped off Pathet Lao troops. The big escape came in 1966. All seven fled the prison and met on a hillside in southern Laos. They could not all go the same direction, so they decided to split up. Martin and Dengler went one direction and encouraged Gene to go with them. The three Thais were to go another direction. That left the Chinese, Chiu, who had become ill. When I later interviewed Indradat, he said Chiu had "big balls," indicating infection, and he had trouble walking. He would be left alone to die. I'm told the seven had quite a discussion over what to do. After years of being together, they didn't want to leave Chiu behind. Gene chose to be the one to stay with Chiu. He encouraged the others to go ahead; he and Chiu would wait for help. Gene told the others he would strip the white, inside bark from a banana tree and place it in the shape of an "X" on the side of a hill. If the others made it to safety, the "X" would pinpoint Gene and Chiu's location.

Indradat told me the last time he saw Gene was on the mountain where the seven had met. I don't know if the signal with the tree bark was ever put in place. When an air crew made a search of the area, they found no white "X."

As the others continued on their way, the three Thais got into a fight over which way to go. Indradat split from Promsuwam and Thanee and wandered through the jungles for forty-five days before collapsing from fatigue and dehydration. The Pathet Lao recaptured him and put him in prison with fifty other political prisoners but a planned raid eventually led to his release. To my knowledge, nothing has ever been heard from the other two Thais.

Dengler and Martin were approaching a village to look for food when Martin was macheteed to death. One report I've received says Martin said hello to a little Lao girl along the trail. An elderly man who thought Martin was going to molest the child ran toward him with a machete and with one swift blow severed his head. Dengler took off in the other direction and was later spotted from the air. Dengler, in the terms of those who rescued him, "lucked out." He was almost dead when he climbed onto a large rock in a stream. The crew overhead spotted him because his dark beard contrasted with the light color of the rock. Dengler tells another version of the story. He told me he found an old white parachute, tore it into the shape of an S.O.S. and placed it on the side of a mountain so a chopper could spot it.

I'm still in limbo about my brother's fate. The U.S. government contends nothing has ever been heard about Gene or Chiu. In 1976, Sonny Montgomery's commission concluded that Gene died in his 1966 escape attempt. I've received five different reports about what happened to my brother . . . reports of how and when he died. None has been verified. It's hard to believe the authenticity of most of them. The most valid one, however, was a report that Gene was tied to a tree in Muong Nong village and remained there from the latter part of 1966 through all of 1967. Then, according to villagers, in January of 1968, shortly before the Tet offensive, Gene and five other Air Force prisoners were taken northward to Hanoi.

The villagers said a North Vietnamese officer named Ong Lui told them the prisoners were being taken away for training. The U.S. government does not consider the 1968 report credible since it did not come from a U.S. source. Nonetheless, when I heard that Gene may have been sent to a camp with other American captives, I decided to contact all the returned POWs to see if they had known of him. In the POW camps, prisoners had developed an intricate communication system and passed names of those known to be in the prison system, as a way of record keeping. I wrote to 594 returnees, getting a seventy-two percent response. Most said they had never seen Gene but had heard of his escape — that was common knowledge. One said, "We didn't see him but heard a lot about him." I was glad to get such a good response from the returned POWs. They took time to write.

In 1971, I traveled to Vientiane, Laos to visit Soth Phetrasi, a Pathet Lao leader. I showed him the photo of Gene and the others in prison and said, "Your people took this photo and published it. I've come half way around the world just to ask you if he's alive." Phetrasi said he was very familiar with the case. "I know of your brother, but do not have any information because American bombs disrupt our communication lines." That ended our conversation.

Phetrasi recommended I talk to the people at the North Vietnamese Embassy. A senior ranking official at the embassy was cordial but told me, "Tell your parents that war brings many tragedies and that many North Vietnamese parents do not know the fates of their loved ones." I left the embassy broken-hearted.

The typical line of the Lao or the Vietnamese is that they have no information or hold no records. I've found the contrary to be true. In many cases they have kept meticulous records and I'm sure they could tell us more about the hundreds of men missing in Laos than they would lead us to believe. I'm also aware that the Lao do not like to lose face. The most uncomfortable situation for a Lao is to be backed into a corner. Their behavior becomes very uncharacteristic if they are pressed for information.

To illustrate their knowledge of American prisoners, specifically Gene's case, I got a report from a Lao official as late as September of 1982. During a visit to Laos by a delegation from the National League of Families, Colonel Khamla Keophithoune approached ABC reporter Ron Miller who was traveling with the League, and out of the blue told him he had news about Gene DeBruin. He read from documents as he told Miller that Gene had died in the summer of 1982. Miller tried to glance at the document but was unable to get a close look at the paper. I'm guessing the news offered about Gene may have been prompted by my inquiries in London the previous spring, when I visited the Lao Embassy, the North Vietnamese Embassy and Amnesty International. This was the last report I've had about Gene . . . that he lived until the summer of 1982.

I base my involvement in Gene's case and the MIA/POW issue on a Gestalt model. It goes in cycles of awareness, excitement, action and withdrawal. I'll reach a new level of awareness, get more excited, then take action and eventually withdraw. Each cycle brings greater awareness of myself and others. I've withdrawn a number of times to reflect. Many withdraw to rest for a period and then jump back into it. Others withdraw permanently, saying life is for the living. I've come to expect myself to go through these stages; I see it as a natural process and an integral part of my life.

I have a great deal of love and respect for the people who have helped me find information about Gene over the years and also for the other families who struggle to know the whereabouts of loved ones. I admire the work of other families who, in some cases, have developed their own sophisticated intelligence networks. Certain families have acquired information the government has not had. The families had a valuable East German source at one time; their having that contact, I think, caused the U.S. government some consternation. Information must be gathered very cautiously. It's easy to make an inference. Without hard data, it's easy to get off course. You have to be careful about letting your personal feelings creep in. After two decades, I can deal with Gene's case more objectively.

Some day my family will learn of Gene's fate. Many people would say he's surely dead by now but I won't believe that. Look at how many years others have lived in captivity. Plus, my brother was a civilian and many civilians are in foreign prisons right now. You only have to refer to the case in which the Chinese held Americans Richard Fecteau and John Downey for twenty years, after the Korean War.

I'll not stop working to find out what happened to my brother Gene. I love him and will always remember one thing he did which represented his love for me. Gene had gone to the University of Montana at Missoula and graduated with a degree in forestry. He worked as a smoke jumper, fighting forest fires by air, before going to work for Air America in Southeast Asia. For three years after high school, I just played baseball, farmed and worked construction. Gene, at that time, was still at the University of Montana. He encouraged me to go to college. He said, "I have about $350.00 in my bank account . . . but if you need it you're welcome to it and you can pay it back any time in the next zillion years." I used the money to go to college and eventually got a Ph.D. I can't forget a brother like that.

Sgt. Peter R. Cressman
U.S. Air Force
Lost: February 5, 1973
Laos

CHAPTER FIFTEEN
ROBERT CRESSMAN

Air Force officials told our family that my brother Pete was killed instantly when his plane crashed in Laos. Apparently they lied. Five years later they told us he had been taken prisoner.

Pete was assigned to a security service detachment at the U.S. Air Base in Udorn, Thailand. He and seven members of his flight crew were on a mission over Laos, flying an EC-47, an electronics warfare surveillance plane. During the night, the aircraft was reportedly shot down, although the cause of the crash was never officially determined. The pilot had reported anti-aircraft fire in the area, but then gave an all clear sign. Five minutes later, the ground base lost radar contact with the aircraft. Ground control heard nothing more from the crew. My family was notified the next day that the plane had gone down, was being considered a combat loss and that everyone on board was considered missing in action.

About seventeen days later, the Air Force sent a chaplain and an officer to my parents' house to report that the EC-47 had been located just outside Saravan, Laos, and that all the crew had perished in the crash.

Five years later, in 1978, we got a call from the National League of Families' attorney, Dermot Foley in New York City, telling us about forthcoming information on my brother's case. Columnist Jack Anderson had uncovered some classified documents which showed that four of the eight crew members of the EC-47 had survived the crash and were taken prisoner by the Pathet Lao or the North Vietnamese.

The documents indicated that U.S. intelligence had intercepted radio transmissions by the Pathet Lao as they talked about four American pilots captured near the crash site. The first enemy radio intercept from the day of the crash read, "Group is holding four pilots captive and the group is requesting orders concerning what to do with them." The fourth and final intercept about the four men was monitored in May. So, the men were known to be in captivity for at least three months.

Also, it was reported to me by several confidential sources that about thirty days after the shootdown, a Lao provided U.S. intelligence with detailed descriptions of the four captives. The four were identified as Sgt. Peter Cressman, Sgt. Dale Brandenburg, Sgt. Joseph Matejon, and Sgt. Todd Melton. Anderson informed the Air Force that he intended to go to press with the story. That's when the Air Force notified my parents.

Up to then, my parents and I had basically believed what we had been told by the military. We knew men were lost in wartime, but always had a faint ray of hope that Pete might have been alive since only one body was recovered from the crash. When we learned that Pete had been taken prisoner and was not killed in action, I exploded with emotion. I was enraged to find we had not been given the known truth about my brother. In addition to my anger, I began to develop a strong curiosity about the kind of justification made to withhold the truth.

I have speculations why the families of the four men were not notified that their relatives were taken captive. First, it was during a time when the U.S. was negotiating with North Vietnam for the release of POWs who were later released during Operation Homecoming. The EC-47 incident could have jeopardized those negotiations. It may have come down to "let's not rock the boat." Another theory has to do with my brother's questioning the legality of his mission. Pete had gone to the base legal office and told an Air Force legal representative that he was concerned about continuing intelligence missions over Laos since the missions were in direct violation of at least one of the articles in the Paris Peace Accords which had been signed on January 27, 1973. When Pete's personal effects were shipped home we found a draft of a letter he had written to a congressman. The letter, outlining his concerns, would have been written between January 27 and February 5, 1973:

> *Dear Sir,*
>
> *On January 26th I read the headlines which hailed the "Peace with honor" agreement, only to wake the next morning to find my situation the same as the day before as though nothing had changed in Southeast Asia.*
>
> *Feeling that I must have missed some of the small print of the agreement, I again read it and found that I had not overlooked anything that was on the printed page. It was then that I realized that I and the others of my unit were in violation of an agreement which I consider to be an order from the Commander in Chief of the Armed Forces of the United States.*
>
> *The impact of this realization was quite intense for me. Not only do I feel that it is morally wrong to participate in activities which may jeopardize a peace which took twelve years to reach, but also because I feel I may be participating actively in an illegal military mission.*
>
> *This thought brought back a memory of another military man who was in a similar situation and made the choice to dutifully carry out his orders even though there was a question of their legality. This man was Lt. William Calley.*
>
> *Not wanting to risk the possibility of being indirectly responsible for the possible results of the orders I am under, I went to seek advice of the base legal office. There I was informed of the consequences for refusing to carry out the*

orders which I consider to be illegal as well as immoral. These consequences instilled in me a fear which has caused me to abandon any thoughts of refusing to obey these illegal orders.

The truly sad part of this situation is that I wonder how many other "Lt. Calleys" there have been because of the same fear that I feel now . . . that fear of being punished for doing what his mind and soul tells him is right.

I regret that I cannot give you any specific details of my unit's violations due to the classification of my work. However, in general terms, violations have been made against (the Peace Agreements) Chapter II, Article 2; Chapter II, Article 3, paragraph A; Chapter II, Article 4; Chapter VII, Article 20, paragraph A; Chapter VII, Article 20, paragraph B.

Perhaps the most disheartening fact is that ever since I entered school and later the military, I have been taught that because of American's firm beliefs in truth and justice we did not break our national promises. However, now I find myself involved in just such an act.

I gratefully appreciate any assistance you can render to help eliviate [sic] this situation for the American servicemen for whom the war has become more frightening. . .for now he has yet another enemy to meet: his conscience.

Yours truly,

Peter R. Cressman
Sgt. United States A.F.S.S.
Det 3 6994 Security Sqdn.
Ubon, RJAFB
A.P.O. San Fran 96304

If my brother was considered a whistle blower and came up missing, someone may have asked the question, "How badly do we want this guy back?" A couple others on his flight, I've been told, also voiced similar objections to the mission.

I can understand how servicemen become missing in a time of war. I know that certain lost individuals can never be found. But what annoys the hell out of me is the fact that the military deliberately lied about this case. Moreover, when confronted with the facts, they had no comment or refused to change policies about notification of families on the fates of missing men.

As a result of the new information about my brother being captured, my family started digging deeper into the case. We've found discrepancies over the years. For example, when we first asked for photos of the crash site, my parents received a letter from Air Force Casualty saying, "We have researched all possibilities in an attempt to locate a photo of your son's crash site and find that none exists." A few months later, I again requested any photos available of the crash site — this time under the Freedom of Information Act. Eight days later I received a packet of fifteen photos which had been declassified. They included high altitude photographs, taken from rescue helicopters which originally surveyed the crash site. I understand the need for classification of documents, but the mishandling of case information is difficult for families, already tormented by the unknown whereabouts of a loved one. With all the changing information, I began to feel like a ping pong ball . . . first my brother was dead . . . then he was captured . . . first there were no photos . . . then there were.

Discrepancies also exist in reports about the investigation at the crash site. We heard that the Air Force didn't find the EC-47 until two days after the crash and that it was four days before a search team made it to the site. However, in the summer of 1982, a retired Air Force Sergeant read an article my mother had written about Pete and the EC-47 incident. He asked to come talk to us, explaining that he had been on the flight line the morning of the crash. He said that right after dawn several helicopters came in and their crews reported being on the crash site. I had no reason to doubt what he had said, but yet I wanted documentation. I started digging back through reports we had collected on my brother's case, and ran across one dated February 5, 1973. It said, "EC-47, Baron 52 (code name) has been located forty-five nautical miles southeast of Saravan, Laos. Aircraft appears to be a combat loss." The document simply verified that a search team found the wreckage the same day it went down, not two days later.

I think if my brother is alive today he's in Russia or China. I'm convinced prisoners were moved to China or Moscow. I've seen reports of prisoners being moved there for interrogation. If my brother's captors had had any awareness of what kind of plane the EC-47 was, I think the crewmen would have been taken somewhere like Peking or Moscow for an intense interrogation. The EC-47 was carrying extremely classified intelligence equipment which the U.S. government would not want to fall into enemy hands. In fact, the plane was designed to explode on impact, destroying everything aboard.

This one, however, did not explode immediately. It figures the enemy would be interested in what the four crewmen could tell them. But if they were sent to China or Russia, I don't think there's a snowball's chance in hell of getting them out. They could have been shipped up to Kalima in northern Siberia to a labor camp where they would eventually die. On the other hand, some Americans may have been detained to maintain and operate the millions of dollars' worth of technical equipment U.S. forces left behind.

Some of the men left behind in Southeast Asia have a good chance of returning if the U.S. government presses the matter. To date, the government has been slow to act on the problem, despite the eyewitness accounts of refugees who say they've seen Americans. I've spent thirteen years as a law enforcement officer and I know if I took existing information into a courtroom, a jury would conclude that live Americans are still being held. The evidence is monumental. The government has, at least, upgraded its policy to now say it doesn't rule out the possibility that Americans are still being held. That's a big turnaround from the 1970's when the policy was that no Americans were still imprisoned in Southeast Asia.

Accounting for the missing in action has been a problem after every war. Sooner or later, we need a policy change for handling the missing. How high a priority should this be? It needs to be a whole lot higher. It scares me the way some cases are mishandled. I'm chairman of the National Forget-Me-Not Association, an organization whose purpose is similar to the National League of Families', and I've had an opportunity to study a lot of MIA cases. In my area alone, six families have missing relatives. I've dug into their cases and found five have major flaws. One man, Jerry Dennis of Florida, received what he thought were his brother's remains but when questions came up about the identity of the remains, he had the body exhumed. The remains were found to be those of a non-American, not his brother's. Because he accepted the body, he can't return it.

Why isn't the government working harder to solve the MIA/POW problem? It's partly because there were major screw-ups during and after the war. Men who were captains and majors made minor mistakes which have now resulted in serious consequences. Today, these men are colonels and generals and they don't want their mistakes uncovered. Some of these guys, along with certain politicians, don't want their careers to go down the drain. I don't know if the military wants to solve the problem.

Maj. Donald E. Shay
U.S. Air Force
Lost: October 8, 1970
Laos

CHAPTER SIXTEEN
SARAH FRANCES SHAY

On a spring evening in 1970, I was fixing dinner and watching the six o'clock news when a story came on about the newly formed National League of Families. They were meeting at Constitution Hall in Washington and talking about their sons and husbands who were missing in action or who were prisoners of war in Southeast Asia. I listened but went ahead with my cooking. Little did I realize that our son would become missing that October and I would spend the next sixteen years working with the National League of Families.

Our son, Don, attended the Air Force Academy and was a career officer, although a very young one. We were shocked when he disappeared but realized anything could happen in time of war. At first, the Air Force and other branches of government appeared to be giving us all available information and were cooperating fully. The Air Force had regular communications with families; they even had a newsletter. This was early in the Vietnam conflict and we pretty much went along with what we were told. We knew other families who had not received as much information as we had.

It was during this time I became active in the League. I lived close to Washington and could afford to leave my teaching job. I was soon elected Assistant National Coordinator. Once I got involved with other families and started working more closely with the military and government agencies, I realized that we weren't getting the entire story. In fact, the most frustrating thing about this whole experience is that I've had to fight my own government.

Before Operation Homecoming, people would come to us and say not enough was being done to obtain the release of prisoners. Some of the folks were Red Cross employees or other government workers, who couldn't comment publicly but were telling us privately that more could be done. Their belief was that if the government wanted to obtain the release of the known prisoners they could push for it.

During the Nixon administration I began to feel the government was cooperating with our organization just to shut us up, to make us believe they were doing everything they could. Maybe they thought if they placated us to a certain extent we would go along with it. Now and then during our frequent discussions with Henry Kissinger he would ask us what we thought the government should do, what we recommended. Well, how did we know? We were civilians with no expertise in war or prisoner negotiations. But again, his meeting with the League was a placating kind of thing.

I can remember some of the career officers' wives becoming furious. Their husbands had been imprisoned for years. One time at the White House, Sybil Stockdale, wife of Jim Stockdale who eventually returned, banged her hand on the table and said to Kissinger, "Don't tell me that a giant of a country like the U.S. can't do something with a little, squirty nation like North Vietnam." Kissinger almost jumped out of his seat. The wives felt there was no reason for their husbands to be held in some foreign prison and they were ready to picket the White House. Some members of the League said we could never do a thing like that; others said to heck with it, we're not getting anywhere as it is. My eyes started to open. I realized more could be done.

During these years, the League board met monthly with Kissinger. It's no secret that I and a majority of other family members fault Kissinger on a number of points. After we learned the Paris Peace Accords had been signed and that prisoners would be returned, we had one of our regular meetings with Kissinger. I asked him what was being done about those still missing. My question seemed to catch him off balance. I'll never forget his answer. He thought for a few seconds and said, "The North Vietnamese have agreed to assume responsibility for accounting for the missing."

It hit me like a ton of bricks. Here he had been sitting, meeting with us for months, telling us not to believe anything the North Vietnamese told us. Now, all of a sudden they were wearing white hats and were going to do the honorable thing and account for our missing men? We questioned, "What about the men in Laos?" Nothing had been done about them. No demands were put on the Vietnamese. I don't remember his exact response but it was evasive. Again, he said something about the North Vietnamese taking responsibility. Even if he had been told this, how could he believe it? After all the times he had met with us, knowing how concerned we were, he gave us no assurance that the government would be doing anything about those still missing. It was the last time we met with Kissinger. He would not agree to see us again. As it turned out, for several years thereafter, little was done to further account for the missing men.

Kissinger's cutting us off was typical of what happened after 1973 through about 1978. After Operation Homecoming, the government went out of its way to shut us down. They were determined to get rid of us and offered no cooperation. Only a few in Congress were interested in our cause. It was discouraging. We couldn't get any kind of public support. Even my friends would say, "What do you expect to get out of this effort . . . you don't think your son is still alive, do you?" I said, "I don't know, but this government, the one he was fighting for, has not done all it could to find out if he's living or dead." For all of us families, it was sheer grit and guts that enabled us to hang together and continue working.

The handling of the men missing in Laos has always been one of my greatest bones of contention. Our government never did pursue the fact that over 560 men were lost in Laos. They would not push it even though the Lao had known prisoners. One Lao official stated that they were holding hundreds of prisoners. Our State Department said it couldn't be. Our government representatives kept coming back to us saying we had no diplomatic relations with North Vietnam; we would have to work through another country to get any reaction from them. Our point, however, was that we always had had diplomatic relations with Laos — those relations have never been severed. Our government had relations with the Royal Lao and a direct line of communication with the Pathet Lao.

To this day, I don't know why the U.S. government didn't want to make waves in Laos, unless it was because they didn't want the world to know about extensive U.S. activities and military presence in Laos. We weren't supposed to be there. But the country was loaded with Americans, training the Royal Lao Air Force and setting up — practically running — the Royal Lao government. Anyone with relatives missing in Laos will agree with me. Emmet Kay, the only man captured in Laos and released by the Lao, told us after his release that he was convinced he was let go because the Pope made a plea for his release. His particular case got a lot of worldwide publicity.

Another story about our son's disappearance illustrates how information was withheld by the military. Now, I understand that some information cannot be released if it would affect national security, but I don't see how my knowing about my son's shootdown would be a threat to national security. We were always told that we knew as much as government agencies or the military knew but that some information may have been withheld for our own sake. Still, we wanted the whole truth, good or bad.

Shortly after Don's plane went down, a good friend in his squadron, who was also stationed at Udorn, Thailand, wrote to Don's fiancee to tell her what he knew of Don's incident. He told her he had heard that two parachutes had been spotted in the area where Don's plane had crashed. The chutes were believed to belong to Don and his pilot. He explained that a Vietnamese informer said that upon landing both were shot and killed by the North Vietnamese.

Immediately, I called Randolph Air Force Base and talked to Col. Joe Luther, who was handling casualty information. He hit the ceiling, insisting the Air Force would have to issue another order, telling servicemen to stop giving such information to families. He pulled Don's file and told me the story was not true. Later, when I went to Laos, I stopped at the Joint Casualty Resolution Center in Thailand and was allowed to see Don's file. In that file was the account of the two parachutes being seen and the two men being shot. I was furious. When I arrived back in the States, I stopped at Randolph Air Force Base unannounced and asked to see my son's file. Surprisingly, a telegram had preceded my arrival. It was from Lt. General Robert Kingston, who was in charge of the Joint Casualty Resolution Center. He recommended that the office at Randolph be prepared for reaction from families who were not being given accurate information.

Well over a decade later, the National League of Families continues to press for information. We've kept going. I doubt the government would have completely changed its stance on this issue if we had backed off years ago.

I feel the work of the League has great historical significance. No organization that I know of has pushed its government so long and so hard to get government policy turned around. Congress has had to listen; the Pentagon has had to listen. It proves to me an average group of American citizens can go bang on the door of the White House and be heard. You won't always get results but you can be heard. When the Israelis were fighting and losing soldiers in their battle with Egypt, some of them came to us to learn what we had done, how we had pushed our government to strive for an accounting of the missing.

For five or six years, all I did was work on League activities. Everything revolved around it. I felt obligated to do it; I'm just lucky our daughter was through college and we could afford for me to devote my time to it. Usually by the time you reach middle age you think of travel and other things, but our lives changed and became geared to this issue. The only good things coming from it are the wonderful people we've met and good friends we've made. I've seen all types, from the high society mother who came to meetings in mink to the young wife with six kids who circled the White House in her camper. People in the League have been blue collar workers as well as Ph.Ds. You name it, we've got it. We are typically American, as truly American as you can find anywhere.

To me, the entire MIA/POW question is synonymous with government responsibility. If the government expects service and loyalty from the fighting men it sends to foreign soil, then it is responsible for them. Just because Vietnam was a quagmire, that responsibility shouldn't be written off. Not all efforts have been exhausted in accounting for the missing in Southeast Asia. I'm of World War Two vintage and can remember what went on when the government and the public were behind the effort wholeheartedly. The men who went to Vietnam went with just as much courage as the men in any other war.

I do feel that finally, more than ever before, our government is putting a sincere step forward, trying to resolve the problem. I think something will happen but I don't know when. I'm convinced some men are still being held over there, against their will. I hope they will be returned. I don't know who they are or where they are but I think our government knows who and where. I believe our government has demonstrated its knowledge of live prisoners being held by its change in policy over the past few years. There's got to be something behind it. If it's just Operation Busywork, our government is in trouble.

Looking back, I wouldn't say time has healed our wounds, but I don't feel I'm in the same state of suspension I once was. In the case of our son, Don, we've accepted the not knowing what happened to him but we're still determined to find out. I have to slow down a little though . . . I'm sixteen years older now.

CHAPTER SEVENTEEN
GEORGE SHINE

My wife Helen and I had four children and all of them served in Vietnam. We lost two of them. Our youngest son, Jonathan, graduated from West Point in 1969 and was killed on the front lines in October of 1970. His body was returned. Our next son, Alexander, currently a Lt. Col. in the Army, served two tours in Vietnam. He was hit by shrapnel and wounded but returned home and fully recovered. Our daughter, Sarah, joined the Red Cross after she finished college and volunteered to go to Vietnam. She served as a recreation director in Saigon. Our oldest son, Anthony, is still missing. He was a "Red River Rat," and was on his second tour, having completed 100 missions over North Vietnam during his first tour.

The day he was lost he was on a mission preparing to make a strike along Route 7, a major highway out of China connecting with the Ho Chi Minh Trail. It was a cloudy day and Tony advised his wingman that he was going down below the cloud cover to take a closer look at the target. That was the last that was ever heard from him. No explosion, no smoke, no radio, no beeper signals. To this day we have no idea what happened. Certainly, the possibilities are limited. He could have crashed and been killed or he could have crashed and been captured. We just don't know. That's the hard part.

Two years before Tony was lost, we had received word that our son Jonathan had been killed in action. At one time I remember thinking, "Thank God he's not missing, but rather well and happy with the Lord." Ironically, by December of 1972, we did have a son listed missing in action.

We've experienced the death of one son in war and have another who's missing. I can tell you it's easier knowing one has died in battle than to live with not knowing. We, like other parents, have always cared so much about our children and their well being. I guess it's part of that parental instinct to wonder if your kids are all right . . . that's what parents need to know. In Tony's case, we think he was killed, but since we don't know, we've had to wonder, to think "what if?" Frequently over the years, I have told myself he was killed, only to hear more stories about American prisoners being spotted or about more bodies being returned to the U.S. Then, it's hard to stop thinking maybe we'll get news about Tony. Every time I think I've given up I find out later that I really haven't.

I went to Southeast Asia twice, once in 1973 and another time in 1974, to prod the Vietnamese government as well as the American government to do more. I'm disappointed the State Department and the Defense Department got off to such a slow start in the 1970s as far as pushing for a greater accounting for the missing. Some bitter feelings have crept into my heart from time to time over the way the government has handled this, but I don't believe in wasting time being bitter.

I guess we've had our emotional ups and downs over how this issue has been treated. Once, during a down time, my wife Helen decided she was going to Laos and tell leaders there that she was going in to look for our son. They could either allow her to do it or shoot her. She later realized the most she would get out of making the trip was headlines. She would be perceived as "one more stupid mother, doing one more stupid thing." We were frustrated then. It was back during the years when the subject was dormant. No one seemed to care.

On the other hand, our family has always felt the Air Force was helpful. For several years, an Air Force representative from Fort Dix called monthly to offer news the military had received and to see if we had any new information. That relationship no longer continues, but we do receive an Air Force newsletter and have access to representatives at Randolph Air Base in Texas.

People have asked us over the years if we ever resisted the idea of all four of our children going to Vietnam. We didn't. Our sons wished to be in the military. I had been a military career man and served in World War Two and the Korean War. It was part of our family heritage. Tony just loved flying. All our kids volunteered for duty in Vietnam. They believed they were doing something for their country; they wanted to be part of the effort. It brings to mind the story about Franklin Roosevelt, who was struggling with the idea of his youngest son going into World War Two. Roosevelt's wife, Eleanor said, "Franklin, if you raise them to behave as eagles, you can't expect them to act like sparrows." We have no regrets. As a matter of fact, we're proud of what our children did. Only, we do miss them so very much.

Lt. Morgan J. Donahue
U.S. Air Force
Date lost: December 13, 1968
Laos

CHAPTER EIGHTEEN
VINCE DONAHUE

My son Morgan volunteered for Vietnam and flew with Scott Albright, one of his best friends and classmates at the Air Force Academy. Ironically, Scott's father, who was a colonel in the Air Force, quietly had the boys' orders changed so they would be sent to an air base in Thailand — an area he thought would be safe. Despite his efforts, both our sons were lost over Laos in December of 1968. Morgan, Scott and the rest of their crew were aboard a C-123 which crashed near Tchepone, Laos, around three o'clock in the morning. They were participating in a bombing mission along the Ho Chi Minh Trail. Morgan's crew was to fly over the area, identify targets, drop slow-descending flares toward the targets and then radio a B-57 or B-26 to make the strike. The bombers would be circling at higher altitudes, waiting for directions. In this particular incident, the descending bomber, a B-57, struck the C-123, sending it spiraling to the ground.

I've carefully researched my son's crash and have been to Southeast Asia ten times in pursuit of information about his capture. My efforts have convinced me that my son survived the crash and that he was taken prisoner by the Pathet Lao. I have several cogent reasons for believing he still might be alive today.

First of all, Morgan was in the safest place in the C-123 when it was struck. I'm not just operating on guesswork, I hold an active transport pilot's license and have a master's degree in criminology from the University of California at Berkley; I did my master's thesis on aircraft accident investigation. So, when I studied the crash of the plane, I had a working knowledge of the subject. Immediately after we were notified of our son's disappearance, I went to the Royal Thai Air Force Base in Nakhon Phanom, Thailand, where Morgan had been stationed. There, I interviewed Lt. Thomas Turner, the sole returnee from the incident.

According to Turner, Morgan was up in the nose of the plane, in a passageway beneath the flight deck, which was not impacted in the collision with the B-57. Incidentally, after the mid-air impact, the B-57 went into a vertical dive, crashed into a river bank and burned. Both pilots were killed. In the meantime, my son's craft was going down in a flat spin to the left, rotating as if it were a propeller on a child's beanie cap. Turner was momentarily knocked out when the C-123 was struck. He said when he came to, no one was in the cockpit. The co-pilot and the flight engineer were gone. Turner was able to pull a side window open and parachute. The plane had to be in a spin to the left; if it had been spinning to the right, he would have been chewed up by the propeller when he jumped. As it was, the propeller was retreating from him.

In what little moonlight there was at three o'clock in the morning, Turner could see two other chutes below him as he descended in his own chute. He couldn't tell who was in them and didn't find out because he never landed on the ground; he landed on top of a multiple canopy tree cover, near an open, grassy field. He remained in the tree, pulled his parachute up around him and stayed quiet. He could hear some scattered ground fire around him but couldn't tell exactly what was happening.

At daybreak, around five o'clock that same morning, a helicopter, a Jolly Green, came in to reconnoiter the area for survivors. It backed off in the face of some ground fire, but then came in and plucked Turner out of the treetop. He told me the rescue was the most dangerous part of the entire incident. The whirling blades of the chopper almost blew him out of the trees.

What a double blow by fate that would have been, but Turner was rescued, uninjured, and returned by the Jolly Green to Nakhon Phanom. Based on the facts I elicited about the crash from Turner during our meeting in Thailand, I knew Morgan had a good chance of surviving the accident. I then returned to the States to get my act together. I knew I had a job to do.

I made all my plans and in 1969, went back to Southeast Asia. I had a thousand flyers printed, bearing Morgan's picture, a description of him and details of the accident. I had them printed in four languages — Chinese, Lao, Thai and English. I went to Laos several times during the next two years. Each time I distributed flyers.

Of course, I wasn't going over there simply to pass out leaflets. I went to make contacts with U.S. Government agencies and with indigenous government leaders. During the first trip of 1969, I sought and obtained an interview with Soth Phetrasi, head of the Pathet Lao contingent in Laos. He invited me to his five-acre villa on the outskirts of Vientiane, the capital of Laos. He had about 100 Pathet Lao soldiers at the villa — they looked very Chinese, with little peaked caps and quilted jackets. Phetrasi was quite courteous and had his house boy serve tea. The house boy packed a Russian AK-47 under one arm and a teapot under the other.

I told Phetrasi of my search for my son, only to have him deliver an hour's lecture about the murderous American pilots who should be tried as war criminals. I had sense enough not to blow my cool, was able to maintain my composure and finally left under ostensibly pleasant terms.

I went back to see him again the following year and also a third time in 1972. This time I took my wife with me. We were invited to his villa and again, he started his spiel about the barbarous American pilots. I noticed my wife was trying to hold back tears.

Then, Phetrasi also noticed she was weeping and, surprisingly, tried to soothe her. He told her that he, too, had lost a son, during a bombing raid by the French near Dien Bien Phu during the French occupation. Apparently out of sympathy he said, "I will tell you this . . . we are holding tens of tens of American pilots whom we have shot down." He continued, "I cannot tell you at this time who they are, but you will be told at such time as we win our just struggle against the American Imperialists."

I considered this pretty important information, but to my disbelief the State Department and other federal agencies were uninterested in my conversation with Phetrasi when I tried to report it to them upon my return to the United States.

Several years later, in 1976, I had an equally disheartening experience when I recounted the Phetrasi conversation before Congressman Sonny Montgomery's commission which looked into the MIA/POW question. I was the last witness called after a full day of testimony before the commission. It was about 4:30 p.m. Montgomery was at a table in the front of the hearing room, leaning back in his chair, his hands behind his head, looking up at the ceiling. After I took the stand and identified myself, he asked me what I had to say. I told of Phetrasi's disclosure and explained that at the time, Phetrasi was "the" man, the head of the Pathet Lao in Vientiane. Montgomery looked at his watch and said, "Who the hell is Soth Phetrasi . . . some Lao we've never heard of? I mean, I'm sorry, I've got to curtail this meeting. I've got a five o'clock engagement. Good day." Montgomery got up and walked out. That's the type of cavalier treatment we families were getting in the early 1970s.

I went back to Laos again during 1972. This time I went to the U.S. AID Mission. There, agronomists were trying to teach the Lao to raise crops. Hydrologists were working with water purification and river flow problems. A public safety unit also operated within the AID Mission in Vientiane. The CIA used it as a cover for years. There, I got to know George Miller, who headed the narcotics branch of the public safety unit. He was a former FBI agent. Because he had a son in the Army, he took an interest in my case and agreed to do all he could to help me. Miller had two Royal Lao police colonels assigned to him, along with some other officers. One of the Lao, Colonel Bhounton, spoke good English and had been born and raised near the village of Tchepone, where my son's craft went down.

Through discussions with Miller, we arranged for Bhounton to penetrate Pathet Lao lines and go south to Tchepone to see if he could learn anything from the indigenous people about my son or about the plane crash. I wanted to know if the villagers might have seen prisoners led away or executed. I paid Bhounton a modest per diem, which was all he would accept, and armed him with a handful of the flyers with Morgan's picture.

When he returned about ten days later, he briefed me and Miller, saying the villagers had welcomed him. They remembered his family and were happy to see him. When he questioned the village elders about the crash of the C-123 in December of 1968, they told Bhounton that an aircraft had crashed a mile or two away from the bank of a nearby river. They had rescued one of the men and had taken him to the village. He had a broken leg but was otherwise in good health. The villagers had cared for him for two days when a Pathet Lao foot patrol came through, probably searching the crash site, and took him away in an ox cart. Bhounton didn't ask the villagers leading questions. He wanted to hear their version of the story. When he asked about the man's physical appearance, their descriptions fit Morgan's. Then, he showed them a picture of Morgan. They unanimously agreed it was Morgan who had been led from their village by the Pathet Lao. I was finally sure my son had been taken into captivity.

I gathered additional evidence that my son was captured when, in 1975, a former CIA agent who had been in Laos contacted me. The agent, Rosemary Conway, was attending a fighter pilot reunion in Las Vegas and asked around if anyone knew me or my son. I'm a retired Air Force Colonel so some people there knew me and told her how to get in touch with me. Her story proved to be extremely valuable.

While working for the CIA in Laos, her cover was Assistant Director of the International School in Vientiane. It was a school for children of ambassadors and their staffs in various embassies there. Her job for the CIA was to persuade Royal Lao Air Force pilots to take their aircraft and defect to Udorn, Thailand. The object was to recover the Royal Lao's American-supplied aircraft, in view of the imminent take over of the Royal Lao Air Force by the Pathet Lao. Conway had managed to get five or six pilots to take their aircrafts and defect from Laos when the Pathet Lao grabbed her. She was held for five months in the Pathet Lao headquarters in Vientiane. The CIA was eventually able to "buy" her release. They wanted her out of there; they were afraid she would be forced to spill information about other CIA activities in Laos. But, while she was incarcerated, she acquired information about my son.

Let me explain how it came about. The headquarters where Conway was held was a square, three-story, white structure. It was made up of large, gray rooms, which were separated by partitions but did not have walls which went all the way to the ceiling. During the day, she was forced to do menial chores, sweep and clean around the building. This gave her a chance to overhear a number of conversations. She told me that once a week, in a room adjacent to where she was kept, the senior staff of the headquarters would assemble; they would review the list of Americans captured, report on any additional Americans captured and list the camps in which prisoners were held.

Each time the roster of names was read, she heard my son's mentioned as one of the captives being held in a camp near Tchepone. She explained that my son's name stood out, because the Lao could pronounce the name "Donahue" quite easily. Even with Lao phonetics, they pronounced the name as an American would. That's why, after hearing the name repeated over the five-month period, she was able to remember it. There were other names, but she could not understand or remember all of them, due to the Lao's bungled pronunciation. However, she also heard the name Albright — Morgan's friend.

I made arrangements to meet with Rosemary Conway in Chicago to take an official deposition from her statement. She met with me and my attorney for two hours, outlining in detail the story of how she had heard my son's name mentioned repeatedly by the Pathet Lao. Later, when I wanted to use her testimony at my son's status review hearing, I asked if she would submit to a polygraph test. She said she would be pleased to do so. I called George Wackenhut of Wackenhut Security, based in Coral Gables, Florida, the largest private security organization in the world. He promised to send me one of his best polygraphers, a man who had been conducting lie detector exams for twenty-five years. He ran Conway through the test three times. The polygraph results showed there had been no deception. Her answers were honest, straightforward.

I introduced this information to Morgan's status review hearing board. It was the second hearing; I had appealed the first one when they declared him killed in action. I was granted a second hearing by the Secretary of the Air Force, Dr. Hans Mark. Unfortunately, we got the same panel of three colonels who declared Morgan KIA during the first hearing. Apparently my evidence didn't weigh very heavily in the minds of the three colonels; they declared Morgan dead on February 2, 1981. Their recommendation was passed on to Dr. Mark. He let Morgan's file sit on his desk for over a year. Then, the day he stepped down from the secretary's post, he signed the recommendation, approving the findings of the review board. The entire status review process had taken over three years to complete.

Later, I ran into one of the colonels on the review panel after he had retired. He told me if he had it to do over, he would not have voted in favor of the presumptive finding of death. Of course, that was easy for him to say then. He was retired, home free, in no danger of ruffling feathers. During most of the status reviews, the military had an assignment: to find there were no Americans being held against their will in Southeast Asia.

I gathered additional information about American POWs in 1981, when I met a Lao Resistance leader, General Vang Pao. A former Hmong leader, Pao is now a refugee, living in Montana, but continues to run a resistance operation in Laos. I met him through the late Pop Buell who was noted for his charitable work with refugees toward the end of the Vietnam War. Pao wrote to me in November of 1981 to say he had learned that a couple months earlier, a group of forty-two prisoners had been transported by air from Phong Saly, a Pathet Lao re-education camp, to another camp at Kham Keut in east central Laos and then moved over land to another camp at Nhom Marrot, not too far from Tchepone. Vang Pao said the men were moved because the Vietnamese in Laos feared that the Chinese, in their incursions across the borders of Laos and Vietnam, would overrun the camps and free the Americans. Vang Pao said that twenty-five of the forty-two prisoners were Royal Lao political figures, the other seventeen were American pilots.

I've collected a lot of evidence over the years; I've taken it to the State Department, to the Defense Intelligence Agency and to Congress, but it's been like talking to the wind. I have strong concerns about the laxness exhibited by the State Department. The career people there strike me as a self-styled intelligensia. They act as if they're omniscient, as if they know what's better for the American people in the area of foreign policy than anyone else in the country. Look what they did for their own people, those who were hostages in Iran. They were State Department employees. I didn't wish the hostages any harm, but look at their comparative treatment. They were housed, fed, allowed visitors, received mail, and watched television. Occasionally, one may have been slapped or kicked around, but it was a Brownie picnic compared to the degradation, the deprivation, the abuse and cruelty the American fighting men suffer as prisoners in Southeast Asia. Still, the State Department made heroes out of the hostages; it was even espoused at the State Department level that they all be given lifetime pensions.

The State Department wants the MIA issue silenced, buried, repressed. Even the POWs who returned in 1973 were ordered not to talk publicly about the possibility of American prisoners being detained in Southeast Asia. I've got a copy of the memo from Air Force Lt. Gen. Chappie James, of the Defense Department, who issued the order and told the returned POWs that the State Department would handle any statements about the MIA/POW issue. It's all so incredible. After eighteen years and no resolution to the problem, with all the evidence, it's as if parts of our government have cooperated in this betrayal, abandonment of young men who answered the call of duty. The men who are left over there are dying, one by one. Will we allow the American government to be co-conspirators in the deaths of Americans at the hands of the enemy? Our men answered the call to fight for their country in a no-win war in a far-off land, and now get their reward in betrayal, abandonment and death.

All past presidents have vowed to resolve the MIA controversy. Nixon promised a prompt resolution. Ford and Carter promised the same. President Reagan has made the most progress, but he, like any president, is surrounded by horse-holders, his own good coterie. He only knows what the State Department is telling him. The State Department has reported for years that it is continuing terribly sensitive, high-level negotiations with the Vietnamese. Well, those negotiations have been ongoing since 1973. How long can this continue? It's the officials at the top of the government bureaucracies who are not moving toward resolution. The people at the bottom are helpful but they're stymied by policy. They often disapprove of the policies levied on them; I have friends in the State Department who are dissatisfied with policies written by the long-term career people who believe in their own insolubility.

I've heard from reliable sources about a master plan by the State Department. It prescribes getting rid of the MIA/POW issue so it can implement its long-held goal to obtain a reproachment with Hanoi. This would permit an exchange of ambassadors, and make Hanoi privilege to all our resources, as we've been known to do with our enemies. According to this plan, Hanoi would be so smitten with our largess that it would forsake the Soviet orbit and gravitate to the bosom of the Western powers. If anyone believes this delusion has merit, then he must also believe in the tooth fairy. No Communist nation would ever be so tempted, especially Vietnam. They hate us. Nearly 900,000 of their people were killed in that war.

I really haven't coped with the loss of our son, especially since I've had good reason to believe he's alive. My heart is broken. My wife's health has declined. She's had two coronaries. The doctors say there's no organic basis for her condition, that it's stress-related. I've had friends who've become alcoholics, friends who've died and friends who've taken to the shrink's couch . . . all were involved in fighting this issue. My wife and I have lost the last eighteen years of our lives being in limbo, but I won't quit fighting. If I'm going to die of a broken heart, I'm going to die fighting. I just wish we could shake some sense into this nation's high-ranking policymakers. They are so far removed, so out of touch with the grass roots people who make this great country what it is.

CHAPTER NINETEEN
MAUREEN DUNN

My husband's case is unusual because he was lost in China. He's the only man presumed captured, but not returned, from that country. Joe was due home in early 1968 but his duty was extended when the Pueblo was captured on January 28, 1968 in Wonson Harbor. His carrier, The Coral Sea, was ordered to cruise around the Korean Harbor to protect other ships which might be attacked by the Koreans. Joe was with a group of fourteen men who had volunteered to fly the A-1s, propeller-driven rescue planes. It was the last time these planes were to be flown, because the U.S. had sold them to South Vietnam. Joe was making a ferry flight, taking a plane which was unarmed from one location to another. About two hours into the flight, he hit typhoon-like winds which caused him to veer off course and stray over Chinese territory. He was shot down by Chinese MiGs over the South China Sea. I later learned that the Chinese tracked his plane by radar for about three hours before the actual shootdown.

The guy in the lead plane, Lt. Bob Stoddard, was ahead of my husband and heard Joe's emergency radio go off. He looked out his window, saw the A-1 going down and saw Joe descending in an open parachute. Stoddard heard Joe's beeper which Joe would have had to operate manually. He said Joe tried to say something, but the drone of the plane's engine made it impossible to hear. Stoddard had to leave the area, taking off into the clouds, when the Chinese MiGs started coming his direction.

Joe managed to land in water and inflate his life raft within a few minutes. Rescue planes took off from carriers in the area within seven minutes after Joe's plane went down; however, one radar plane radioed that he had gone down over North Vietnam and the search planes spent three hours looking in the wrong place. I was told by a communications officer that when U.S. pilots did locate the right spot they sent in F-4s to do a low-flying search. He said they were unable to get close because Chinese MiGs were circling the area, almost like vultures over their prey. They were watching, protecting something. They were likely preparing to capture Joe or pick up his body. Because of the heavy activity over the area, the F-4s were ordered back.

Seven hours after the shootdown, which occurred at nine o'clock in the morning, Joe's beeper signal was picked up for twenty minutes. If the U.S. forces were monitoring his signal, the Chinese could have as well. There's little question that he would have been captured.

Unfortunately, I learned of my husband's shootdown from a newspaper. The paper boy came around about five o'clock. An article said an A-1 carrier plane had been shot down by the Chinese. It went on to describe the plane, saying it belonged to the carrier, The U.S.S. Coral Sea, based at Subic Bay near the Philippines. I had talked to Joe by phone the day before and he had told me he would be making a ferry flight to the Philippines, flying an A-1 from his carrier The Coral Sea in Subic Bay. The only thing that wasn't in the paper was his name. I began putting one and one together and started making phone calls. I knew, I just knew something was wrong.

I could find out nothing by phone. Luckily, a friend of ours named Jack McDermott who was on the carrier, had come back to our hometown to visit his father who was ill so I called him and said, "Jack, I'm worried . . . and don't understand what's going on. I think Joe's plane may have been shot down." He said, "If it is Joe, don't worry. If it's China, he'll be picked up right away . . . if they can get in there immediately, say within twenty minutes." He explained that search planes had a certain amount of time to go in before their presence was acknowledged and that he had done many pickups like it in the past, and had guys out in fifteen minutes.

By this time, it was six o'clock in the evening. I was alone with my one-year-old son. I decided to call the First Naval District in Boston. I asked if they had a casualty from a shootdown in China. The officer on the other end of the phone asked for a name. I asked, "Do you have a listing for a Lt. Joseph Dunn?" When he replied, "Do you have a middle initial?" I knew it was Joe.

We later learned Joe was shot down about five miles from the northeast coast of Hainan Island, right off the southeast coast of mainland China. It was near Nanning Province, county of Guan Phong. The search for Joe was called off on February 16, two days later.

So, my encounters with the military and my battle with government red tape began. An important anecdote to relate is an early experience I had with the Navy. I went to the First Naval District office to see a Naval adjudicative officer and write a will. I was still stunned from hearing that Joe had disappeared, but was trying to go through the motions with the Navy's paper work.

After we finished the legal papers, I couldn't believe what the officer said to me. He said, "You know Mrs. Dunn, there are three things that can happen here. First, your husband could have been killed . . . I've seen more bad chutes make it than good chutes. Just because your husband's beeper went off doesn't mean he survived. Secondly, the Chinese could be using his body for fertilizer in a rice paddy and thirdly, keep in mind that if he was captured he may decide to stay there, marry someone and have five Chinese children." The young enlisted man who had escorted me probably could have gotten into trouble but he interrupted with, "I think she's heard enough." I thought it was ironic that the adjudicative officer's name was Commander Fink.

By the next Friday, other reports were coming out about whether or not my husband had been captured. The case was getting a lot of publicity and reporters were calling. I told the Navy I wanted to be better informed. So, on Friday evening a Navy public affairs officer was sent to the house to update me. It was about eight o'clock and the guy had apparently come from one of the local happy hours because he was nothing less than drunk. To top it off, his wife somehow tracked him to my house, called on the phone and gave him a tongue-lashing, demanding that he get home. I don't hate the Navy, but I had some discouraging moments with them during the first few days after my husband's incident.

I started becoming more aggressive in my effort to research the case. In 1969, I got an appointment with then-Secretary of State Dean Rusk. My Congressman, Jim Burke, and my attorney accompanied me. Our meeting went well, although Mr. Rusk told me that nothing had been learned from inquiries made at a meeting of the International Red Cross in Geneva. It was at this point Mr. Rusk was called out of the office momentarily. Joe's file was on his desk so I opened it. On one page, in large black letters it said, "DO NOT TELL MRS. DUNN." It didn't make sense to me. Why would they withhold anything? I still wonder what it was they weren't supposed to tell me. I read only a bit further in the file, enough to see something about requesting that Pakistan get involved in asking about Joe Dunn. Why shouldn't I know that?

All these kinds of things fueled me on . . . I realized I had to do more on Joe's behalf. During that same trip to Washington, my congressman got some material from the State Department which proved to be interesting. It was a package of daily newspapers from Southeast Asia. They all contained articles about my husband's shootdown. The papers included the *New China News Agency*, the *Liberation Army Daily* and the *People's Daily*.

Not only did the articles talk about Joe's plane crash, they also praised the two Chinese pilots who shot him down and mentioned the awards they had received. But most importantly, they listed the names of these pilots. Out of the scores of men who were shot down in Southeast Asia, my husband's case is the only one we know of in which the names of the enemy pilots are known. At that point, I told myself . . . someday I'll meet face to face with these pilots, look into their eyes and ask them if they know what happened to Joe Dunn. If they were watching him for three hours before the shootdown, they surely kept an eye on him afterwards. I realize their planes would have been traveling with great speed at high altitudes and they may not have had a bird's-eye view of Joe in a life raft, but they would have received radio messages from prop planes sent in.

By this time, it was 1970. Our country had no diplomatic relations with China, so pursuing any contact with China was next to impossible. I became actively involved with the National League of Families. I had set up the Joe Dunn Committee and had good participation, but decided to channel all that effort into the League. I sometimes think I hurt my own case by blending into another organization, but I realized we all needed to work together. I wanted satisfaction for myself, and for the other families as well. I sort of put my husband's case aside even though I was still convinced that he was alive. Four U.S. pilots had seen his open parachute and the Destroyer McCord picked up his beeper signal seven hours later.

I kept a keen focus on China. I tried to talk to anyone going that direction or anyone coming into the U.S. from China. When a Chinese delegation arrived at the Roosevelt Hotel in New York, I tried to pass myself off as a waitress and get to the sixteenth floor where they were staying. I would have done anything to talk with them. Twice I got to the floor, but when I got off the elevator, security was so heavy I couldn't get through. The employees in the hotel were really nice to me. Since I had made several attempts to make contact with the Chinese, they were beginning to recognize me. They thought it was a humanitarian issue and pretended not to notice as I went about my business. However, I was never able to talk to members of the Chinese delegation.

Shortly thereafter, Gerald Ford, who was then a congressman, went to China. I had friends who knew Ford. They briefed him on Joe's case and gave him a case file to take along. When he brought up the subject, the Chinese handed out the same line, saying they had no information. They were unwilling to discuss it.

Then, in 1975 Henry Kissinger and President Ford went to China. By now, I knew Kissinger fairly well because during the last three years of the Vietnam War we members of the League had met with him or a National Security Council representative every six weeks. Kissinger told me he would call me when he returned from China. Well, before I got that call, a reporter approached me one afternoon as I pulled into my driveway. He said, "What do you think of the news the President and Mr. Kissinger have come back with?" "What news?" I asked. "That your husband's name is on the dead list," he said.

My immediate thought was that I wanted to choke everyone in the Navy because I had not been notified before the press approached me. I called the Navy office. An officer informed me that he had received a list of four men who had been killed, but that Joe Dunn's name was not among them. As it turned out, an aide in Senator Ted Kennedy's office had confused the details, thinking my husband's name was on the list, and released the story to the news media. So, by the time my son got home from school, the afternoon paper was out with an 8 x 10 photo of Joe, above which the headline read: "Dunn is Dead." It took a long time to undo that one.

Later, Kissinger did call me. He told me he felt the Chinese knew what had happened to Joe, but that I probably shouldn't expect him to ever walk through my door again. He explained the Chinese told him the exact location of the shootdown, the province and county and the depth of the water. However, they insisted that they had no further knowledge and refused to discuss the case.

Another incident in 1973 convinced me that Joe was alive
and about to be freed. The Chinese released a statement saying they
were going to release an American captured in 1968. I was excited
because Joe was the only man shot down in that area in 1968. I
even made a close check with all the military service secretaries to
make sure that Joe had been the only shootdown in that location that
year. My son and I were just waiting for the name to be released . .
. it was like we already knew it was Joe.

But, my hopes were dashed; the prisoner released was a
young American woman, Mary Ann Harbert. She and her companion had been sailing near Macao and were presumed to have
drowned when their boat capsized. However, they were captured.
The man later died and she was held for five years. Kept under
heavy guard, she saw no other Americans but said she had heard of
them. For five years, the Chinese did not let it be known that she
was imprisoned.

It was 1979 when the U.S. announced the beginning of diplomatic relations with China. I got excited; I thought this is it for
me. I'm going to China to meet with the two pilots. I wrote a letter
to the Chinese but got no reply. I kept writing. Finally, I got an
answer, instructing me to meet with Chai Zemin, Chinese Ambassador to the U.S. in Washington. Zemin agreed to the meeting. I
went to Washington in August and met with him for nearly two
hours, explaining my situation. He listened intently, then asked,
"What can I do?" I said, "You can grant me and my son visas to
your country and arrange a meeting with these two Chinese pilots.
When I meet them face to face I will know if they are telling the
truth, if they saw Joe or know what happened."

As we talked, I noticed the ambassador was impressed to
learn that the Navy considered my husband on active duty, and that
Joe would still be presumed alive until we gained an accounting or
he was declared dead. Also, I could tell Ambassador Zemin really
liked my son, who at that time was a chubby little kid. So I tried to
play on his feelings about family. "I know the Chinese are a family-

loving people," I said, "and a unit is missing from our family. Please help us bring him back or close the memory of him." I told him I would return again and again until the meeting was granted. I think he believed me, since I and 500 others had once picketed the Chinese Embassy. Finally he responded, "I think I can help." Then in his broken English he said, "You will be back, you will be back."

I left, feeling the leverage I had with Zemin was the fact that the U.S. military was operating as if Joe were alive, even though we didn't know for sure. I waited and waited for a response from Zemin. I got one in March, seven months later, saying they were declining the meeting with the two pilots. I called the embassy and told them I would not accept that answer. I further explained that I would be back with the press and that it would not look good for a country wishing to normalize relations with the U.S. In May of 1981 they called and said they would help me set up the meeting.

In May, I went back to the Chinese Embassy in Washington to make arrangements for the trip to Peking in early September. But later in May my plans started going downhill. I received a notice from the Navy, informing me that a status review hearing had been scheduled to declare my husband dead. I contacted Navy officials and asked them to please postpone the hearing until October. I explained that I was going to China to meet with the pilots who shot down Joe's plane and that I might in fact come back with information which would be valuable in the hearing. The answer was "No." The hearing was scheduled for September 11. I had to cancel my trip to China; I wanted to be present at the hearing.

During the hearing, several professional people testified that Joe could have survived, but because the evidence was inconclusive, the review board changed his status. On December 1, 1981, the Navy declared Joe Dunn dead.

So, that's my story. It's unique because of where Joe was lost, but don't get the idea I think my husband is some superhero. He had his faults. He was just another human whom I loved very much. I used to chuckle to myself sometimes in meetings with other wives because somehow the husbands always got put up on pedestals.

I have mixed emotions about my country's system of government. My niece married recently, to the class president at Annapolis. I had introduced them. When my son Joe and I went to the wedding, one relative said to me, "Oh, wouldn't you just love to have your Joe go to Annapolis?" It really made me stop and think. When I heard "Pomp and Circumstance" being played, saw the dress parade and the uniforms, it was so patriotic. I felt like standing up and singing "God Bless America." I love my country. But when I think about the chance of giving my son to a country that never did justice to his father and hundreds of others, I have strong reservations.

Col. Charles E. Shelton
U.S. Air Force
Lost: April 29, 1965
Laos

CHAPTER TWENTY
MARIAN SHELTON

My husband is the only man the U.S. government still carries on record as a POW. He never has been declared dead. I think it's because so much was known about his being in captivity; he's one of many men we know the Vietnamese could readily account for. They held Charles as a prisoner for years, ever since he was shot down over Laos on his thirty-third birthday in 1965.

I should have known something was about to happen the night his plane went down. It had been a bad week. We were living in Okinawa at the time. I had been hit on the head by a burglar the night before and had eleven stitches in my head. My daughter had broken her leg that week and was in a cast. The last time I talked to Charles by phone he teased us about nursing each other back to good health. He said he would call the next night to see how we were doing. And, since it was his birthday, I was expecting his call that evening; however, the call I got was not from Charles. Two Air Force officers came to the house to tell me that Charles' plane had been hit by ground fire during a reconnaisance mission but that Charles had ejected safely. They thought he would be rescued by midnight so I had high hopes. Unfortunately with the darkness and cloud cover, they weren't able to approach the crash site. I later learned Charles had hidden that night, but was captured the next day.

I've learned a lot about Charles' case over the years, mostly through declassified intelligence reports, but I've also had some classified information leaked to me. The most tragic story I've heard about Charles' captivity had to do with a secret CIA operation code-named "Duck Soup." It was a rescue plan by the CIA, Air Force and Hmong villagers, indigenous people who were working for the CIA. During the mission, in the fall of 1965, Charles was actually rescued. However, about ten days later, the group of Hmong villagers who had assisted in his rescue were going to be compromised; they were surrounded by Pathet Lao. So, they struck a deal and gave Charles back to the enemy. I don't know if any American officers were directly involved in the barter that went on, but it's heartbreaking just the same. I learned about the mission from a reliable military source so I have reason to believe it's true.

Charles was known to be in captivity for at least three years. For a while, he was held in a cave near Sam Neua, Laos. I've seen pictures of those caves. Laos has hundreds of caves, some large enough to drive into with a semi-truck. Other reports indicate Charles had been shot twice but recovered; he also supposedly contracted malaria. I've been told that Charles escaped several times but was recaptured each time. Once, when Vietnamese guards tried to chain him to a desk, he overturned the desk on them and killed three of them with his bare hands before he could be subdued. After that, he was held in a cage-like area, actually a shallow ditch with bars over the top. A guard would stand by with a live grenade in case he tried to escape. The Pathet Lao termed him "incorrigible." He was a resister, a fighter. The last report I got was that he had been sent "up North," probably Hanoi. I think if he was sent to a regular prison in Hanoi he could be alive, but if he was forced to live in a cave in Laos, I don't believe he could have survived.

I cried for years, thinking about the horrible conditions he had to endure. I agonized to think he was in such misery and state of mind that he would kill three men with his bare hands. I just couldn't imagine the horrors of it. I guess over the years, I learned not to think about it all the time. Twenty years later, I've learned how to cope but I've never forgotten.

I recall my husband talking to me about what to do if anything ever happened to him. Shortly before he left for his tour in Vietnam, he remarked, "Marian, be sure to teach those children how to do everything . . . cook, clean, play ball, do everything. I'm sure you could do things around the house much easier yourself, but I want my boys to know all of that, too." The night before he left he made out a list of things — what kind of house to buy if anything happened to him, where to settle, what kind of car to get and who to use as a financial advisor. It was the kind of information you think you'll never need. I don't know if he thought there was a strong chance of his not returning. I think his talking to me about the house and everything was precipitated by an incident that had happened a week earlier. He was flying an RF-101 and had to make an emergency landing when his landing gear stuck. He circled the airstrip for about an hour, dumped his fuel and finally managed to land on a foamed runway. I think it made him aware of how quickly something could happen. That incident occurred on a Thursday. He left the next Tuesday.

I have survived because of my five children. Staying involved with them helped so much. My faith has sustained me, too; I'm a strong Catholic. These past few years have been difficult for me though because we've had so many family affairs — affairs I would like to have shared with Charles. For example, my youngest daughter got married. My oldest son is a priest so he performed the wedding ceremony. I have another son who is an actor and singer so he sang at the wedding. My third son gave the bride away and my other daughter was a bridesmaid. Now that's what I call a family affair. It was really hard not having Charles there.

Also, one of my sons and his wife had a baby, the first grandchild. I remember the day I shopped for a baby gift, I couldn't help thinking of Charles — it was our wedding anniversary. We would have been married for thirty-two years. I found a little wooden music box, shaped like an airplane. It played "Somewhere Over the Rainbow," and I knew I had to buy it. I said to myself, "If Charles were home, this is what he would buy."

I'm still working with the League of Families and have been to Southeast Asia. I was with the first group of American family members to visit there after the war in 1973. However, I had to curtail my League work from time to time as my responsibilities grew with my children and my business. A few times I've had to back away, then later jump back in with both feet. I stay abreast of what's happening. I am not pleased with the lack of progress made by past administrations or by the State Department, but President Reagan has shown more promise than any of his predecessors. I have confidence in what he's doing to achieve a further accounting of the missing.

I operate on the belief that Charles is still alive. I know there's a good chance that he's dead, but I've worked hard with my attorney to keep the military from changing his status to dead or killed in action. I think it really takes the pressure off the Vietnamese when our government declares men dead. It makes them think we're not pushing for the return of any live men. So, I've fought to keep Charles' records intact; we presume he's alive. I would want him to do the same for me. Sometimes I talk as if he were gone. I guess I talk both ways. Mostly, I think of him as being alive but sometimes I say, "Well, you know, it's been twenty years. The man's not going to live forever."

Lt. Col. Robert Standerwick
U.S. Air Force
Lost: February 3, 1971
Laos

CHAPTER TWENTY-ONE
LYNN STANDERWICK

I was thirteen when I first learned that my father was missing in action. My mother waited to tell us kids until we were all home together, after we had gotten out of school for the day and I had finished my piano lesson. She said that Air Force officials had come that morning and reported that my father was missing. At first, I wasn't too worried, mostly because I didn't understand what it meant to be missing in action, and I didn't even understand what the war was all about. Still, we were all concerned and hopeful that we'd get good news. But, the news never came, and we were left with many unanswered questions. I never dreamed my search for answers would eventually lead me to Southeast Asia and to a jail in Thailand.

I tried to grow up and lead a normal life the best I could under the circumstances; I was active in high school and went on to college with career goals in mind. But several years ago, around Christmas time, my goals changed. I was home for the holidays and had been sorting through the files on my dad's case, and it just made me realize how long we had been waiting for answers about what happened to him. That's when I decided to invest my full time and resources to working on the MIA/POW issue.

At the time, several POW advocacy groups were active across the nation. I thought it might help if we all joined forces to make the effort stronger. I traveled around the country and talked with members of various organizations, attended League meetings and wrote editorials. I launched an effort to raise funds by selling silver MIA/POW commemorative medallions; the POW bracelets weren't available then. I met Bo Gritz in 1982 and later joined him on what some people call the "controversial" POW rescue mission into Laos in 1983.

I had heard about Bo's active involvement with the POW issue, but was still quite skeptical about him and his ideas. However, the first time I heard him talk about POWs, I was impressed with how much he knew and how well he understood the issue. Having had a long military career and having served in Vietnam, he knew a lot about the war and the history of the POW situation. And, I could tell he was a man of action — someone who was willing to do something about the problem. That appealed to me after all the years of watching my mom trying in vain to enlist the support of others to fight for this issue.

I got to know Bo over the course of a year, through League meetings and fundraisers; later in 1982, another MIA daughter, Janet Townley, and I started helping him with plans for a rescue mission into Laos. We started the mission in January 1983, but were forced to abort it several weeks later.

Janet and I had gone to Washington, D.C., where we stayed from October 1982 to December. We were the communications contacts here in the states for Bo who had headed for Thailand with his team — Lance Trimmer, Gary Goldman, Chuck Patterson and Scott Weekly. Janet and I had been trained to operate an electronic communications device, a burst-code transmitter; we maintained constant contact with the team in the field. They sent back coded messages about their location, what their needs were and their plan of action. If they discovered any camps with American prisoners, they were to radio us and we were to notify certain officials in

Washington. The team was moving toward a target when they had to scrub the mission. One of the team members, Chuck Patterson, had become anxious about the mission and left the team. Bo and the others were concerned about the possible impact of his abrupt departure and decided to put the mission on hold. We were really disappointed. Initially, I thought we would have some POWs home by Christmas.

The team came back to the states and we all returned to California and began planning our next attempt at the mission. Janet and I let it be known that we were willing to go to Southeast Asia the next time. And, so it was in January 1983, that we all headed for Thailand, leaving in small groups at different intervals.

Once in Thailand, Janet stayed in Bangkok, while Lance and I went to Nakhon Phanom, on the Thai-Laotian border, where we set up a base station in a rented house. Once again, we took care of radio communications. Bo and the rest of the team loaded the boats one night and crossed the Mekong River, slipping quietly over the border into Laos. They began moving toward a site where we believed prisoners were being held. The plan called for rescuing POWs or coming back with proof that prisoners were there.

Up to this point, all was going well, but in mid-February, everything collapsed. A leak to the American media had alerted Thai authorities. We had known about the leak and sensed that our being discovered was inevitable, but we persevered, hoping to accomplish as much as we could. Then, on February 13, a knock came at the door. It was Thai police. Within moments, the house was swarming with police and Thai military men. I think they were searching for weapons, but of course, we had none. They were all chattering in Thai — none spoke English; the landlord who had been summoned, translated for us. When police found the radio transmitter, we were arrested; it was against the law to have possession of such equipment. Lance and I were taken to jail where we stayed for three days. We weren't too worried about ourselves, but were concerned about the team out in the field with no radio contact. Within several days, though, they figured out what had happened. The team decided to come back and report to Thai police.

Meanwhile, as I sat in the jail which overlooked the Mekong, I could see across the border into Laos. It was ironic — there I sat in jail, looking into the very jungle where my dad's plane had gone down. I wondered if I might be stuck there for years. You can never tell what could happen in foreign jails or prisons. You play only by their rules. I had moments when I thought about being caged like that indefinitely. The thought was overwhelming.

Lance and I ended up paying a bond — "bribe" is a better word for it — and were released. We returned to the house but could not leave it without permission. Once the team had returned, we all appeared before a three-judge Thai court. On March 11, we were each fined $130.00 and given one-year suspended sentences.

Our objective had been to rescue POWs. Although we did not succeed, we did build public awareness. The POW issue got more media attention than it had received in a decade. The story was blasted across newspapers and airwaves so you had to be living under a rock not to hear about MIAs or POWs and the Gritz mission.

A lot of the media coverage was critical of our mission, and attempts were made to discredit Bo. The government denouncement of the mission was certainly something we expected. It came as no surprise. Even though we had government assistance with some planning and equipment, the U.S. Government could not publically endorse such a private, cross-border foray. But, none of the criticism hindered our resolve.

As for me, there's no question about my involvement in the POW issue. I'm in for the distance. I think more people would be if they fully understood the problem. The hardest thing over the years has been getting people informed. If they understood, I don't think most could turn their backs on it. I can't. And, I have faith that our efforts will bring men home. I operate on the premise that a

POW is coming home tomorrow. If I didn't, I'd have no business doing what I'm doing.

Col. Farrell J. (Sully) Sullivan
U.S. Air Force
Lost: June 27, 1972, North Vietnam
Remains returned July 2, 1983

CHAPTER TWENTY-TWO
SUE SULLIVAN

I began working on my husband's case the day I learned he was shot down. His aircraft was hit in the tail section by a surface-to-air missile and crashed in downtown Hanoi. Initial reports from the Air Force indicated he may have gotten out of the plane, although I have received conflicting reports over the years. Sully was never a known prisoner. I could never find a returned POW who had known my husband or had witnessed his crash, which occurred close to Hoa Lo Prison in Hanoi where many American prisoners were held. When the Air Force changed Sully's status to killed in action, a casualty officer did tell me an American prisoner had been an eyewitness to the incident.

Later, I wrote to that prisoner after he had returned and asked about the crash. He was dumbfounded to hear that he had been listed as an eyewitness and explained it would have been impossible for him to see the crash from his location in the prison compound. The Air Force report also conflicted with an account of the crash I received from the wingman flying in Sully's formation. Given the inconclusive evidence I was able to piece together, I hoped that Sully had managed to get out of the plane. My hopes were finally snuffed when his remains were returned to the U.S.

and positively identified on June 27, 1983 — eleven years to the day that his plane was shot down.

In March of 1983, the Vietnamese announced they were releasing the remains of twelve men. I had a gut feeling that Sully's could be among them because during the past two years, whenever various groups, both government and National League of Family delegations, had made trips to Southeast Asia to speak with Vietnamese leaders, I would send along a folder of information about him. I knew his name had been brought up to the Vietnamese on more than one occasion. It's hard to say if my inquiries influenced the return of his remains. The Vietnamese could have randomly selected those returned from over 400 sets of remains we know they are harboring.

When an Air Force casualty officer called me to confirm that Sully's remains had been identified, I can't describe the feeling of relief, the sense of peace it gave me. I felt grief, too. It was almost like someone walking in telling me my husband had just been killed.

But even though it wasn't the answer I had prayed for, it was an answer . . . finally, after eleven years. Along with my mixed feelings of grief and relief, I also felt anger and bitterness — not only toward the Vietnamese but toward my own government for allowing the Vietnamese to withhold remains. My husband's plane crashed into downtown Hanoi, not into some triple canopy jungle, so the Vietnamese had had him or his remains from the very beginning.

When Sully's remains arrived home in July of 1983, I decided I wanted to view them. It was something I had to do for myself. I had seen the dental X-rays and it was clear to me that the remains were his but I had to satisfy myself that the remains were in the casket. I didn't want to go through the rest of my life wondering what I had buried. An Air Force casualty officer had shown me photographs of the remains so I knew what I was going to see. My children chose not to view the remains but didn't want me to view them alone, so a family friend went with me.

The funeral director removed the military uniform which was placed on top of the casket and opened the lid. The remains were arranged in the same order I had seen in the photograph. It was sort of a numbing experience; I didn't feel a lot of emotion. I did touch the bones and place in the casket Sully's MIA bracelet I had worn. Viewing the remains was a personal decision. It was something I had to do.

During the years I worked to find out what happened to my husband, I had one other major goal — to raise our three children in the very best way I could. They were sixteen, thirteen, and eight when Sully was lost. It was difficult for them growing up, not knowing what happened to their father. It was especially hard for them to explain that their father was still missing when the U.S. prisoners came home in 1973. People just assumed he was dead. Finally, the children got to where they didn't want to discuss it much. They stopped wearing their MIA bracelets. Experiencing the loss of Sully made us a closer-knit family. We were drawn even closer when my son Tom was almost killed six months after my husband was reported missing. He was on a ski trip with a group of church kids in December of 1972 when their bus was hit by a cattle truck on a narrow bridge. Nineteen people were killed. We didn't expect Tom to live and were told if he did survive he would likely be paralyzed. Although he fully recovered, losing Sully and having Tom's accident at the same time drew us together. Now we have a bond that's probably not common to all families.

We've had our fun times, too. I made sure that sometime during each year we had all left the house for some type of vacation — to get away and have some fun, even if it was only for a few days. I tried to carry on a normal household, observing the holidays, keeping the kids in scouts and participating in school and community activities. I remember going to Dad's Day at my son's university. It flustered the guy at the door when he found out I was standing in for Tom's dad. I just slapped on a name tag which read,

"Hi, I'm Tom Sullivan's Father." I've learned how to see the humor in things.

I also went to work about a year after Sully was reported missing. It helped me cope if I got up to a schedule every day. I made new friends. The friends Sully and I had together faded away, but any widow can tell you that's to be expected.

Right now, I don't think I could encourage my children to enter the military. I believe this country needs to reconsider the honor of its fighting men before getting into future conflicts. We've lost some of our commitment to them. I still think this is the greatest country in the world; I don't know of many countries where you can stand up and criticize the government the way I have and still be a free person. But I do think some things need to change if we're going to ask individuals to put their lives on the line. We must stand behind them. If you can't have your loved one home, you're entitled to know as much as the government knows. The military and other government agencies should be honest and open their files. I still don't understand why documents relating to Col. Sullivan's case are classified. I would like to know everything the U.S. government knows about his crash and subsequent return of his remains.

I continue holding down a job, and try to stay active in my community. I want to keep growing as a person. I stay involved, too with the League of Families because I want to return the support others gave me all those years. I realize all the men can't be accounted for, but the Vietnamese could release information on hundreds of them. We cannot abandon these men or their families who are living out their lives not knowing what happened. As for me, I'm at peace. It's a lot easier knowing some of my questions have been answered. I no longer have that feeling that when the phone rings it might be about Sully.

Maj. Michael J. Bosiljevac
U.S. Air Force
Lost: September 29, 1972
North Vietnam

CHAPTER TWENTY-THREE
KAY BOSILJEVAC

I know the Vietnamese can account for my husband whether he's alive or dead. They knew things about him before he was ever shot down. The last time I saw him was during his R&R in Hawaii in August of 1972, and he talked to me very seriously about combat and the possibility of his coming up missing or being captured. He said if he were shot down it would be naive to assume that the Vietnamese didn't know about him or his fate.

He explained that the Vietnamese used Soviet intelligence and that the Soviets carried fairly comprehensive files on certain individuals, including the American pilots who were flying missions in Vietnam. They acquired this information from various sources, sometimes through clipping services taking information from hometown newspapers. Mike told me something he would never forget was the way he learned about the birth of our second child, Michael John. Before the Red Cross or Air Force could notify him that he had a new son, he heard it broadcast by Radio Hanoi. It was a mind game the Communists were playing. It seemed pretty astounding, but showed their capability for acquiring information.

Mike's plane was shot down the first day the F-111s were making bombing strikes into the northern part of North Vietnam. Mike was flying an F-105G, as part of the Wild Weasel Squadron.

His job was to provide protective cover for the F-111s. His plane carried sophisticated electronic equipment which served as an electronic blanket to confuse enemy missiles being fired.

Mike's craft and three others were flying in a formation of four when a surface-to-air missile was fired from near the western gates of Hanoi. Pilots have explained to me the typical procedure for dodging one of these missiles. They simply take the aircraft up, then down and make an S-turn — a series of maneuvers which causes the missile tracking them to overstress and destroy itself. But this missile was apparently more sophisticated than those previously used; it compensated. It tracked the plane and exploded about twenty feet behind the craft, blowing off part of the tail section.

Mike and his co-pilot, Lt. Col. Jim O'Neil, flew for about five minutes, which is a long time in a crippled aircraft. They tried to move out toward the ocean but couldn't make it, so they went southwest until the craft started to lose stability. That's when they punched out. Other pilots in the formation kept circling above, watching and fixing the points as the two went down to see exactly where they were landing. They could see their parachutes as they descended. O'Neil, being smaller and lighter than Mike, descended more slowly and could see Mike in the chute below. As he was still coming down, he noticed Mike's chute billowing on the ground.

Both Mike and O'Neil landed at the base of Mt. Bavi in North Vietnam. O'Neil says he was captured within an hour, but because he and Mike had been separated by a stream and were a quarter mile apart, they couldn't see each other. About four days later in Hoa Lo Prison, also known as the Hanoi Hilton, O'Neil asked a guard who spoke fluent English about Mike Bosiljevac. The guard wrote the last name down since it was difficult for him. He later returned and reported to O'Neil that Mike was "alive, well, uninjured and luckier than you."

Now, I don't know what "luckier" meant and I don't believe everything the Vietnamese guard might have said, but that's the story. It's obvious to me that in a densely populated area like Mt. Bavi, far from any friendly forces, there's no way a tall, fair-haired Caucasian could walk away unnoticed. The area was filled with Vietnamese people who most likely had been evacuated from their villages in anticipation of the air strikes.

I've worked for over a decade trying to find out what happened to Mike. In the beginning, I was basically stunned over the whole incident but my main focus was on gathering as much information as I could to try to put pieces together in some way.

I happened to get ahold of a *New York Times* article which referred to my husband's capture. I thought it strange that this information could appear in newspapers, yet the Air Force had never mentioned these details to me. When I made an inquiry about it, Air Force officials replied that they had no information. I sent them a copy of the article and then, like magic, they informed me that they did have information about the incident. I know the Air Force had a lot of cases to manage, but it was disappointing to have information withheld at such a critical time. It made me wonder what was going on.

I later learned part of the problem resulted from poor management of the casualty branch at Randolph Air Force Base. The following summer another MIA wife, Carolyn Standerwick, and I made a visit to the casualty branch office to see what was on record. An elderly man in charge, Col. Joe Luther, said to me abruptly, "Listen little girl, I handled the missing in World War Two. I handled the missing in Korea and by God I'm going to handle it now." I began to feel like I was dealing with individuals who were either pushing a Kleenex box at me and telling me to go away or who weren't being very thorough in their work. Later, when I continued to press Luther for details, he became irritated and shouted, "Your husband's dead! Got it? Dead!" Their attitudes made me angry and again, I wondered what was going on.

I have had some unusual bits of information leaked to me over the years. One time, in 1973, shortly after Operation Homecoming, we families were brought together in five regional meetings throughout the country. General Russell Ogen of IPWIC (Interagency Prisoner of War Intelligence Committee) spoke to us. He essentially explained that within a year and a day our guys would be declared legally dead. I thought it was especially interesting that after the meeting General Ogen pulled some of us aside and told us not to lose hope, not to quit and to press harder than ever for information. I saw a genuine sincerity in his eyes. He wasn't lying. He knew what we felt. He felt bad.

Another time, when I was traveling in Southeast Asia in 1973, I was in touch with people who were affiliated with sensitive military sourcing. One gentleman asked me if I would mind stepping outside my hotel to talk. He told that he had seen my husband's name on a list with the names of twenty-two other individuals who had been taken into Hunan Province in Southern China. Although I realized the paper could have been just a working document or speculation, when I traveled on to Paris, I related the story to Mark Pratt, first secretary for Indochina Affairs at the American Embassy. Pratt said, "It's more likely that your husband was taken to Russia, rather than China." He explained that it was probable the Vietnamese had either kept the men or given them to their allies.

I've been to Southeast Asia a total of three times and to Paris once. When I went to Southeast Asia the first time in the fall of 1973, I found it helpful to talk to some of the support personnel in American stations, but I decided to also make contact with the Vietnamese and the Lao. I traveled from Bangkok, Thailand to Vientiane, Laos, which was then under a coalition government — part free, part Communist. I was led, under guard, into the North Vietnamese Embassy in Vientiane, where I spoke with officials. They made some surprising admissions. They claimed they were in control of Americans being held in Laos. The chargé told me that my husband would be released upon the fulfillment of certain conditions. He rambled on about some fifteen conditions and also stated that I would have to return to America and work with the peace movement if I ever wanted to have contact with my husband.

I went back to Southeast Asia in 1975 and visited with Army Col. Pat Volmar, the man in charge of the JCRC (Joint Casualty Resolution Center). I walked in, sat down in his office and without my saying a word, he closed the door and said, "Ah, I agree. That's a good idea, Mrs. Bosiljevac. We'll make an offer to pay for the maintenance and medical care of the prisoners to keep them alive until we can get them out." He knew that I knew prisoners were being detained. I don't know if any efforts were ever made to furnish medical supplies to the POWs.

Working with various government officials over the years has been both helpful and frustrating. Some people have worked hard and helped me along the way. A few were quiet plodders within the system, others put their careers on the line to make a point. On the other hand, I feel some individuals have made poor political decisions. I guess a number of those decisions were made early on because the country was trying to move beyond the stigma of the Vietnam War. I'm not interested in casting blame on who did what to whom but I think these early policies set the scene. Politicians were afraid that even talking about the war would rile the public and change the nation's political climate. I think the State Department was genuinely hostile. I imagine some people there were given the job of eliminating the issue.

A man whom I respected a great deal was Ed Manny. He served on the MIA/POW Task Force at the Defense Department in the early 1970s. I admired him for being truthful and straightforward in explaining the government line — that the missing men were being considered a "reasonable level of casualty." He pointed out, "If 25,000 men were still missing, the Defense Department would get excited about it, but 2,500 men is considered a reasonable level of casualty. The irony is that, statistically, it makes sense. But, if you look at it on a human level it's different."

It was my impression that the people working in the intelligence community were having a hard time accepting the decision to presume all the missing men dead. They were the ones dealing with the facts, getting the information and sorting it out. Declaring all the men dead certainly didn't fit with what they were seeing. If they looked at the wall map, pinpointing where these men went down, it appeared that the men crashed in areas where they likely would have been captured or their bodies recovered. The classification of these men then as "reasonable casualties" no longer seemed justified. I think it was hard for them to sit back and listen to government policy, especially when the families started to fight back.

It was a surprise to the administration when we started to fight because essentially, in all previous wars people had been told to go away and they did. In our cases, the National League of Families decided declarations of death by the military were occurring too rapidly for us to accept. Families of other veterans were coming to us, reminding us that live Americans had been left behind in the Korean War and that it shouldn't be allowed to happen in this war.

The Departments of State and Defense held differing opinions over what to do about this problem. The basic resolve, however, was to get rid of it. We families kept the concern alive and showed our determination even through some very hard years when people like Congressman Sonny Montgomery showed up to do his hatchet work on the missing men and their families. When he led the 1976 House Select Committee on Missing Persons in Southeast Asia, we were accused of all kinds of things, like being involved in this issue for the money. It was incredible. I couldn't understand it.

Even though Montgomery's committee finally concluded that no living Americans were being detained in Southeast Asia, we continued to try to educate congressmen and make trips to foreign embassies, letting it be known that we intended to persevere. We were trying to point out that the Vietnamese had withheld French prisoners and then used them for bargaining tools. In the case of the

American prisoners, the Vietnamese were demanding war reparations. They consistently linked the return of men to the Paris Peace Accords, Articles, 8a, 8b and Article 22, which dealt with reparations and an accounting of prisoners and the missing. It was tied together into one package.

I think we can look back and see how some very poor decisions were made at a critical time. Not only were government agencies disagreeing, it all came at a time when Watergate was breaking. It was a confusing period in America. Henry Kissinger may have had some pragmatic attitudes about the war, but he was careless in negotiating for American prisoners. The Defense Department was helpful, but locked into policy. The State Department people were simply not willing to cooperate. We families were considered radicals. If you get to know the families, you'll find we're hardly a group of radicals. It was a bad situation and bad decisions were made. I believe the families have made progress, however, and the government realizes trying to eliminate the problem was probably the worst avenue it could have taken. It was a different type of war. Whitewash wouldn't make it go away.

Basically, I feel we have a sound government. Even when policy is against you, it's possible to work on things through channels . . . if you can stay around long enough to get the task accomplished. In this situation, time is critical. The best thing we can do now to help the men, the government and the families of these men is to unite and not waste our time going back over the past. It's useful to understand it and report it so it won't happen again but you can't take it back or dwell on it. What does it change? When I look back and recall how I reacted to certain things, it makes me wish I could change them. There were times when I showed a lot of anger and frustration. As soon as I got to the point where I could forgive people, life became a lot easier. I knew I had done the best I could to get answers and I would continue working to get more answers.

The families have a combined hope. We hope that some of the men in captivity can come out. We'd rejoice at seeing anyone who made it, whether it's our relative or not. I think the important thing is that the public understands the issue. Block out, if you will, our comfortable surroundings, microwave ovens, expressways, the good life . . . and try to imagine being imprisoned in Vietnam or Laos. Every generation in those countries has lived with war but we as Americans must stretch our imaginations to realize the types of cruelties that have been perpetrated on our men — being detained, called war criminals, being sentenced for undetermined numbers of years, being given away as payments to benefactors. We must realize these things really happen in this world. It's hard to comprehend. In fact, the biggest frustration I've encountered is people saying, "Na, it's not possible — they couldn't be holding prisoners. It just can't be." So, it's forgotten. It's a natural reaction for a Western mind. However, as a nation, I fear we set ourselves up for future terrorist activity if we're unwilling to understand Communist tactics. I consider withholding live Americans a terrorist tactic and it's one they've gotten away with so far.

I predict that eventually the Vietnamese will want to deal . . . to straighten out the situation. I believe the Vietnamese are intent on getting their demands met, even if they have to angle it through another country. I don't know exactly what they'll do but I suspect they'll do something. Otherwise, why would they have warehoused remains? I think they'll turn them over but will command a price for them. It's always concerned me that this country declared the men dead. It sends a signal that we're not expecting the men to return or that we're interested only in their remains. It indicates almost a preference for remains over live men. However, it wouldn't surprise me to see live prisoners coming out. Survivability is possible. They can keep the prisoners alive if they wish. It's hard to believe they would use them that way but like it or not, we're in a pretty hostile world.

Col. Brendan Foley
U.S. Air Force
Lost: November 24, 1967
Border of Laos and North Vietnam

CHAPTER TWENTY-FOUR
DERMOT FOLEY

The years of effort I've contributed to the MIA/POW cause were motivated by my brother's loss, and as an attorney I've been deeply involved in the legal aspects of the issue. For years, I served as the legal counsel for the National League of Families. However, my interest in POWs goes beyond the Vietnam conflict. Back at Columbia Law School, my roommate was a POW in the Korean War. We were also classmates in undergraduate school and are still best friends. The day my brother, Brendan, became missing he told me that Brendan and others in his position were going to be in a "very bad way" and that I should be aware the government would give the issue lip service but be basically unconcerned. At the time, it didn't seem possible but I knew the guy well enough to give credence to what he said. I decided I wouldn't prejudge the situation adversely but would certainly keep an eye on it.

As the years went by, the very things my friend had predicted began coming true. The families of the missing men have been on the front lines of their own battle with the government and military establishment for more than a decade. We families, have sought, with little or no success, to penetrate the massive government bureaucracy and produce some changes in attitude and policy on the subject of MIA/POWs.

Unfortunately, we have collided with the arrogantly ineffec-
tual bureaucracy which has been long on bromides and
blandishments but short on objective accomplishments. We have
found and exposed dismal failures in bureaucratic performance but
we have not found anyone who is able and willing to truly remedy
the problem or even remove the incompetents who remain on the
job.

It's important to look at the makeup of the MIA/POW
families. Not everyone would have kept up the battle like these
folks. While many of them describe themselves as typically American, I'm not so sure they are. Ninety-five percent of the missing
men are college graduates; eighty- eight percent were officers or
airmen. Their families represent a similar distinction from what you
might call the average American. I would say, by and large, they
are above average in education and probably above average in career
position and earning power. They are pro-government, pro-military
and quite conservative. There are few exceptions.

Toward the end of the Vietnam conflict, family members
began to seriously question the way our government was treating the
MIA issue. We were giving a lot and getting damn little back except
for vague rhetoric. One of the first things military officials mention
when they come to your house to tell you someone is missing is that
"everything possible" is being done. It's a totally meaningless
phrase, straight out of the regulation book, by the way. That entire
performance is spelled out in regulations. We families have had to
deal with built-in vagueness and meaningless phrases every step of
the way. Even now, you hear such words as "commitment" . . .
"We're committed to do something." It goes beyond MIAs; it's one
of the meaningless phrases in American politics today. It means
"get lost." It says, "Hey, I'm on your side, now you've won the
argument, go home and leave me alone. Get lost."

As early as 1972, some families were beginning to sense the
government couldn't be trusted. They were afraid the government
would let them down. There aren't words around to describe the ill

will heaped on some of the family members by pro-government people who were in control of the National League of Families at that time.

In the early fall of 1972, I was not getting too involved in politics and public statements. I tend to feel those things don't help. But what I did do was begin in-depth research into what happened after the Korean War. I found two things that disturbed me quite a bit. First I learned that after the Korean War, the federal government, under the Missing Persons Act, simply and arbitrarily declared dead anyone the North Koreans did not send back to us. This was done administratively, without a hearing, a notice or any inquiry or participation by families involved. It was over and done with. Looking over the Missing Persons Act, I immediately saw grave constitutional problems. The second thing that alarmed me was the language of the Paris Peace Accords. Sections of the document were a stunning disappointment to me, particularly the language of Article 8b, the section which provides for return of prisoners, repatriation of remains and accounting for the missing.

To my amazement, I found it followed the precise pattern that led to failure in getting a full accounting for the missing after the Korean War. The agreement at the end of the Korean War contained the same defects. The same mistake had been repeated. I'll never forget the night I first read that agreement and realized immediately what it meant — the peace accords were written to be violated. It's not fair to say the violation was one sided. Both sides violated it. Everyone involved knew that at the time. The agreement was a way for the U.S. to get out. The Vietnamese saw it as the end of the trail, with victory at hand.

At this point, I wanted to dig in with every ounce of legal expertise I could muster to fight what I knew was about to come . . . declarations of death for all those still missing. Soon enough, we were told of the government plan to do just that.

In preparation for Operation Homecoming, in 1972, the Defense Department arranged regional meetings across the country for the MIA families. The purpose was to have experts brief us on details of Operation Homecoming and describe the problems to be anticipated. I think they were expecting the returned POWs to be a group of mutilated, mentally disturbed catastrophies. There were plenty of those, but they were never returned. The returned POWs were in much better shape than anticipated.

Although most aspects of Operation Homecoming were handled well, I do have one bone to pick about the debriefings of the returned prisoners. I think the debriefings were a great way for them to ventilate, get things off their chests. But the information was never fully used. In a lot of cases, the tape recordings of their debriefings were never transcribed. I happen to know of the basement where many of those tapes are still kept today.

Anyway, during our regional meeting, I asked a question, "You've told us what you're going to do with those people who are coming home . . . now tell us what you're going to do about the people who don't come home." After some hesitation, one of the military officers responded, "We're going to declare them dead, under the Missing Persons Act." The legal battle was about to begin.

We joined forces with a group based in California called VIVA, Voices in Vital America. They too were concerned about missing men being declared dead. After a couple of meetings to get organized, we decided to take the matter to court. We believed constitutional problems existed with the way the Missing Persons Act was written and the way it was being implemented. We started drafting the lawsuit that summer and filed it in September of 1973. The first case was *McDonald vs. McLucas*. We filed in the U.S. District Court for the Southern District of New York. It was a class action suit seeking a declaratory judgment of unconstitutionality, and an injunction prohibiting the military from making any further declarations of death. The whole purpose was to have the declaration of death provisions in the Missing Persons Act declared unconstitutional in two ways — on its face, as written and in the manner in

which it was applied. The most important basis for unconstitutionality was the absence of a hearing.

We struck luck right at the start of the lawsuit. The judge,
Charles M. Metzner, conducted a hearing on the preliminary injunction and granted it. He not only granted it, but wrote a long decision
on why he granted it, buying our cases right down the line. The day
I read that decision I knew we could not lose the lawsuit. The judge
had painted himself into a corner, but an appropriate corner. It was
then I realized the lawsuit was really over. It was just a matter of
carrying on with it. The case was then assigned to a panel of three
federal judges — a standard procedure for resolution of constitutional challenges at that time, but one which has since been changed.

In February of 1974, the court came down with a decision
holding the statute unconstitutional as applied because of the absence
of a hearing. Having done this, the court decided that it was not
necessary to review the other constitutional issues. The decision
meant the military could resume status reviews but would have to
incorporate new procedures which, for the first time, included a
hearing. The government had to go about the business of redrafting
the regulations and deciding how to set up hearings.

Another important case is *Hopper vs. Carter*, filed in 1977.
It was the first case in which we named the president as a defendant.
The case is still in court, but dormant for now. It was August of
1977 when President Jimmy Carter announced the government was
going to proceed with declarations of death. Up to then, the government had put an informal hold on determinations of death except in
the cases where primary next of kin had requested them. In the
Hopper case, we weren't successful in stopping the status changes.
I think the judge is disturbed and concerned by the case. I know the
judge, Jack B. Weinstein, a remarkably intelligent and sensitive
individual. I took classes under him at Columbia Law School. I
think he feels the need to get past the emotionalism before he can
decide if there's really a case. He's basically inclined to think
there's not, but has been willing to keep an open mind. Essentially

he is saying if you need a case, this one is here. For example, if a prisoner does come out of Southeast Asia, a lot of legal implications would have to be considered. The case is still there but no one's pushing it right now.

Politics, of course, have had an influence on the MIA problem. I see the League's own internal politics having had some negative effects. In the early 1970s, many of us felt the people in charge of the League were too pro-government. I believe everyone has a right to his or her opinion, but this issue called for a "healthy" adversarial relationship with the government. Nothing was being accomplished. Everyone was nice to everyone else. League representatives were, in a mild, inoffensive way urging the government to pursue an accounting, but the approach was openly nonadversarial. There's nothing nonadversarial about whether a guy is alive or dead. But, many of the League people felt it would have been disloyal to challenge the government. So, during a 1974 League meeting in Omaha, Nebraska, with the vigorous support of over ninety percent of the League membership, the pro-government leadership was replaced.

Oddly enough, almost overnight, we began to pay the price. Our volunteer lawyer quit. Our headquarters' free WATS lines were cut off. One good development was the loss of our advisory committee, made up of folks supplied by the government, who were supposed to know how to get things done. These included such illustrious figures as E. Howard Hunt and Fletcher Prouty who was a CIA operative. They all had been there to "help us." Well, we may have been alone, but we weren't beholden to anyone. We were poor, but better off because at least we owned our own outfit. I know other family members disagreed with me, insisting the government operation was the only show in town so we should have cooperated. I believed in affirmative, aggressive cooperation but not in domination.

Reflecting over my fifteen years of involvement with the MIA/POW issue, several individuals and events stand out in my mind. The "mortician" who came out of Vietnam as a refugee in 1980 was a major development in the course of events. Now, I've always kept a pretty close ear to the ground. I knew about the mortician before the U.S. government or the League did and even had his name, which no one else did at the time. I got my information from my own sources who also told me about the military unit he belonged to in Vietnam. The mortician was a bigger wheel in Vietnam than many people realized. When Congressman Lester Wolff used to go to Vietnam for meetings as a representative of the House Subcommittee on Asian and Pacific Affairs, the mortician would always be among those in the welcoming committee. You can see him in pictures. He's very obese. He was in charge of a hell of a lot more than processing remains.

I think we need to ask ourselves if the mortician was a refugee, a defector or a messenger. I say he was a messenger, that the Vietnamese sent him here with a message about American remains. It was a subtle offer to make a deal. Unfortunately, the U.S. position has been: no deals. That's easy to say if you're sitting behind a desk in Washington; it wouldn't be so easy if you were sitting in some cell in a remote area of Laos. I consider it indisputable that the Vietnamese have been sending messages for several years and our bureaucracy has refused to hear them.

Another peculiar experience had to do with an individual named Sean Toolis, who showed up in Chicago in December of 1980. He told me that he had just come out of Vietnam and that he had seen my brother in a gun factory. He explained that my brother Brendan, who was working in the factory, had slipped him a note saying, "Contact my brother, D. Foley, attorney, New York City." Toolis says my brother spoke to him in Gaelic. Now my brother and I spent a lot of time in Ireland when we were kids. We both spoke Gaelic but I would never go up to someone and say something in Gaelic, and find it difficult to visualize my brother doing so. Toolis said after he translated the note into Gaelic in his notebook, he destroyed the original copy so he wouldn't be caught with it. He claimed he was in Vietnam as a smuggler, buying arms for the I.R.A. Toolis also brought out a fingerprint he said was Brendan's, but it proved not to be.

Toolis was, however, able to identify my brother in a group photo. But in short, Toolis hasn't given me enough evidence. I don't want to condemn him, but I'll need more before I can go any further with him. I don't totally discount what he says but don't believe all he's told me. I've spent thousands of dollars checking out Toolis and his goods. I had to pursue it — it's another case where the government refused to investigate effectively.

I'm still curious about how my brother was lost. I don't believe I've been given the straight facts. The story goes that he was flying a reconnaisance aircraft, doing weather reconnaisance. By the way, "weather reconnaisance" is one of the great euphemisms of the Vietnam War. It doesn't mean a thing. We lost so many guys doing weather reconnaisance. We may have lost the war but we sure knew a lot about the weather. I think it's what people were told in some cases where the military didn't want to say what was really going on. My brother is alleged to have gone out over a route leading from Thailand to Laos then northwest of Hanoi and back. Radar tracked him for about 105 miles then lost him. He was never heard from again.

I don't know if we'll ever see a resolution to this problem. I'm convinced men are still being held in Southeast Asia but I don't know if we'll ever get them back. The government says it's committed again, but I'm not sure that says anything more than, "Hey folks, we're committed. You can go home happy now because we're going to start doing things differently." It's that type of reasoning that will preclude the problem's being solved. To my way of thinking, if our government wanted to seriously undertake the responsibility of completing the accounting of those missing, it would have to do several things. First, it would assess what went wrong with the accounting process and determine who was responsible. Secondly, if the persons responsible were still around, as many of them are, they would be ousted so that they could cause no further harm. Then, in a businesslike manner, a plan of action would be developed and those in charge would be responsible for accomplishing the goal. The possibility of failure would be deemphasized. The will to succeed would be emphasized. Performance accountability would be a reality. In short, the enterprise, finally, would begin to look as though it was being conducted by people with the ability and determination to succeed. At long last, the "commitment" and "priority" would be real.

A big part of the problem all along has been denial. Many in the U.S. feel bad about the possibility of men being withheld. They feel so bad about it they choose to believe it can't be true. Bureaucratic inertia feeds on this.

Still, there's only one message here. No one has ever gotten serious about this issue. Nothing will happen until someone does.

AFTERWORD

Over a decade after the Vietnam War, MIA families and concerned citizens have scored a partial victory in the battle to create greater public awareness about the POW issue. Perhaps at no time since the war's end have more Americans, including lawmakers and members of the media, been more aware of the POW controversy. With some of the war's painful memories behind, the nation has not only come back to honor its veterans who returned from Vietnam, but also has begun asking questions about those who didn't return. Unfortunately, the search for answers is ongoing and difficult, hindered by the tangled rhetoric exchanged between two former enemies.

Just as the MIA/POW issue is complex, so is a resolution to the problem. Based on the premise that Americans are still being held against their will in Southeast Asia, how does the U.S. gain the release of these men? Several possible outcomes exist.

Diplomatic negotiations, through which the Vietnamese would agree to release prisoners to the U.S., would be the most desirable way to resolve the crisis; however, the diplomatic process is painfully slow and, historically, U.S. diplomacy with Communist governments has been largely ineffective. Ongoing diplomatic talks have been further hampered by the Vietnamese' continued denial that they hold any Americans. Without such an admission, even the most skilled U.S. diplomats are left with no foothold in discussions, and direct negotiation for the prisoners' release is virtually impossible.

From the Vietnamese point of view, economic assistance may be the key to the deadlock in negotiations. The Vietnamese have, since the war's end, considered economic aid as a pre-condition to their accounting for America's missing servicemen, but U.S. foreign policy prohibits responding to blackmail — paying for the release of hostages or prisoners. Even though the Vietnamese have not, in recent years, linked the MIA/POW issue to economic assistance, it would be contrary to their nature to take actions which would benefit another government unless they were able to profit from the move themselves. In fact, they sit patiently, waiting for the best deal, ultimately seeking normalized relations with the U.S.

The subject of normalization sparks another argument; currently, the accounting issue is one of several factors precluding normalized relations with Vietnam. The U.S. could normalize relations with the Vietnamese, anticipating that Hanoi would then turn over American prisoners, but opponents argue that such action by the U.S. would relieve Hanoi of any pressure to release their captives. Then the Vietnamese, no longer needing POWs for bargaining power, could dispose of them, never admitting that they held prisoners. On the other hand, American recognition of Vietnam, along with economic aid, could result in their giving up the men they withheld. Between these two possibilities lies the delicacy of negotiation.

Even though diplomatic talks have moved slowly, U.S.-Vietnamese technical talks have not been without some progress. Most notably, in February 1986, the Vietnamese for the first time ever, began talking about the possibility of American prisoners still in Southeast Asia. Vietnamese officials told a U.S. congressional delegation that it was possible some Americans, of whom they were not aware, could be held in remote areas. The Vietnamese willingness to discuss this possibility was a major departure from their previous position that no Americans were being held in Vietnam.

Further, as a result of diplomatic talks, the Vietnamese stated during the summer of 1985 that they wished to resolve the MIA/POW controversy within two years. This apparent change in the Hanoi government's attitude could be a sign that the Vietnamese are positioning themselves for the release of prisoners, or it could mean only that they intend to return more of the human remains they harbor. Despite their stated intention to be more forthright, the Vietnamese have frequently canceled MIA/POW talks on a whim and have backed away from pledges to furnish MIA/POW information. They have routinely cited poor U.S. attitude as reason for such postponements.

Perhaps a more expedient solution, the U.S. could independently confirm the existence and location of POWs in Southeast Asia through intelligence sources. Such confirmation would leave the U.S. with several options, depending on the status of negotiations at the time. Basically, the options range from immediate negotiations in which release is demanded within hours to a military rescue.

Understandably, a military rescue operation can tolerate only minimal risk of casualties for both prisoners and a rescue force. As with the Son Tay raid, which was a well-planned exercise, the risk of failure is constant. Highly perishable intelligence information on prison locations is one of the most crucial factors. Typically, the Vietnamese have held prisoners in small groups, in camps scattered throughout the thick jungle, and they have moved the prisoners regularly. During the war, even the prisoners within the impenetrable walls of Hoa Lo were moved around inside the prison to thwart escape and disrupt communications. Consequently, a rescue attempt might require updating intelligence reports on prison camp locations several times a day.

Whether a military rescue would be undertaken also depends on other factors such as location and terrain. Are the prisoners heavily guarded or are they moving about relatively freely? Are they being held near a coast or deep within the jungle?

In any case, confirmation of the POWs' existence would not necessarily be made public. Pentagon sources have said that the U.S. likely would not admit the existence of prisoners until a plan is in place to retrieve them or until they have been freed. According to other intelligence experts the government would not make an admission if it might endanger the lives of prisoners. Unfortunately, it is this need for classifying information that has also left the American public with unanswered questions about the government commitment to strengthen intelligence capabilities in order to obtain confirmation.

The government's failure to bring out any prisoners has strengthened the call, in some circles, for a private rescue — a rescue planned and executed by civilians. It is possible that non-military personnel could develop intelligence information that could verify the prisoners' existence; however, military experts criticize the concept of a private rescue operation, arguing that a civilian group would lack the sophisticated equipment needed to execute such an exercise.

Finally, despite the hard work by increasing numbers of Americans concerned about the return of POWs, the possibility exists that no additional Americans will come out of Southeast Asia. The U.S. could be left with a bitter lesson — that some men fell through the cracks in a system which had no means for retrieving them.

But the indomitable will of the American people is the force that can prevent this outcome. Persistent Americans, demanding the return of their countrymen, can influence politics in Washington and Hanoi as well as affect world opinion.

Without a clamorous appeal by the American public, the worst outcome will be realized. This scenario is best described by Alexander Solzhenitsyn, now an American citizen, who spent years in Soviet prisons as a political prisoner. Through his words we can

understand the possible fates of those men who have not yet
returned from Vietnam:

> *"If the government of North Vietnam has difficulty explain-*
> *ing to you what happened with your brothers, with your*
> *American POWs who have not yet returned, I, on the basis of*
> *my experience in the Archipelago, can explain this quite clearly.*
> *There is a law in the Archipelago that those who have been*
> *treated the most harshly and who have withstood the most*
> *bravely, the most honest, the most courageous, the most*
> *unbending, never again come out into the world. They are never*
> *again shown to the world because they will tell such tales as the*
> *human mind cannot accept.*
>
> *A part of your returned POWs told you that they were tor-*
> *tured. This means that those who have remained were tortured*
> *even more, but did not yield an inch. These are your best*
> *people. These are your first heroes, who, in a solitary combat,*
> *have stood the test. And today, unfortunately, they cannot take*
> *courage from our applause. They can't hear it from their solitary*
> *cells where they may either die or sit thirty years . . ."*

> *Alexander Solzhenitsyn*
> *Washington, D.C.*
> *June 30, 1975*

BIBLIOGRAPHY

Boettcher, Thomas D. "We Can Keep You...Forever." *National Review*, August 1981, pp. 958-962.

Clarke, Douglas L. *The Missing Man, Politics and the MIA*. Washington, D.C.: National Defense University, 1979.

Clark, Mark W. *From the Danube to the Yalu*. New York: Harper & Brothers, 1954.

Copulos, Milt. "The French Experience." *Soldier of Fortune*, Spring 1983, pp. 66-67.

Defense Intelligence Agency. "DIA Findings on the Report of US PWs in Vietnam from Refugee Ngo Phi Hung." Washington, D.C., [1978].

Department of Defense. *POW-MIA Fact Book*. Washington, D.C.: February 1985.

Department of Press and Information, Ministry of Foreign Affairs, Socialist Republic of Vietnam. *On the Question of Americans Missing in the Vietnam War*. Hanoi: [1980].

Dimas, David D. *Missing in Action/Prisoner of War, A Report to the American People.* La Mirada, Cal.: By the Author, 1984.

Groom, Winston. *Conversations With The Enemy.* New York: Putnam, 1983.

Halloran, Bernard F. "Intelligence Watch." *Army Reserve Magazine*, May 1977, p. 32.

Heller, Bruce L. "Pathet Lao Knowledgeability on U.S. PWs." Washington, D.C.: Defense Intelligence Agency, [1977].

Hubbell, John G. *P.O.W.* New York: Reader's Digest Press, 1976.

Hunter, Edna J. *Prolonged Separation: The Prisoner of War and His Family.* San Diego, California: Center for Prisoner of War Studies, Naval Health Research Center, [1977].

"Laos Tribe Likely Led MIA Hunt." *Omaha World Herald*, May 21, 1981, p. 1.

"Missing: Search for American MIAs in Southeast Asia Goes On." *Los Angeles Times*, March 29, 1983, Part 1, p. 8.

National League of Families. "Analysis of the Final Report of the House Select Committee on Missing Persons in Southeast Asia." Washington, D.C.: [1977].

National League of Families. *Report Concerning Misinformation On The Issue Of American Prisoners of War And Missing In Action In Southeast Asia.* Washington, D.C.: [1985].

"Robert Garwood Says Vietnam Didn't Return Some American POWs." *Wall Street Journal*, December 4, 1984; April 24, 1985.

Roberts, James C. *Missing in Action.* Washington, D.C.: The Fund for Objective News Reporting, 1980.

"Trial Documents Suggest Army Left POWs in Korea." *Omaha World Herald* (Associated Press), July 17, 1983.

U.S. Congress. House. Select Committee on Missing Persons in Southeast Asia. *Americans Missing in Southeast Asia, Hearings before the House Select Committee on Missing Persons in Southeast Asia* (5 vols.), 94th Congress, 2nd sess., 1976.

U.S. Congress. House. Subcommittee on Asia and Pacific Affairs. *POW-MIAs: Oversight, Hearing before the House Subcommittee on Asian and Pacific Affairs*, 96th Congress, 2nd sess., 1980.

U.S. Congress. House. Subcommittee on Asian and Pacific Affairs. *Prisoners of War/Missing in Action: Oversight, Hearing before the Subcommittee on Asian and Pacific Affairs*, 97th Congress, 1st sess., 1981.

U.S. Congress. House. Subcommittee on Asian and Pacific Affairs. *New Information on U.S. MIA-POW's in Indochina? Hearing before the Subcommittee on Asian and Pacific Affairs*, 98th Congress, 1st sess., 1983.

U.S. Congress. House. Subcommittee on Asian and Pacific Affairs. *MIA/POW's in Southeast Asia: A Continuing*

National Priority, Hearing before the Subcommittee on Asian and Pacific Affairs, 98th Congress, 1st sess., 1983.

U.S. Congress. House. Subcommittee on Asian and Pacific Affairs. *MIA/POWs: Oversight, Hearing before the House Subcommittee on Asian and Pacific Affairs* , 99th Congress, 1st sess., 1985.

U.S. Congress. Senate. Committee on Judiciary. *Communist Treatment of Prisoners of War, A Historical Survey Prepared for the Committee on the Judiciary, United States Senate*, 92nd Congress, 2nd sess., 1972.

U.S. Department of State. *Report of the Presidential Commission's Trip to Vietnam and Laos*, March 16-20, 1977.

The Washington Post, May 25, 1973; December 23, 1976; February 26, 1977; March 17, 18, 19, 20, 21, 24, 1977; May 21, 1981.

APPENDIX

U.S. SERVICEMEN
UNACCOUNTED FOR BY STATE*

Alabama - 43	Nebraska - 24
Alaska - 3	Nevada - 10
Arizona - 24	New Hampshire - 10
Arkansas - 27	New Jersey - 63
California - 244	New Mexico - 17
Colorado - 41	New York - 157
Connecticut - 39	North Carolina - 61
Delaware - 5	North Dakota - 17
District of Columbia - 9	Ohio - 128
Florida - 80	Oklahoma - 49
Georgia - 48	Oregon - 46
Hawaii - 11	Pennsylvania - 119
Idaho - 12	Rhode Island - 10
Illinois - 100	South Carolina - 30
Indiana - 70	South Dakota - 9
Iowa - 39	Tennessee - 44
Kansas - 38	Texas - 159
Kentucky - 22	Utah - 23
Louisiana - 34	Vermont - 4
Maine - 17	Virginia - 61
Maryland - 37	Washington - 60
Massachusetts - 59	West Virginia - 26
Michigan - 75	Wisconsin - 37
Minnesota - 47	Wyoming - 6
Mississippi - 18	Puerto Rico - 2
Missouri - 51	Virgin Islands - 1
Montana - 21	Other - 7

*DoD figures, June, 1986.

MISSING U.S. SERVICEMEN

COUNTRY	UNACCOUNTED FOR/PFOD	*KIA (BNR)**	CIVILIANS	
			Missing	Presumed Dead
North Vietnam	442	253	0	0
South Vietnam	442	675	13	12
Laos	351	205	7	4
Cambodia	34	48	6	0
China	4	2	0	0
Sub-totals	Total 1,253	Total 1,183	26	16
TOTALS	2,436			42

*Presumptive Finding of Death
**Killed in Action--Body not Recovered

DoD figures, June, 1986

U.S. CASUALTIES IN SOUTHEAST ASIA
(MISSING IN ACTION)
MILITARY PERSONNEL

Name	Military Service	Country of Casualty	Date of Incident
Abrams, Lewis H.	Marine Corps	N. Vietnam	11-25-67
Acalotto, Robert J.	Army	Laos	2-20-71
Acosta-Rosario, Humberto	Army	S. Vietnam	8-22-68
Adachi, Thomas Y.	Air Force	Laos	4-22-70
Adam, John Q.	Air Force	Laos	5-22-68
Adams, John R.	Army	S. Vietnam	11-08-67
Adams, Lee A.	Air Force	N. Vietnam	4-19-66
Adams, Oley N.	Air Force	S. Vietnam	6-17-66
Adams, Samuel	Air Force	S. Vietnam	10-31-65
Adams, Steven H.	Air Force	N. Vietnam	10-18-66
Adkins, Charles L.	Army	S. Vietnam	2-02-68
Adrian, Joseph D.	Air Force	S. Vietnam	3-12-67
Ahlmeyer, Heinz, Jr.	Marine Corps	S. Vietnam	5-10-67
Alberton, Bobby J.	Air Force	N. Vietnam	5-31-66
Albright, John S., II	Air Force	Laos	12-13-68
Aldern, Donald D.	Navy	Laos	6-29-70
Aldrich, Lawrence L.	Army	S. Vietnam	5-06-68
Alford, Terry L.	Army	S. Vietnam	11-04-69
Alfred, Gerald O., Jr.	Air Force	N. Vietnam	12-11-66
Algaard, Harold L.	Army	N. Vietnam	3-04-71
Allard, Michael J.	Navy	N. Vietnam	8-30-67
Allard, Richard M.	Army	S. Vietnam	8-24-67
Allee, Richard K.	Air Force	Laos	12-21-68
Allen, Henry L.	Air Force	Laos	3-26-70
Allen, Merlin R.	Marine Corps	S. Vietnam	6-30-67
Allen, Thomas R.	Air Force	N. Vietnam	7-31-67
Allen, Wayne C.	Army	S. Vietnam	1-10-70
Alley, Gerald W.	Air Force	N. Vietnam	12-22-72
Alley, James H.	Air Force	S. Vietnam	4-06-72
Allgood, Frankie E.	Marine Corps	S. Vietnam	3-26-68
Allinson, David J.	Air Force	N. Vietnam	8-12-66

Name	Military Service	Country of Casualty	Date of Incident
Alloway, Clyde D.	Air Force	S. Vietnam	6-07-70
Alm, Richard A.	Marine Corps	N. Vietnam	2-01-66
Almendariz, Samuel	Army	Laos	7-12-67
Altizer, Albert H.	Army	S. Vietnam	10-08-69
Altus, Robert W.	Air Force	Laos	11-23-71
Alwan, Harold J.	Marine Corps	S. Vietnam	2-27-67
Amesbury, Harry A., Jr.	Air Force	S. Vietnam	4-26-72
Amos, Thomas H.	Air Force	S. Vietnam	4-20-72
Amspacher, William H.	Navy	N. Vietnam	6-02-65
Anderson, Denis L.	Navy	Laos	1-11-68
Anderson, Gregory L.	Air Force	N. Vietnam	1-28-70
Anderson, Robert D.	Air Force	N. Vietnam	10-06-72
Anderson, Thomas E.	Marine Corps	S. Vietnam	10-06-62
Anderson, Warren L.	Air Force	N. Vietnam	4-26-66
Andre, Howard V., Jr.	Air Force	Laos	7-08-69
Andrews, Stuart M.	Air Force	S. Vietnam	3-04-66
Andrews, William R.	Air Force	N. Vietnam	10-05-66
Angell, Marshall J.	Army	S. Vietnam	12-12-63
Angstadt, Ralph H.	Air Force	N. Vietnam	10-18-66
Anselmo, William F.	Air Force	S. Vietnam	3-06-68
Anspach, Robert A.	Army	S. Vietnam	9-11-67
Antunano, Gregory A.	Army	Cambodia	7-24-71
Apodaca, Victor J., Jr.	Air Force	N. Vietnam	6-08-67
Appleby, Ivan D.	Air Force	N. Vietnam	10-07-67
Applehans, Richard D.	Air Force	Laos	10-16-67
Ard, Randolph J.	Army	Laos	3-07-71
Armitstead, Steven R.	Marine Corps	Laos	3-17-69
Armond, Robert L.	Air Force	S. Vietnam	6-18-65
Armstrong, Frank A., III	Air Force	Laos	10-06-67
Armstrong, John W.	Air Force	Laos	11-09-67
Arnold, William T.	Navy	N. Vietnam	11-18-66
Ashall, Alan F.	Navy	N. Vietnam	8-29-68
Ashby, Clayborn W., Jr.	Navy	Laos	2-17-68
Ashby, Donald R., Sr.	Navy	S. Vietnam	1-19-67
Ashlock, Carlos	Marine Corps	S. Vietnam	5-12-67
Asire, Donald H.	Air Force	N. Vietnam	12-08-66
Asmussen, Glenn E.	Navy	S. Vietnam	2-05-66
Aston, Jay S.	Army	S. Vietnam	7-18-71
Austin, Carl B.	Navy	N. Vietnam	12-02-65
Austin, Charles D.	Air Force	N. Vietnam	4-24-67
Austin, Ellis E.	Navy	N. Vietnam	4-21-66
Austin, Joseph C.	Air Force	N. Vietnam	3-19-67
Auxier, Jerry E.	Army	S. Vietnam	7-29-68
Avery, Allen J.	Air Force	S. Vietnam	4-06-72

Name	Military Service	Country of Casualty	Date of Incident
Avery, Robert D.	Marine Corps	N. Vietnam	5-03-68
Avolese, Paul A.	Air Force	S. Vietnam	7-07-67
Avore, Malcolm A.	Navy	S. Vietnam	7-18-65
Ayers, Darrell E.	Marine Corps	S. Vietnam	3-19-70
Ayers, Richard L.	Air Force	Laos	4-16-70
Ayres, Gerald F.	Air Force	S. Vietnam	6-18-72
Ayres, James H.	Air Force	Laos	1-03-71
Babcock, Ronald L.	Army	Laos	2-27-71
Babula, Robert L.	Marine Corps	S. Vietnam	8-28-66
Bacik, Vladimir H.	Marine Corps	N. Vietnam	8-27-67
Backus, Kenneth F.	Air Force	N. Vietnam	5-22-67
Bader, Arthur E., Jr.	Army	Laos	11-30-68
Badley, James L.	Air Force	N. Vietnam	3-27-68
Badolati, Frank N.	Army	S. Vietnam	1-29-66
Bailey, John E.	Air Force	N. Vietnam	5-10-66
Bailey, John H.	Marine Corps	S. Vietnam	5-01-67
Baker, Arthur D.	Air Force	Laos	4-07-65
Balamoti, Michael D.	Air Force	Laos	11-24-69
Balcom, Ralph C.	Air Force	N. Vietnam	5-15-66
Baldridge, John R., Jr.	Air Force	Laos	11-20-69
Bancroft, William W., Jr.	Air Force	N. Vietnam	11-13-70
Bankowski, Alfons A.	Air Force	Laos	3-23-61
Bannon, Paul W.	Air Force	Laos	7-12-69
Barber, Robert F.	Navy	N. Vietnam	9-18-65
Barber, Thomas D.	Navy	N. Vietnam	3-17-68
Barden, Howard L.	Air Force	Laos	1-31-67
Bare, William O.	Air Force	N. Vietnam	7-27-67
Barker, Jack L.	Army	Laos	3-20-71
Barnes, Charles R.	Army	S. Vietnam	3-16-69
Barnett, Charles E.	Navy	N. Vietnam	5-23-72
Barnett, Robert R.	Air Force	Laos	4-07-66
Barr, John F.	Navy	N. Vietnam	10-18-67
Barras, Gregory I.	Air Force	Laos	12-18-68
Bartocci, John E.	Navy	S. Vietnam	8-31-68
Bates, Paul J., Jr.	Army	S. Vietnam	8-10-71
Batt, Michael L.	Army	S. Vietnam	3-16-69
Bauder, James R.	Navy	N. Vietnam	9-21-66
Bauman, Richard L.	Army	Cambodia	3-17-71
Baxter, Bruce R.	Army	Laos	11-09-67
Beach, Arthur J.	Marine Corps	S. Vietnam	3-20-66
Beals, Charles E.	Army	S. Vietnam	7-07-70
Bebus, Charles J.	Air Force	N. Vietnam	12-21-72
Beccera, Rudy M.	Army	Cambodia	3-24-70
Beck, Edward E., Jr.	Marine Corps	S. Vietnam	8-09-69

Name	Military Service	Country of Casualty	Date of Incident
Beck, Terry L.	Navy	N. Vietnam	10-02-69
Becker, James C.	Army	Laos	8-15-70
Beckwith, Harry M., III	Army	S. Vietnam	3-24-71
Bednarek, Jonathan B.	Air Force	N. Vietnam	5-18-72
Beecher, Quentin R.	Army	S. Vietnam	6-11-67
Beene, James A.	Navy	N. Vietnam	10-05-66
Begley, Burriss N.	Air Force	N. Vietnam	12-05-66
Behnfeldt, Roger E.	Air Force	N. Vietnam	8-19-72
Belcher, Glenn A.	Air Force	Laos	12-31-67
Belcher, Robert A.	Air Force	S. Vietnam	3-28-69
Belknap, Harry J.	Navy	N. Vietnam	6-23-66
Bell, Holly G.	Air Force	N. Vietnam	1-28-70
Bell, Marvin E.	Air Force	Laos	6-30-70
Bell, Richard W.	Navy	N. Vietnam	10-02-69
Benedett, Daniel A.	Marine Corps	Cambodia	5-15-75
Bennefled, Steven H.	Marine Corps	S. Vietnam	7-29-67
Bennett, Harold G.	Army	S. Vietnam	12-29-64
Bennett, Robert E., III	Air Force	S. Vietnam	12-13-67
Bennett, Thomas W., Jr.	Air Force	N. Vietnam	12-22-72
Bennett, William G.	Air Force	N. Vietnam	9-02-67
Benson, Lee D.	Navy	N. Vietnam	3-17-68
Benton, Gregory R., Jr.	Marine Corps	S. Vietnam	5-23-69
Benton, James A.	Marine Corps	S. Vietnam	4-27-67
Berdahl, David D.	Army	S. Vietnam	1-20-72
Beresik, Eugene P.	Air Force	N. Vietnam	5-31-68
Berg, Bruce A.	Army	S. Vietnam	8-07-71
Berg, George P.	Army	Laos	2-18-71
Bergevin, Charles L.	Air Force	N. Vietnam	8-23-68
Berry, John A.	Army	S. Vietnam	12-05-68
Berube, Kenneth A.	Marine Corps	S. Vietnam	8-11-67
Bessor, Bruce C.	Army	Laos	5-13-69
Beutel, Robert D.	Air Force	Laos	11-26-71
Beyer, Thomas J.	Air Force	S. Vietnam	7-30-68
Bezold, Steven N.	Army	N. Vietnam	10-29-68
Bibbs, Wayne	Army	S. Vietnam	6-11-72
Biber, Gerald M.	Army	Laos	4-22-61
Bidwell, Barry A.	Navy	N. Vietnam	6-18-71
Bifolchi, Charles L.	Air Force	S. Vietnam	1-08-68
Biggs, Earl R.	Army	S. Vietnam	1-16-68
Billipp, Norman K.	Marine Corps	S. Vietnam	5-06-69
Bingham, Klaus J.	Army	S. Vietnam	5-10-71
Birchim, James D.	Army	S. Vietnam	11-15-68
Bird, Leonard A.	Marine Corps	S. Vietnam	7-13-68
Biscailuz, Robert L.	Marine Corps	S. Vietnam	7-30-67

Name	Military Service	Country of Casualty	Date of Incident
Bischoff, John M.	Army	Laos	4-22-61
Bishop, Edward J., Jr.	Army	S. Vietnam	4-29-70
Bisz, Ralph C.	Navy	N. Vietnam	8-04-67
Bittenbender, David F.	Air Force	S. Vietnam	7-07-67
Bivens, Herndon A.	Army	S. Vietnam	4-15-70
Bixel, Michael S.	Navy	N. Vietnam	10-24-72
Black, Paul V.	Army	Cambodia	3-01-71
Blackburn, Harry L., Jr.	Navy	N. Vietnam	5-10-72
Blackman, Thomas J.	Marine Corps	S. Vietnam	5-10-68
Blackwood, Gordon B.	Air Force	N. Vietnam	5-27-67
Blair, Charles E.	Air Force	S. Vietnam	3-19-68
Blankenship, Charles H.	Air Force	S. Vietnam	7-07-67
Blanton, Clarence F.	Air Force	Laos	3-11-68
Blassie, Michael J.	Air Force	S. Vietnam	5-11-72
Blessing, Lynn	Marine Corps	Cambodia	5-15-75
Blodgett, Douglas R.	Army	S. Vietnam	4-19-68
Bloodworth, Donald B.	Air Force	Laos	7-24-70
Bloom, Darl R.	Marine Corps	S. Vietnam	11-13-64
Bloom, Richard M.	Marine Corps	S. Vietnam	9-20-66
Bobe, Raymond E.	Army	S. Vietnam	3-16-69
Bodahl, Jon K.	Air Force	Laos	11-12-69
Bodden, Timothy R.	Marine Corps	Laos	6-03-67
Bodenschatz, John E., Jr.	Marine Corps	S. Vietnam	8-28-66
Boffman, Alan B.	Army	Laos	3-18-71
Bogard, Lonnie P.	Air Force	Laos	5-12-72
Boggs, Paschal G.	Marine Corps	N. Vietnam	8-27-67
Bogiages, Christos C., Jr.	Air Force	Laos	3-02-69
Bohlig, James R.	Marine Corps	S. Vietnam	8-19-69
Bohlscheid, Curtis R.	Marine Corps	S. Vietnam	6-11-67
Bois, Claire R.	Navy	N. Vietnam	8-25-67
Boles, Warren W.	Navy	N. Vietnam	1-18-68
Bollinger, Arthur R.	Air Force	Laos	2-05-73
Bolte, Wayne L.	Air Force	S. Vietnam	4-02-72
Boltze, Bruce E.	Marine Corps	S. Vietnam	10-06-72
Bond, Ronald D.	Air Force	S. Vietnam	3-11-68
Bond, Ronald L.	Air Force	Laos	9-30-71
Bookout, Charles F.	Army	Laos	7-04-70
Booth, Gary P.	Army	S. Vietnam	12-23-70
Booth, James E.	Air Force	N. Vietnam	6-23-68
Booth, Lawrence R.	Army	Laos	10-16-69
Booze, Delmar G.	Marine Corps	S. Vietnam	1-24-66
Borah, Daniel V., Jr.	Navy	S. Vietnam	9-24-72
Borden, Murray L.	Air Force	N. Vietnam	10-13-66
Borja, Domingo R.	Army	Laos	2-21-67

Name	Military Service	Country of Casualty	Date of Incident
Boronski, John A.	Army	Cambodia	3-24-70
Bors, Joseph C.	Air Force	S. Vietnam	4-28-68
Borton, Robert C., Jr.	Marine Corps	S. Vietnam	8-28-66
Bosiljevac, Michael J.	Air Force	N. Vietnam	9-29-72
Bossio, Galileo F.	Air Force	N. Vietnam	7-29-66
Bossman, Peter R.	Navy	S. Vietnam	9-25-66
Boston, Leo S.	Air Force	N. Vietnam	4-29-66
Bott, Russell P.	Army	Laos	12-02-66
Bouchard, Michael L.	Navy	Laos	12-20-68
Bower, Irvin L., Jr.	Marine Corps	S. Vietnam	10-06-69
Bower, Joseph E.	Air Force	N. Vietnam	8-03-65
Bowers, Richard L.	Army	S. Vietnam	3-24-69
Bowles, Dwight P.	Air Force	N. Vietnam	11-03-65
Bowman, Frank	Navy	N. Vietnam	7-16-68
Bowman, Michael L.	Navy	N. Vietnam	10-02-69
Boyanowski, John G.	Army	S. Vietnam	12-14-71
Boyd, Walter	Marine Corps	Cambodia	5-15-75
Boyer, Alan L.	Army	Laos	3-28-68
Boyle, William	Army	Laos	2-28-70
Bradshaw, Robert S., III	Marine Corps	S. Vietnam	2-12-70
Bram, Richard C.	Marine Corps	S. Vietnam	7-08-65
Branch, James A.	Air Force	N. Vietnam	9-04-65
Brandenburg, Dale	Air Force	Laos	2-05-73
Brandt, Keith A.	Army	Laos	3-18-71
Brashear, William J.	Air Force	Laos	5-08-69
Brasher, Jimmy M.	Army	N. Vietnam	9-28-66
Brassfield, Andrew T.	Army	Laos	4-06-70
Brauner, Henry P.	Air Force	Laos	3-29-72
Brazik, Richard	Air Force	N. Vietnam	7-26-67
Breeding, Michael H.	Marine Corps	S. Vietnam	2-12-70
Breiner, Stephen E.	Marine Corps	S. Vietnam	9-24-68
Bremmer, Dwight A.	Army	S. Vietnam	12-14-71
Brennan, Herbert O.	Air Force	N. Vietnam	11-26-67
Brenning, Richard D.	Navy	N. Vietnam	7-26-69
Brett, Robert A., Jr.	Air Force	N. Vietnam	9-29-72
Breuer, Donald C.	Marine Corps	Laos	11-20-72
Brice, Eric P.	Navy	N. Vietnam	6-04-68
Bridges, Jerry G.	Army	S. Vietnam	10-20-68
Bridges, Philip W.	Army	S. Vietnam	6-30-71
Briggs, Ernest F., Jr.	Army	Laos	1-05-68
Briggs, Ronald D.	Army	S. Vietnam	2-06-69
Brigham, Albert	Marine Corps	S. Vietnam	12-14-66
Brinckmann, Robert E.	Air Force	N. Vietnam	11-04-66
Broms, Edward J., Jr.	Navy	N. Vietnam	8-01-68

Name	Military Service	Country of Casualty	Date of Incident
Brooks, John H.R.	Army	S. Vietnam	5-13-69
Brooks, William L.	Air Force	Laos	4-22-70
Brower, Ralph W.	Air Force	Laos	11-09-67
Brown, Donald A.	Air Force	Laos	7-30-70
Brown, Earl C.	Air Force	Laos	11-24-69
Brown, Edward D., Jr.	Navy	S. Vietnam	7-29-65
Brown, Frank M., Jr.	Navy	S. Vietnam	9-19-66
Brown, George R.	Army	Laos	3-28-68
Brown, Harry W.	Army	S. Vietnam	2-12-68
Brown, James A.	Army	S. Vietnam	8-12-70
Brown, James W.	Marine Corps	S. Vietnam	5-05-66
Brown, Joseph O.	Air Force	Laos	5-19-66
Brown, Robert M.	Air Force	Laos	11-07-72
Brown, Thomas E.	Navy	N. Vietnam	5-29-66
Brown, Wayne G., II	Air Force	S. Vietnam	7-17-72
Brown, Wilbur R.	Air Force	S. Vietnam	2-03-66
Brown, William T.	Army	Laos	11-03-69
Brownlee, Charles R.	Air Force	Laos	12-24-68
Brownlee, Robert W.	Army	S. Vietnam	5-25-72
Bruch, Donald W., Jr.	Air Force	N. Vietnam	5-29-66
Brucher, John M.	Air Force	N. Vietnam	2-18-69
Brunson, Jack W.	Army	Laos	5-31-71
Bucher, Bernard L.	Air Force	S. Vietnam	5-12-68
Buck, Arthur C.	Navy	Laos	1-11-68
Buckley, Louis, Jr.	Army	S. Vietnam	5-21-66
Buckley, Victor P.	Navy	N. Vietnam	12-16-69
Buell, Kenneth R.	Navy	N. Vietnam	9-17-72
Buerk, William C.	Air Force	S. Vietnam	4-11-71
Bullard, William H.	Navy	S. Vietnam	8-25-66
Bullock, Larry A.	Army	S. Vietnam	1-01-67
Bundy, Norman L.	Navy	N. Vietnam	9-06-66
Bunker, Park G.	Air Force	Laos	12-30-70
Burd, Douglas G.	Air Force	S. Vietnam	8-01-69
Burgess, John L.	Army	S. Vietnam	6-30-70
Burkart, Charles W., Jr.	Air Force	Laos	6-13-66
Burke, Michael J.	Marine Corps	S. Vietnam	10-19-66
Burnes, Robert W.	Marine Corps	Laos	1-05-80
Burnett, Donald F.	Navy	S. Vietnam	2-06-68
Burnett, Sheldon J.	Army	Laos	3-07-71
Burnham, Donald D.	Army	S. Vietnam	2-02-68
Burnham, Mason I.	Air Force	S. Vietnam	4-20-72
Burns, Frederick J.	Marine Corps	S. Vietnam	12-25-67
Burns, John R.	Air Force	Laos	8-04-66
Burns, Michael P.	Army	Laos	7-31-69

Name	Military Service	Country of Casualty	Date of Incident
Burris, Donald D., Jr.	Army	Laos	12-22-69
Busch, Jon T.	Air Force	N. Vietnam	6-08-67
Bush, Elbert W.	Army	S. Vietnam	1-08-73
Bush, John R.	Air Force	N. Vietnam	7-24-68
Bush, Robert E.	Air Force	N. Vietnam	3-24-66
Bush, Robert I.	Air Force	N. Vietnam	6-09-66
Bushnell, Brian L.	Navy	N. Vietnam	4-09-70
Butler, Dewey R.	Army	S. Vietnam	7-14-69
Butler, James E.	Army	S. Vietnam	3-20-70
Butt, Richard L.	Air Force	N. Vietnam	11-11-66
Byars, Earnest R.	Marine Corps	S. Vietnam	7-30-67
Bynum, Neil S.	Air Force	Laos	10-26-69
Byrd, Hugh M., Jr.	Army	S. Vietnam	1-09-69
Byrne, Joseph H.	Air Force	Laos	3-13-68
Cadwell, Anthony B.	Army	S. Vietnam	10-17-67
Caffarelli, Charles J.	Air Force	S. Vietnam	11-21-72
Cairns, Robert A.	Air Force	S. Vietnam	6-17-66
Caldwell, Floyd D.	Army	S. Vietnam	12-14-71
Calfee, James H.	Air Force	Laos	3-11-68
Calhoun, Johnny C.	Army	S. Vietnam	3-27-68
Call, John H., III	Air Force	S. Vietnam	4-06-72
Callahan, David F., Jr.	Navy	N. Vietnam	9-23-68
Callanan, Richard J.	Air Force	S. Vietnam	1-07-66
Callies, Tommy L.	Air Force	S. Vietnam	8-01-69
Calloway, Porter E.	Army	S. Vietnam	3-11-68
Cameron, Virgil K.	Navy	N. Vietnam	7-29-66
Campbell, Clyde W.	Air Force	Laos	3-01-69
Campbell, William E.	Air Force	Laos	1-29-69
Caniford, James K.	Air Force	Laos	3-29-72
Canup, Franklin H., Jr.	Navy	S. Vietnam	1-14-67
Cappelli, Charles E.	Air Force	N. Vietnam	11-17-67
Caras, Franklin A.	Air Force	N. Vietnam	4-28-67
Carlock, Ralph L.	Air Force	Laos	3-04-67
Carlson, John W.	Air Force	S. Vietnam	12-07-66
Carlson, Paul V.	Navy	S. Vietnam	2-12-67
Carlton, James E., Jr.	Marine Corps	N. Vietnam	4-17-67
Carpenter, Howard B.	Army	Laos	3-06-67
Carpenter, Nicholas M.	Navy	N. Vietnam	6-24-68
Carpenter, Ramey L.	Navy	Laos	3-31-69
Carr, Donald G.	Army	Laos	7-06-71
Carrier, Daniel L.	Air Force	N. Vietnam	6-02-67
Carroll, John L.	Air Force	Laos	11-07-72
Carroll, Patrick H.	Air Force	Laos	11-02-69
Carroll, Roger W., Jr.	Air Force	Laos	9-21-72

Name	Military Service	Country of Casualty	Date of Incident
Carter, Dennis R.	Marine Corps	S. Vietnam	8-28-66
Carter, George W.	Army	S. Vietnam	4-24-72
Carter, Gerald L.	Navy	N. Vietnam	1-26-71
Carter, James D.	Army	S. Vietnam	6-24-68
Carter, James L.	Air Force	S. Vietnam	2-03-66
Carter, William T.	Navy	N. Vietnam	11-10-66
Cartwright, Billie J.	Navy	N. Vietnam	12-22-65
Cartwright, Patrick G.	Navy	S. Vietnam	1-31-71
Carver, Harry F.	Army	S. Vietnam	4-10-68
Case, Thomas F.	Air Force	N. Vietnam	5-31-66
Casey, Donald F.	Air Force	N. Vietnam	6-23-68
Cassell, Robin B.	Navy	N. Vietnam	7-15-67
Castillo, Richard	Air Force	Laos	3-29-72
Castro, Reinaldo A.	Marine Corps	S. Vietnam	4-27-67
Causey, John B.	Air Force	N. Vietnam	2-25-66
Cavalli, Anthony F.	Air Force	Laos	6-28-66
Cavender, Jim R.	Army	S. Vietnam	11-04-69
Cayce, John D.	Navy	N. Vietnam	11-12-67
Cecil, Alan B.	Army	Laos	9-21-69
Cestare, Joseph A.	Marine Corps	S. Vietnam	4-20-68
Chambers, Jerry L.	Air Force	Laos	5-22-68
Champion, James A.	Army	S. Vietnam	4-24-71
Chan, Peter	Navy	S. Vietnam	9-25-72
Chandler, Anthony G.	Navy	S. Vietnam	6-16-68
Chaney, Arthur F.	Army	S. Vietnam	5-03-68
Chapa, Armando, Jr.	Navy	S. Vietnam	2-06-68
Chapman, Peter H., II	Air Force	S. Vietnam	4-06-72
Chapman, Rodney M.	Navy	N. Vietnam	2-18-69
Charvet, Paul C.	Navy	N. Vietnam	3-21-67
Chavez, Gary A.	Air Force	Laos	7-30-70
Chavira, Stephen	Army	S. Vietnam	5-28-71
Cherry, Allen S.	Air Force	N. Vietnam	8-09-67
Chestnut, Joseph L.	Air Force	Laos	10-13-70
Chiarello, Vincent A.	Air Force	N. Vietnam	7-29-66
Chipman, Ralph J.	Marine Corps	N. Vietnam	12-27-72
Chomel, Charles D.	Marine Corps	S. Vietnam	7-11-67
Chomyk, William	Air Force	S. Vietnam	4-22-68
Chorlins, Richard D.	Air Force	Laos	1-11-70
Christensen, Allen D.	Army	S. Vietnam	4-03-72
Christensen, John M.	Marine Corps	N. Vietnam	4-13-72
Christensen, William M.	Navy	N. Vietnam	3-01-66
Christian, David M.	Navy	N. Vietnam	6-02-65
Christiano, Joseph	Air Force	Laos	12-24-65
Christiansen, Eugene F.	Army	S. Vietnam	2-06-69

Name	Military Service	Country of Casualty	Date of Incident
Christie, Dennis R.	Marine Corps	S. Vietnam	6-11-67
Christopherson, Keith A.	Navy	N. Vietnam	1-21-73
Chubb, John J.	Army	Laos	3-20-71
Churchill, Carl R.	Air Force	Laos	5-03-70
Cichon, Walter A.	Army	S. Vietnam	3-30-68
Clack, Cecil J.	Army	S. Vietnam	1-01-69
Claflin, Richard A.	Air Force	N. Vietnam	7-26-67
Clapper, Gean P.	Air Force	N. Vietnam	12-29-67
Clark, Jerry P.	Army	S. Vietnam	12-15-65
Clark, John C., II	Air Force	Laos	12-05-69
Clark, Lawrence	Air Force	N. Vietnam	10-18-66
Clark, Phillip S., Jr.	Navy	N. Vietnam	12-24-72
Clark, Richard C.	Navy	N. Vietnam	10-24-67
Clark, Robert A.	Navy	N. Vietnam	1-10-73
Clark, Stanley S.	Air Force	Laos	2-14-69
Clark, Stephen W.	Marine Corps	S. Vietnam	5-03-68
Clark, Thomas E.	Air Force	Laos	2-08-69
Clarke, Fred L.	Air Force	Laos	12-13-68
Clarke, George W., Jr.	Air Force	Laos	10-16-67
Claxton, Charles P.	Air Force	N. Vietnam	12-29-67
Clay, Eugene L.	Air Force	Laos	11-09-67
Clay, William C., III	Marine Corps	S. Vietnam	4-12-67
Cleary, Peter M.	Air Force	N. Vietnam	10-10-72
Clem, Thomas D.	Marine Corps	N. Vietnam	5-03-68
Cleve, Reginald D.	Army	Laos	3-22-71
Cline, Curtis R.	Army	S. Vietnam	9-18-69
Clinton, Dean E.	Army	S. Vietnam	6-11-67
Clydesdale, Charles F.	Navy	S. Vietnam	3-15-65
Coady, Robert F.	Air Force	Laos	1-18-67
Coakley, William F.	Navy	N. Vietnam	9-13-66
Coalston, Echol W., Jr.	Army	S. Vietnam	1-21-68
Coates, Donald L.	Marine Corps	N. Vietnam	2-01-66
Cobbs, Ralph B.	Navy	S. Vietnam	6-17-66
Cochran, Isom C., Jr.	Army	S. Vietnam	5-23-68
Cochrane, Deverton C.	Army	Cambodia	6-17-70
Cody, Howard R.	Air Force	S. Vietnam	11-24-63
Coen, Harry B.	Army	S. Vietnam	5-12-68
Cogdell, William K.	Air Force	Laos	1-17-67
Cohron, James D.	Army	Laos	1-12-68
Cole, Legrande, O., Jr.	Navy	N. Vietnam	6-30-67
Cole, Richard M., Jr.	Air Force	S. Vietnam	6-18-72
Coleman, Jimmy L.	Army	S. Vietnam	3-06-69
Collamore, Allan P., Jr.	Navy	N. Vietnam	2-04-67
Collazo, Raphael L.	Army	S. Vietnam	3-17-68

Name	Military Service	Country of Casualty	Date of Incident
Collette, Curtis D.	Navy	S. Vietnam	6-17-66
Collins, Arnold	Marine Corps	S. Vietnam	12-04-67
Collins, Guy F.	Air Force	Laos	3-13-68
Collins, Richard F.	Navy	Laos	11-22-69
Collins, Theothis	Marine Corps	S. Vietnam	8-19-68
Collins, Willard M.	Air Force	S. Vietnam	3-09-66
Colombo, Gary L.	Marine Corps	S. Vietnam	3-06-68
Coltman, William C.	Air Force	N. Vietnam	9-29-72
Colwell, William K.	Air Force	Laos	12-24-65
Comer, Howard B., Jr.	Army	S. Vietnam	11-24-69
Compa, Joseph J., Jr.	Army	S. Vietnam	6-10-65
Compton, Frank R.	Navy	N. Vietnam	3-21-66
Conaway, Lawrence Y.	Air Force	Laos	5-03-70
Condit, Douglas C.	Air Force	N. Vietnam	11-26-67
Condit, William H., Jr.	Air Force	S. Vietnam	6-23-69
Condrey, George T., III	Army	S. Vietnam	5-08-68
Confer, Michael S.	Navy	N. Vietnam	10-10-66
Conger, John E.	Army	S. Vietnam	1-27-69
Conklin, Bernard	Air Force	N. Vietnam	7-29-66
Conley, Eugene O.	Air Force	N. Vietnam	1-21-67
Conlon, John F., III	Air Force	S. Vietnam	3-04-66
Conner, Edwin R.	Navy	S. Vietnam	5-16-70
Conner, Lorenza	Air Force	N. Vietnam	10-27-67
Conner, Charles R.	Marine Corps	S. Vietnam	10-28-68
Consolvo, John W., Jr.	Marine Corps	S. Vietnam	5-07-72
Conway, James B.	Army	S. Vietnam	4-12-66
Cook, Dennis P.	Navy	S. Vietnam	5-06-66
Cook, Donald G.	Marine Corps	S. Vietnam	12-31-64
Cook, Dwight W.	Air Force	Laos	9-21-72
Cook, Glen R.	Air Force	S. Vietnam	10-21-69
Cook, Joseph F.	Marine Corps	S. Vietnam	5-10-68
Cook, Kelly F.	Air Force	N. Vietnam	11-10-67
Cook, William R.	Air Force	S. Vietnam	4-28-68
Cook, Wilmer P.	Navy	N. Vietnam	12-22-67
Cooke, Calvin C., Jr.	Air Force	S. Vietnam	4-26-72
Cooley, David L.	Navy	N. Vietnam	4-22-68
Cooley, Orville D.	Navy	N. Vietnam	1-16-68
Coons, Chester L.	Navy	Laos	2-17-68
Coons, Henry A.	Navy	N. Vietnam	2-28-68
Cooper, Daniel D.	Navy	N. Vietnam	2-04-72
Cooper, Richard W., Jr.	Air Force	N. Vietnam	12-19-72
Cooper, William E.	Air Force	N. Vietnam	4-24-66
Copack, Joseph B., Jr.	Air Force	N. Vietnam	12-22-72
Copenhaver, Gregory S.	Marine Corps	Cambodia	5-15-75

Name	Military Service	Country of Casualty	Date of Incident
Copley, William M.	Army	Laos	11-16-68
Corbitt, Gilland W.	Air Force	N. Vietnam	7-27-67
Cordova, Robert J.	Navy	N. Vietnam	1-27-68
Cordova, Sam G.	Marine Corps	Laos	8-26-72
Corefield, Stan L.	Marine Corps	S. Vietnam	5-01-67
Corle, John T.	Marine Corps	S. Vietnam	12-08-65
Cornelius, Johnnie C.	Air Force	N. Vietnam	6-26-68
Cornelius, Samuel B.	Air Force	Cambodia	6-16-73
Cornwell, Leroy J., III	Air Force	Laos	9-10-71
Corona, Joel	Army	S. Vietnam	11-08-70
Cota, Ernest K.	Navy	S. Vietnam	5-14-68
Cotten, Larry W.	Air Force	Laos	3-09-70
Cozart, Robert G., Jr.	Army	S. Vietnam	3-20-70
Craddock, Randall J.	Air Force	N. Vietnam	12-21-72
Craig, Phillip C.	Navy	N. Vietnam	7-04-67
Crain, Carroll O.	Navy	N. Vietnam	3-08-67
Cramer, Donald M.	Army	S. Vietnam	1-05-71
Crandall, Gregory S.	Army	Laos	2-18-71
Craven, Andrew J.	Army	S. Vietnam	5-12-68
Creamer, James E.	Army	S. Vietnam	4-21-68
Crear, Willis C.	Army	Laos	2-15-71
Creed, Barton S.	Navy	Laos	3-13-71
Cressman, Peter R.	Air Force	Laos	2-05-73
Crew, James A.	Air Force	N. Vietnam	11-10-67
Crews, John H., III	Air Force	N. Vietnam	5-22-68
Cristman, Frederick L.	Army	Laos	3-19-71
Crockett, William J.	Air Force	S. Vietnam	8-22-72
Crody, Kenneth L.	Marine Corps	S. Vietnam	7-11-72
Crone, Donald E.	Army	Laos	2-15-71
Crook, Elliott	Army	S. Vietnam	5-16-71
Cropper, Curtis H.	Navy	N. Vietnam	4-05-70
Crosby, Bruce A., Jr.	Army	S. Vietnam	3-30-72
Crosby, Frederick P.	Navy	N. Vietnam	6-01-65
Crosby, Herbert C.	Army	S. Vietnam	1-10-70
Crosby, Richard A.	Army	S. Vietnam	12-02-67
Cross, Ariel L.	Marine Corps	S. Vietnam	7-17-68
Cross, James E.	Air Force	Laos	4-24-70
Crossman, Gregory J.	Air Force	N. Vietnam	4-25-68
Crosson, Gerald J., Jr.	Air Force	N. Vietnam	5-16-68
Crow, Raymond J., Jr.	Air Force	Cambodia	3-27-72
Crowley, John E.	Army	Laos	8-10-70
Croxdale, Jack L., II	Army	S. Vietnam	11-19-67
Crumm, William J.	Air Force	S. Vietnam	7-07-67
Cruz, Carlos R.	Air Force	Laos	12-29-67

Name	Military Service	Country of Casualty	Date of Incident
Cruz, Raphael	Air Force	S. Vietnam	9-02-63
Cudlike, Charles J.	Army	S. Vietnam	5-18-69
Cunningham, Carey A.	Air Force	N. Vietnam	8-02-67
Cunningham, Kenneth L.	Army	S. Vietnam	10-03-69
Curlee, Robert L., Jr.	Army	S. Vietnam	6-10-65
Curran, Patrick R.	Marine Corps	Laos	9-29-69
Curry, Keith R.W.	Navy	N. Vietnam	1-08-71
Cushman, Clifton E.	Air Force	N. Vietnam	9-25-66
Cuthbert, Bradley G.	Air Force	N. Vietnam	11-23-68
Cuthbert, Stephen H.	Air Force	N. Vietnam	7-03-72
Cutrer, Fred C., Jr.	Air Force	S. Vietnam	8-06-64
Czerwiec, Raymond G.	Army	S. Vietnam	3-27-69
Czerwonka, Paul S.	Marine Corps	S. Vietnam	5-10-68
Daffron, Thomas C.	Air Force	Laos	2-18-70
Dahill, Douglas E.	Army	S. Vietnam	4-17-69
Dailey, Douglas V.	Air Force	Laos	12-13-68
Dale, Charles A.	Army	S. Vietnam	6-09-65
Dallas, Richard H.	Marine Corps	S. Vietnam	4-27-67
Dalton, Randall D.	Army	Cambodia	7-24-71
Danielso, Benjamin F.	Air Force	Laos	12-05-69
Danielson, Mark G.	Air Force	S. Vietnam	6-18-72
Darcy, Edward J.	Air Force	N. Vietnam	12-29-67
Dardeau, Oscar M., Jr.	Air Force	N. Vietnam	11-18-67
Darr, Charles E.	Air Force	N. Vietnam	12-21-72
Davidson, David A.	Army	Laos	10-05-70
Davies, Joseph E.	Air Force	N. Vietnam	5-19-68
Davis, Brent E.	Marine Corps	N. Vietnam	3-18-66
Davis, Charlie B., Jr.	Air Force	Laos	4-22-70
Davis, Daniel R.	Air Force	Laos	8-18-69
Davis, Donald V.	Navy	N. Vietnam	7-25-67
Davis, Edgar F.	Air Force	Laos	9-17-68
Davis, Francis J.	Navy	N. Vietnam	6-14-72
Davis, Gene E.	Air Force	S. Vietnam	3-13-66
Davis, James W.	Air Force	Laos	3-11-68
Davis, Ricardo G.	Army	Laos	3-20-69
Davis, Robert C.	Air Force	Laos	3-23-69
Dawes, John J.	Army	S. Vietnam	5-05-66
Dawson, Daniel G.	Army	S. Vietnam	11-06-64
Dawson, Frank A.	Navy	Laos	2-17-68
Dawson, James V.	Air Force	S. Vietnam	7-16-69
Day, Dennis I.	Army	S. Vietnam	11-03-70
Dayao, Rolando C.	Navy	N. Vietnam	10-02-69
Dayton, James L.	Army	S. Vietnam	5-08-68
De Herrera, Benjamin D.	Army	S. Vietnam	11-19-67

Name	Military Service	Country of Casualty	Date of Incident
DeSota, Ernest L.	Air Force	S. Vietnam	4-12-69
Dean, Donald C.	Navy	N. Vietnam	10-02-69
Dean, Michael F.	Air Force	Laos	6-30-70
Deane, William L.	Army	S. Vietnam	1-08-73
Deblasio, Raymond V., Jr.	Navy	N. Vietnam	6-18-71
Decaire, Jack L.	Army	S. Vietnam	11-03-71
Deere, Donald T.	Army	S. Vietnam	5-17-66
Deichelmann, Samuel M.	Air Force	S. Vietnam	9-06-68
Deitsch, Charles E.	Army	S. Vietnam	10-20-68
Deleidi, Richard A.	Marine Corps	S. Vietnam	2-07-69
Delong, Joe L.	Army	S. Vietnam	5-18-67
Demmon, David S.	Army	S. Vietnam	6-09-65
Dempsey, Jack I.	Navy	S. Vietnam	6-17-66
Demsey, Walter E., Jr.	Army	Laos	2-18-71
Dennany, James E.	Air Force	Laos	11-12-69
Dennis, William R.	Army	S. Vietnam	4-19-68
Dennison, James R.	Navy	N. Vietnam	1-01-68
Denton, Manuel R.	Navy	S. Vietnam	10-08-63
Derby, Paul D.	Marine Corps	S. Vietnam	11-17-68
Derrickson, Thomas G.	Air Force	N. Vietnam	10-12-67
Deuso, Carroll J.	Navy	N. Vietnam	12-15-70
Deuter, Richard C.	Navy	Laos	11-22-69
Dewberry, Jerry D.	Marine Corps	S. Vietnam	7-05-68
Dewispelaere, Rexford J.	Air Force	Laos	11-24-69
Dexter, Bennie L.	Air Force	S. Vietnam	5-09-66
Dexter, Ronald J.	Army	Laos	6-03-67
DiTommaso, Robert J.	Air Force	N. Vietnam	7-29-66
Dibble, Morris F.	Army	S. Vietnam	12-05-65
Dickson, Edward A.	Navy	N. Vietnam	2-07-65
Dilger, Herbert H.	Navy	N. Vietnam	10-02-69
Dillender, William E.	Army	Laos	3-20-71
Dillon, David A.	Army	S. Vietnam	7-20-66
Dinan, David T., III	Air Force	Laos	3-17-69
Dingwall, John F.	Marine Corps	S. Vietnam	7-08-65
Dion, Laurent N.	Navy	N. Vietnam	8-17-67
Dix, Craig M.	Army	Cambodia	3-17-71
Dixon, David L.	Navy	S. Vietnam	9-28-68
Dodge, Edward R.	Army	S. Vietnam	12-31-64
Dolan, Thomas A.	Army	S. Vietnam	8-10-71
Donahue, Morgan J.	Air Force	Laos	12-13-68
Donato, Paul N.	Navy	Laos	2-17-68
Donnelly, Verne G.	Navy	N. Vietnam	9-17-72
Donovan, Leroy M.	Army	S. Vietnam	5-19-65
Donovan, Michael L.	Air Force	Laos	9-30-71

Name	Military Service	Country of Casualty	Date of Incident
Dooley, James E.	Navy	N. Vietnam	10-22-67
Dority, Richard C.	Army	S. Vietnam	10-03-70
Dotson, Jefferson S.	Air Force	Laos	8-09-69
Doughtie, Carl L.	Navy	N. Vietnam	6-10-65
Douglas, Thomas E.	Marine Corps	S. Vietnam	11-22-65
Dove, Jack P., Sr.	Air Force	N. Vietnam	7-12-67
Downing, Donald W.	Air Force	N. Vietnam	9-05-67
Draeger, Walter F., Jr.	Air Force	N. Vietnam	4-04-65
Drake, Carl W.	Air Force	Cambodia	6-18-70
Dreher, Richard E.	Air Force	Cambodia	3-27-72
Driver, Dallas A.	Army	S. Vietnam	10-09-69
Dubbeld, Orie J., Jr.	Army	S. Vietnam	3-03-71
Ducat, Phillip A.	Marine Corps	S. Vietnam	9-25-66
Duckett, Thomas A.	Air Force	Laos	12-12-70
Dudley, Charles G.	Air Force	Laos	6-28-66
Duensing, James A.	Navy	N. Vietnam	1-30-73
Duffy, John E.	Air Force	S. Vietnam	4-04-70
Dugan, John F.	Army	Laos	3-20-71
Dugan, Thomas W.	Air Force	Laos	12-13-68
Duggan, William Y.	Air Force	Laos	12-31-71
Duncan, James E.	Army	S. Vietnam	3-03-71
Duncan, Robert R.	Navy	N. Vietnam	8-29-68
Dunlap, William C.	Army	S. Vietnam	12-02-69
Dunlop, Thomas E.	Navy	N. Vietnam	4-06-72
Dunn, Joseph P.	Navy		2-14-68
Dunn, Michael E.	Navy	N. Vietnam	1-26-68
Dunn, Richard E.	Air Force	S. Vietnam	4-26-72
Dusing, Charles G.	Air Force	S. Vietnam	10-31-65
Duvall, Dean A.	Air Force	S. Vietnam	3-13-66
Dyczkowski, Robert R.	Air Force	N. Vietnam	4-23-66
Dye, Melvin C.	Army	Laos	2-19-68
Dyer, Blenn C.	Marine Corps	S. Vietnam	4-27-67
Dyer, Irby, III	Army	Laos	12-02-66
Eads, Dennis K.	Army	S. Vietnam	4-23-70
Earle, John S.	Navy	S. Vietnam	6-22-70
Earll, David J.	Air Force	N. Vietnam	10-21-66
Earnest, Charles M.	Navy	N. Vietnam	11-28-72
East, James B., Jr.	Air Force	Laos	4-26-69
Eaton, Curtis A.	Air Force	N. Vietnam	8-14-66
Eaton, Norman D.	Air Force	Laos	1-13-69
Echanis, Joseph Y.	Air Force	Laos	11-05-69
Echevarria, Raymond L.	Army	Laos	10-03-66
Eckley, Wayne A.	Air Force	N. Vietnam	12-29-67
Ecklund, Arthur G.	Army	S. Vietnam	4-03-69

Name	Military Service	Country of Casualty	Date of Incident
Edgar, Robert J.	Air Force	Laos	2-05-68
Edmondson, William R.	Air Force	N. Vietnam	5-31-66
Edmunds, Robert C., Jr.	Air Force	N. Vietnam	10-27-68
Edwards, Harry J.	Army	S. Vietnam	1-20-72
Edwards, Harry S., Jr.	Navy	N. Vietnam	10-20-66
Egan, James T., Jr.	Marine Corps	S. Vietnam	1-21-66
Egan, William P.	Navy	Laos	4-29-66
Egger, John C., Jr.	Air Force	N. Vietnam	11-03-67
Ehrlich, Dennis M.	Navy	S. Vietnam	1-19-67
Eidsmoe, Norman E.	Navy	N. Vietnam	1-26-68
Eilers, Dennis L.	Air Force	Laos	12-24-65
Eisenberger, George J.	Army	S. Vietnam	12-05-65
Eisenbraun, William F.	Army	S. Vietnam	7-05-65
Elkins, Frank G.	Navy	N. Vietnam	10-12-66
Ellen, Wade L.	Army	S. Vietnam	4-24-72
Ellerd, Carl J.	Navy	N. Vietnam	10-02-69
Elliot, Robert M.	Air Force	N. Vietnam	2-14-68
Elliott, Andrew J.	Army	S. Vietnam	6-09-70
Elliott, Jerry W.	Army	S. Vietnam	1-21-68
Ellis, Billy J.	Army	S. Vietnam	1-03-68
Ellis, Randall S.	Army	S. Vietnam	4-18-69
Ellis, William, Jr.	Army	S. Vietnam	6-24-66
Ellison, John C.	Navy	N. Vietnam	3-24-67
Elzinga, Richard G.	Air Force	Laos	3-26-70
Emrich, Roger G.	Navy	N. Vietnam	11-17-67
Engen, Robert J.	Army	Laos	2-18-71
Englander, Lawrence J.	Army	S. Vietnam	5-02-68
Entrican, Danny D.	Army	S. Vietnam	5-18-71
Erickson, David W.	Marine Corps	S. Vietnam	3-16-68
Erwin, Donald E.	Navy	N. Vietnam	10-02-68
Escobedo, Julian, Jr.	Marine Corps	S. Vietnam	9-01-69
Espenshied, John L.	Air Force	S. Vietnam	10-21-69
Estocin, Michael J.	Navy	N. Vietnam	4-26-67
Evancho, Richard	Marine Corps	S. Vietnam	3-26-68
Evans, Billy K., Jr.	Army	S. Vietnam	12-05-68
Evans, Cleveland, Jr.	Marine Corps	S. Vietnam	3-13-68
Evans, William A.	Army	Cambodia	3-02-69
Eveland, Mickey E.	Army	S. Vietnam	10-26-71
Evert, Lawrence G.	Air Force	N. Vietnam	11-08-67
Fallon, Patrick M.	Air Force	Laos	7-04-69
Fanning, Joseph P.	Air Force	Laos	12-13-68
Farlow, Craig L.	Army	S. Vietnam	5-16-71
Farris, William F.	Navy	S. Vietnam	2-06-68
Featherston, Fielding W., III	Air Force	Laos	12-30-69

Name	Military Service	Country of Casualty	Date of Incident
Fegan, Ronald J.	Navy		4-09-65
Feldhaus, John A.	Navy	N. Vietnam	10-08-66
Fellenz, Charles R.	Air Force	Laos	11-24-69
Fellows, Allen E.	Air Force	Laos	3-20-68
Feneley, Francis J.	Air Force	N. Vietnam	5-11-66
Ferguson, Douglas D.	Air Force	Laos	12-30-69
Ferguson, Walter, Jr.	Army	S. Vietnam	8-23-68
Fickler, Edwin J.	Marine Corps	S. Vietnam	1-17-69
Fieszel, Clifford W.	Air Force	N. Vietnam	9-30-68
Finger, Sanford I.	Army	S. Vietnam	10-26-71
Finley, Dickie W.	Army	S. Vietnam	10-21-68
Finn, William R.	Air Force	Laos	12-24-71
Finney, Charles E.	Marine Corps	Laos	3-17-69
Fischer, John R.	Marine Corps	S. Vietnam	9-09-66
Fischer, Richard W.	Marine Corps	S. Vietnam	1-08-68
Fisher, Donald E.	Air Force	N. Vietnam	12-29-67
Fisher, Donald G.	Air Force	Laos	4-22-70
Fitts, Richard A.	Army	Laos	11-30-68
Fitzgerald, Joseph E.	Army	S. Vietnam	5-31-67
Fitzgerald, Paul L., Jr.	Army	S. Vietnam	10-17-67
Fivelson, Barry F.	Army	Laos	2-15-71
Flanagan, Sherman E., Jr.	Air Force	S. Vietnam	7-21-68
Flanigan, John N.	Marine Corps	N. Vietnam	8-19-69
Fleming, Horace H., III	Marine Corps	S. Vietnam	5-10-68
Fobair, Roscoe H.	Air Force	N. Vietnam	7-24-65
Foley, Brendan P.	Air Force	Laos	11-24-67
Foley, John J., III	Marine Corps	S. Vietnam	6-11-67
Forame, Peter C.	Army	Cambodia	12-19-71
Ford, Edward	Army	S. Vietnam	12-09-68
Forman, William S.	Navy	N. Vietnam	1-22-66
Forrester, Ronald W.	Marine Corps	N. Vietnam	12-27-72
Fors, Gary H.	Marine Corps	Laos	12-22-67
Fortner, Frederick J.	Navy	N. Vietnam	10-17-67
Foster, Marvin L.	Army	S. Vietnam	3-16-69
Foster, Paul L.	Air Force	Laos	12-29-67
Foster, Robert E.	Air Force	S. Vietnam	3-09-66
Foulks, Ralph E., Jr.	Navy	N. Vietnam	1-05-68
Fowler, Donald R.	Army	S. Vietnam	8-01-68
Fowler, James A.	Air Force	N. Vietnam	6-06-72
Fowler, James J.	Navy	N. Vietnam	10-02-69
Fowler, Roy G.	Navy	N. Vietnam	10-02-69
Frakes, Dwight G.	Navy	S. Vietnam	2-24-65
Francisco, San DeWayne	Air Force	N. Vietnam	11-25-68
Franklin, Charles E.	Air Force	N. Vietnam	8-14-66

Name	Military Service	Country of Casualty	Date of Incident
Franks, Ian J.	Army	S. Vietnam	3-23-68
Fransen, Albert M., Jr.	Navy	S. Vietnam	7-02-69
Frawley, William D.	Navy	N. Vietnam	3-01-66
Frazier, Paul R.	Army	S. Vietnam	9-03-68
Frederick, David A.	Marine Corps	S. Vietnam	7-30-67
Frederick, Peter J.	Air Force	N. Vietnam	3-15-67
Frederick, William V.	Air Force	N. Vietnam	7-05-67
Freng, Stanley J.	Navy	S. Vietnam	6-17-66
Frenyea, Edmund H.	Navy	N. Vietnam	1-22-66
Frink, John W.	Army	S. Vietnam	4-02-72
Fritsch, Thomas W.	Marine Corps	S. Vietnam	5-10-68
Frosio, Robert C.	Navy	S. Vietnam	11-12-66
Fryar, Bruce	Navy	Laos	1-02-70
Fryer, Charles W.	Navy	N. Vietnam	8-07-66
Fullam, Wayne E.	Air Force	N. Vietnam	10-07-67
Fuller, William O.	Air Force	N. Vietnam	8-26-67
Fullerton, Frank E.	Navy	N. Vietnam	7-27-68
Gage, Robert H.	Marine Corps	S. Vietnam	7-03-66
Galbraith, Russell D.	Air Force	Laos	12-11-68
Gallagher, Donald L.	Navy	S. Vietnam	2-06-68
Gallagher, John T.	Army	Laos	1-05-68
Gallant, Henry J.	Army	S. Vietnam	7-13-65
Galvin, Ronald E.	Navy	N. Vietnam	3-08-67
Gan, Leonard M.	Navy	N. Vietnam	10-02-69
Gande, Berman, Jr.	Army	Cambodia	3-24-70
Ganley, Richard O.	Air Force	Laos	11-24-69
Garbett, Jimmy R.	Army	S. Vietnam	10-09-69
Garcia, Andres	Marine Corps	Cambodia	5-15-75
Garcia, Ricardo M.	Army	Laos	3-19-71
Gardner, Glenn V.	Army	S. Vietnam	11-25-66
Gardner, John G.	Marine Corps	Laos	6-03-67
Garner, John H.	Navy	S. Vietnam	5-29-67
Garrett, Maurice E., Jr.	Army	S. Vietnam	10-22-71
Garside, Frederick T.	Air Force	Laos	3-23-61
Gassman, Fred A.	Army	Laos	10-05-70
Gates, Albert H., Jr.	Marine Corps	S. Vietnam	3-07-70
Gates, James W.	Army	Laos	4-06-66
Gatewood, Charles H.	Marine Corps	S. Vietnam	5-31-68
Gatwood, Robin F., Jr.	Air Force	S. Vietnam	4-02-72
Gaughan, Roger C.	Marine Corps	S. Vietnam	5-01-67
Gauley, James P.	Air Force	Laos	1-10-67
Gause, Bernard, Jr.	Navy	Cambodia	5-15-75
Gauthier, Dennis L.	Army	S. Vietnam	10-31-69
Gee, Paul S.	Marine Corps	S. Vietnam	1-16-68

Name	Military Service	Country of Casualty	Date of Incident
Gehrig, James M., Jr.	Air Force	S. Vietnam	6-18-65
Geist, Stephen J.	Army	S. Vietnam	9-26-67
George, James E., Jr.	Army	S. Vietnam	2-08-68
Gerstel, Donald A.	Navy	N. Vietnam	9-08-72
Gervais, Donald P.	Army	S. Vietnam	5-01-68
Getchell, Paul E.	Air Force	Laos	1-13-69
Giammerino, Vincent F.	Army	S. Vietnam	6-27-68
Giannangeli, Anthony R.	Air Force	S. Vietnam	4-02-72
Gierak, George G., Jr.	Navy	N. Vietnam	6-13-66
Gilbert, Paul F.	Air Force	S. Vietnam	6-18-72
Gilchrist, Robert M.	Air Force	N. Vietnam	10-07-66
Gillen, Thomas E.	Air Force	Laos	2-18-70
Ginn, David L.	Army	S. Vietnam	11-03-70
Gish, Henry G.	Air Force	Laos	3-11-68
Gist, Tommy E.	Air Force	N. Vietnam	5-18-68
Glandon, Gary A.	Air Force	S. Vietnam	5-26-66
Glanville, John T., Jr.	Navy	N. Vietnam	6-13-66
Glasson, William A., Jr.	Navy	China	4-12-66
Glover, Calvin C.	Air Force	Laos	5-22-68
Glover, Douglas J.	Army	Laos	2-19-68
Godfrey, Johnny H.	Air Force	S. Vietnam	1-11-66
Godwin, Solomon H.	Marine Corps	S. Vietnam	2-05-68
Goeden, Gene W.	Navy	N. Vietnam	3-17-67
Goeglein, John W.	Air Force	Laos	6-30-70
Goetsch, Thomas A.	Navy	N. Vietnam	9-17-72
Goff, Kenneth B.	Army	S. Vietnam	8-24-67
Gold, Edward F.	Navy	N. Vietnam	12-22-65
Gollahon, Gene R.	Navy	N. Vietnam	8-13-65
Golz, John B.	Navy	Laos	4-22-70
Gomez, Robert A.	Air Force	Laos	4-23-70
Gonzales, David	Marine Corps	Laos	3-32-70
Gonzalez, Jesus A.	Army	S. Vietnam	4-19-68
Gonzalez, Jose J.	Marine Corps	S. Vietnam	6-11-67
Goodman, Russell C.	Air Force	N. Vietnam	2-20-67
Goodwin, Charles B.	Navy	N. Vietnam	9-08-65
Gopp, Thomas A.	Marine Corps	S. Vietnam	8-03-67
Gore, Paul E.	Navy	N. Vietnam	10-02-69
Gorsuch, William D.	Navy	N. Vietnam	10-02-69
Gorton, Thomas F.	Air Force	S. Vietnam	12-06-63
Gosen, Lawrence D.	Navy	S. Vietnam	7-23-68
Gould, Frank A.	Air Force	Laos	12-21-72
Gourley, Laurent L.	Air Force	Laos	8-09-69
Govan, Robert A.	Air Force	Laos	4-01-67
Grace, James W.	Air Force	Laos	6-14-69

Name	Military Service	Country of Casualty	Date of Incident
Graf, Albert S.	Marine Corps	S. Vietnam	8-29-69
Graf, John G.	Navy	S. Vietnam	11-15-69
Graffe, Paul L.	Army	S. Vietnam	10-03-69
Graham, Dennis L.	Air Force	N. Vietnam	3-28-68
Graham, Gilbert J.	Navy	S. Vietnam	9-28-67
Graniela, Jose A., Jr.	Army	S. Vietnam	8-16-68
Grantham, Robert E.	Army	S. Vietnam	3-08-71
Grauert, Hans H.	Navy	S. Vietnam	11-03-67
Graves, Richard C.	Navy	N. Vietnam	5-25-67
Gravitte, Connie M.	Air Force	S. Vietnam	6-17-66
Gray, Harold E., Jr.	Navy	N. Vietnam	8-07-65
Grayson, William R.	Navy	S. Vietnam	4-01-66
Graziosi, Francis G.	Army	S. Vietnam	1-10-70
Green, Donald G.	Air Force	N. Vietnam	11-16-65
Green, Frank C., Jr.	Navy	N. Vietnam	7-10-72
Green, George C., Jr.	Army	Laos	12-04-70
Green, Gerald	Navy	N. Vietnam	9-12-65
Green, James A.	Army	Cambodia	6-18-70
Green, Larry E.	Marine Corps	S. Vietnam	3-26-68
Green, Norman M.	Air Force	Laos	1-09-68
Green, Robert B.	Air Force	Laos	10-25-66
Green, Thomas F.	Army	S. Vietnam	10-26-71
Greenleaf, Joseph G.	Navy	S. Vietnam	4-14-72
Greenley, Jon A.	Air Force	S. Vietnam	1-07-66
Greenwood, Robert R., Jr.	Air Force	Laos	9-02-72
Greer, Robert L.	Marine Corps	S. Vietnam	6-07-64
Gregory, Paul A.	Navy	N. Vietnam	7-25-70
Gregory, Robert R.	Air Force	N. Vietnam	12-02-66
Greiling, David S.	Navy	N. Vietnam	7-24-68
Grella, Donald C.	Army	S. Vietnam	12-28-65
Grenzebach, Earl W.	Air Force	N. Vietnam	5-12-67
Grewell, Larry I.	Air Force	Laos	11-24-69
Griffey, Terrence H.	Air Force	S. Vietnam	5-26-66
Griffin, Rodney L.	Army	Cambodia	5-02-70
Griffith, John G.	Navy	N. Vietnam	3-12-68
Griffith, Robert S.	Army	Laos	2-19-68
Grissett, Edwin R., Jr.	Marine Corps	S. Vietnam	1-22-66
Grosse, Christopher A., Jr.	Army	S. Vietnam	3-28-68
Groth, Wade L.	Army	S. Vietnam	2-12-68
Grubb, Peter A.	Air Force	N. Vietnam	9-17-67
Guajardo, Hilario H.	Marine Corps	S. Vietnam	5-01-67
Guerra, Raul A.	Navy	S. Vietnam	10-08-67
Guillermin, Louis F.	Air Force	Laos	4-30-68
Guillet, Andre R.	Air Force	Laos	5-18-66

Name	Military Service	Country of Casualty	Date of Incident
Guillory, Edward J.	Army	S. Vietnam	6-18-67
Guillory, Hubia J.	Army	S. Vietnam	4-25-68
Gumbert, Robert W., Jr.	Army	S. Vietnam	6-22-70
Gunn, Alan W.	Army	S. Vietnam	2-12-68
Haas, Leon F.	Navy	N. Vietnam	7-17-72
Hackett, Harley B., III	Air Force	N. Vietnam	7-24-68
Hackett, James E.	Army	S. Vietnam	6-11-72
Hagan, John R.	Marine Corps	S. Vietnam	5-06-69
Hagen, Craig L.	Army	S. Vietnam	6-10-65
Haight, Stephen H.	Army	S. Vietnam	5-09-70
Hail, William W.	Air Force	S. Vietnam	8-02-65
Hale, John D.	Army	S. Vietnam	3-08-71
Hall, Donald J.	Air Force	N. Vietnam	2-06-67
Hall, Fredrick M.	Air Force	S. Vietnam	4-12-69
Hall, Gary L.	Marine Corps	Cambodia	5-15-75
Hall, Harley H.	Navy	S. Vietnam	1-27-73
Hall, James S.	Air Force	N. Vietnam	7-29-66
Hall, James W.	Navy	N. Vietnam	10-28-72
Hall, Walter L.	Army	S. Vietnam	6-10-65
Hall, Walter R.	Army	Laos	3-22-71
Hall, Willis R.	Air Force	Laos	3-11-68
Hallberg, Roger C.	Army	S. Vietnam	3-24-67
Halpin, David P.	Navy	S. Vietnam	9-28-68
Halpin, Richard C.	Air Force	Laos	3-29-72
Hamilton, Dennis C.	Army	Laos	1-05-68
Hamilton, Eugene D.	Air Force	N. Vietnam	1-31-66
Hamilton, John S.	Air Force	N. Vietnam	4-19-67
Hamilton, Roger D.	Marine Corps	S. Vietnam	4-21-67
Hamm, James E.	Air Force	S. Vietnam	3-14-68
Hammond, Dennis W.	Marine Corps	S. Vietnam	2-08-68
Handrahan, Eugene A.	Army	S. Vietnam	10-10-68
Hanley, Larry J.	Air Force	Laos	11-04-69
Hanley, Terrence H.	Navy	N. Vietnam	1-01-68
Hanna, Kenneth	Army	S. Vietnam	2-07-68
Hanratty, Thomas M.	Marine Corps	S. Vietnam	6-11-67
Hansen, Lester A.	Army	S. Vietnam	8-13-69
Hanson, Robert T., Jr.	Navy	N. Vietnam	2-03-66
Hanson, Stephen P.	Marine Corps	Laos	6-03-67
Hanson, Thomas P.	Air Force	N. Vietnam	9-05-67
Harber, Stephen J.	Army	S. Vietnam	7-02-70
Hardie, Chales D.	Navy	N. Vietnam	7-27-67
Hardy, John K., Jr.	Air Force	N. Vietnam	10-12-67
Hargrove, Joseph N.	Marine Corps	Cambodia	5-15-75
Hargrove, Olin, Jr.	Army	S. Vietnam	10-17-67

Name	Military Service	Country of Casualty	Date of Incident
Harley, Lee D.	Air Force	Laos	5-18-66
Harned, Gary A.	Army	Cambodia	3-24-70
Harper, Ralph L.	Marine Corps	S. Vietnam	6-06-68
Harper, Richard K.	Army	S. Vietnam	5-19-65
Harris, Bobby G.	Army	Cambodia	3-17-71
Harris, Gregory J.	Marine Corps	S. Vietnam	6-12-66
Harris, Harold L.	Army	S. Vietnam	10-22-66
Harris, Jeffrey L.	Air Force	N. Vietnam	5-10-72
Harris, Paul W.	Marine Corps	S. Vietnam	3-13-67
Harris, Reuben B.	Navy	China	4-12-66
Harris, Stephen W.	Air Force	Laos	4-22-70
Harrison, Donald L.	Army	N. Vietnam	10-29-68
Harrison, Larry G.	Army	Cambodia	2-26-71
Harrison, Robert H.	Air Force	S. Vietnam	6-18-72
Harrold, Patrick K.	Air Force	Laos	12-05-69
Hart, Joseph L.	Air Force	Laos	2-25-67
Hartness, Gregg	Air Force	Laos	11-26-68
Hartney, James C.	Air Force	N. Vietnam	1-05-68
Hartzheim, John F.	Navy	Laos	2-27-68
Harvey, Jack R.	Air Force	S. Vietnam	11-28-72
Harwood, James A.	Army	S. Vietnam	1-15-71
Harworth, Elroy E.	Air Force	N. Vietnam	5-31-66
Hasenback, Paul A.	Army	S. Vietnam	4-21-67
Hassenger, Arden K.	Air Force	Laos	12-24-65
Hastings, Steven M.	Army	S. Vietnam	8-01-68
Hatley, Joel C.	Army	Laos	3-05-71
Hattori, Masaki	Army	S. Vietnam	3-23-68
Hauer, Leslie J.	Air Force	N. Vietnam	11-18-67
Hauer, Robert D.	Air Force	S. Vietnam	9-05-70
Haviland, Roy E.	Navy	N. Vietnam	1-30-73
Havranek, Michael W.	Marine Corps	S. Vietnam	6-11-67
Hawkins, Edgar L.	Air Force	N. Vietnam	9-20-65
Hawthorne, Richard W.	Marine Corps	S. Vietnam	9-12-67
Hayden, Glenn M.	Navy	Laos	2-17-68
Heep, William A.	Navy	N. Vietnam	8-24-68
Heideman, Thomas E.	Air Force	Laos	10-24-70
Heiskell, Lucius L.	Air Force	N. Vietnam	2-06-67
Heitman, Steven W.	Army	S. Vietnam	3-13-68
Helber, Lawrence N.	Marine Corps	S. Vietnam	1-24-66
Held, John W.	Air Force	S. Vietnam	4-17-68
Hellbach, Harold J.	Marine Corps	S. Vietnam	5-19-67
Helmich, Gerald R.	Air Force	Laos	11-12-69
Helwig, Roger D.	Air Force	Laos	9-11-69
Hemmel, Clarence J.	Air Force	S. Vietnam	10-21-67

Name	Military Service	Country of Casualty	Date of Incident
Hempel, Barry L.	Marine Corps	S. Vietnam	5-10-68
Hendrix, Jerry W.	Marine Corps	S. Vietnam	7-11-72
Henn, John R., Jr.	Army	S. Vietnam	5-24-72
Henninger, Howard W.	Air Force	S. Vietnam	3-13-66
Henry, David A.	Navy	S. Vietnam	9-19-66
Hensley, Ronnie L.	Air Force	Laos	4-22-70
Hensley, Thomas T.	Air Force	Laos	3-17-68
Hentz, Richard J.	Army	N. Vietnam	3-04-71
Hepler, Frank M.	Air Force	S. Vietnam	5-12-68
Hernandez, Frank S.	Army	S. Vietnam	5-06-70
Herold, Richard W.	Air Force	Laos	9-02-72
Herreid, Robert D.	Army	S. Vietnam	10-10-68
Herrera, Frederick D.	Army	S. Vietnam	3-25-69
Herrick, James W., Jr.	Air Force	Laos	10-27-69
Herrin, Henry H., Jr.	Navy	N. Vietnam	1-01-68
Herrold, Ned R.	Air Force	N. Vietnam	5-31-66
Hesford, Peter D.	Air Force	Laos	3-21-68
Hess, Frederick W., Jr.	Air Force	Laos	3-29-69
Hess, Gene K.	Air Force	S. Vietnam	6-17-66
Hessom, Robert C.	Navy	N. Vietnam	3-05-66
Hestle, Roosevelt, Jr.	Air Force	N. Vietnam	7-06-66
Hetrick, Raymond H.	Air Force	Laos	2-24-66
Hewitt, Samuel E.	Marine Corps	S. Vietnam	3-23-66
Heyne, Raymond T.	Marine Corps	S. Vietnam	5-10-68
Hickman, Vincent J.	Air Force	S. Vietnam	1-14-64
Hicks, Prentice W.	Army	S. Vietnam	3-25-69
Hicks, Terrin D.	Air Force	N. Vietnam	8-15-68
Hiemer, Jerry A.	Army	S. Vietnam	11-17-65
Hilbrich, Barry W.	Army	S. Vietnam	6-09-70
Hill, Arthur S., Jr.	Navy	Laos	12-29-65
Hill, Billy D.	Army	S. Vietnam	1-21-68
Hill, Charles D.	Navy	N. Vietnam	5-15-67
Hill, Gordon C.	Air Force	Laos	6-30-70
Hill, John R.	Army	S. Vietnam	4-27-70
Hill, Joseph A.	Marine Corps	S. Vietnam	5-28-68
Hill, Rayford J.	Navy	N. Vietnam	10-02-69
Hill, Richard D.	Air Force	S. Vietnam	12-06-63
Hill, Robert L.	Air Force	N. Vietnam	10-18-66
Hills, John R.	Air Force	Laos	2-14-66
Hilton, Robert L.	Air Force	N. Vietnam	3-14-66
Hines, Vaugh M.	Army	S. Vietnam	11-08-67
Hise, James H.	Navy	S. Vietnam	3-25-67
Hodges, David L.	Navy	N. Vietnam	10-07-67
Hodgson, Cecil J.	Army	S. Vietnam	1-29-66

Name	Military Service	Country of Casualty	Date of Incident
Hoeffs, John H.	Army	S. Vietnam	11-28-66
Hoff, Michael G.	Navy	Laos	1-07-70
Hoff, Sammie D.	Air Force	N. Vietnam	8-30-66
Hoffman, Terry A.	Marine Corps	S. Vietnam	8-19-68
Hogan, Jerry F.	Navy	N. Vietnam	1-21-67
Holdeman, Robert E.	Marine Corps	N. Vietnam	11-25-67
Holden, Elmer L.	Air Force	S. Vietnam	6-09-68
Holguin, Luis G.	Army	S. Vietnam	1-03-71
Holland, Lawrence T.	Air Force	S. Vietnam	6-12-65
Holland, Melvin A.	Air Force	Laos	3-11-68
Holley, Tilden S.	Air Force	N. Vietnam	1-20-68
Hollinger, Greg N.	Army	S. Vietnam	12-14-71
Hollingsworth, Hal T.	Navy	S. Vietnam	1-16-66
Holm, Arnold E., Jr.	Army	S. Vietnam	6-11-72
Holman, Gerald A.	Navy	S. Vietnam	12-14-66
Holmes, David H.	Air Force	Laos	3-15-66
Holmes, Frederick L.	Navy	N. Vietnam	12-30-71
Holmes, Lester E.	Air Force	N. Vietnam	5-22-67
Holt, James W.	Army	S. Vietnam	2-07-68
Holt, Robert A.	Marine Corps	N. Vietnam	9-19-68
Holton, Robert E.	Air Force	Laos	1-29-69
Holtzman, Ronald L.	Army	S. Vietnam	8-24-67
Hom, Charles D.	Navy	N. Vietnam	8-17-67
Homuth, Richard Wendal	Navy	N. Vietnam	5-23-67
Hopper, Earl P., Jr.	Air Force	N. Vietnam	1-10-68
Hopps, Gary D.	Navy	N. Vietnam	2-10-66
Horchar, Andrew A.J.	Navy	N. Vietnam	4-09-70
Horney, Stanley H.	Air Force	N. Vietnam	1-14-68
Hosken, John C.	Army	Cambodia	3-24-70
Hoskins, Charles L.	Air Force	Laos	2-16-71
Hoskins, Donald R.	Air Force	S. Vietnam	4-26-72
Hoskinson, Robert E.	Air Force	N. Vietnam	7-29-66
House, John A., II	Marine Corps	S. Vietnam	6-30-67
Housh, Anthony F.	Army	S. Vietnam	4-19-68
Howard, Lewis, Jr.	Army	S. Vietnam	7-07-70
Howard, Luther H.	Army	S. Vietnam	6-30-67
Howell, Carter A.	Air Force	Laos	3-07-72
Howes, George A.	Army	S. Vietnam	1-10-70
Hrdlicka, David L.	Air Force	Laos	5-18-65
Huard, James L.	Air Force	N. Vietnam	7-12-72
Hubbs, Donald R.	Navy	N. Vietnam	3-17-68
Huberth, Eric J.	Air Force	Cambodia	5-13-70
Hubler, George L.	Marine Corps	S. Vietnam	2-23-68
Huddleston, Lynn R.	Army	S. Vietnam	9-26-67

Name	Military Service	Country of Casualty	Date of Incident
Hudgens, Edward M.	Air Force	Laos	3-21-70
Huggins, Bobby G.	Air Force	S. Vietnam	6-04-70
Huie, Litchfield P.	Navy	S. Vietnam	2-27-67
Hull, James L.	Air Force	Laos	2-19-71
Hume, Kenneth E.	Navy	N. Vietnam	3-29-65
Hummel, John F.	Army	Laos	3-06-71
Humphrey, Galen F.	Marine Corps	N. Vietnam	2-01-66
Huneycutt, Charles J., Jr.	Air Force	N. Vietnam	11-10-67
Hunsicker, James E.	Army	S. Vietnam	4-24-72
Hunt, James D.	Navy	N. Vietnam	10-13-68
Hunt, Leo A.	Air Force	S. Vietnam	6-18-72
Hunt, Robert W.	Army	S. Vietnam	2-28-68
Hunt, William B.	Army	S. Vietnam	11-04-66
Hunter, James D.	Army	S. Vietnam	10-29-68
Hunter, Russell P., Jr.	Air Force	Laos	2-10-66
Huntley, John N.	Army	Laos	9-27-69
Hurst, John C.	Marine Corps	S. Vietnam	7-13-68
Huss, Roy A.	Navy	S. Vietnam	2-06-68
Huston, Charles G.	Army	Laos	3-28-68
Hyde, Jimmy D.	Navy	S. Vietnam	12-05-65
Hyde, Michael L.	Air Force	S. Vietnam	12-08-66
Hynds, Wallace G., Jr.	Air Force	N. Vietnam	8-02-67
Iandoli, Donald	Army	S. Vietnam	11-19-67
Ibanez, Di Reyes	Marine Corps	S. Vietnam	6-05-67
Innes, Roger B.	Navy	N. Vietnam	12-27-67
Ireland, Robert N.	Air Force	Laos	4-22-70
Irsch, Wayne C.	Air Force	Laos	1-09-68
Irwin, Robert H.	Air Force	N. Vietnam	2-17-72
Ivan, Andrew, Jr.	Air Force	Laos	9-10-71
Jablonski, Michael J.	Army	S. Vietnam	6-27-69
Jackson, Carl E.	Air Force	S. Vietnam	6-27-65
Jackson, James T.	Air Force	Laos	3-23-72
Jackson, James W., Jr.	Marine Corps	S. Vietnam	9-21-69
Jackson, Paul V., III	Air Force	Laos	12-24-72
Jacobs, Edward J., Jr.	Navy	N. Vietnam	8-25-67
Jacobsen, Timothy J.	Army	S. Vietnam	5-16-71
Jacques, James J.	Marine Corps	Cambodia	5-15-75
Jakovac, John A.	Army	S. Vietnam	5-31-67
Jamerson, Larry C.	Army	S. Vietnam	4-21-68
James, Samuel L.	Air Force	Cambodia	4-18-73
Janousek, Ronald J.	Marine Corps	S. Vietnam	8-09-69
Jarvis, Jeremy M.	Air Force	N. Vietnam	7-25-67
Jefferson, James M.	Air Force	N. Vietnam	5-12-67
Jefferson, Perry H.	Air Force	S. Vietnam	4-03-69

Name	Military Service	Country of Casualty	Date of Incident
Jeffords, Derrell B.	Air Force	Laos	12-24-65
Jeffs, Clive G.	Air Force	S. Vietnam	3-12-71
Jenkins, Paul L.	Air Force	Laos	6-30-70
Jenne, Robert E.	Army	S. Vietnam	5-08-68
Jensen, George W.	Air Force	Laos	5-15-66
Jerome, Stanley M.	Navy	N. Vietnam	2-18-69
Jewell, Eugene M.	Air Force	N. Vietnam	9-04-65
Jimenez, Juan M.	Army	S. Vietnam	5-11-68
Johns, Paul F.	Air Force	Laos	6-28-68
Johns, Vernon Z.	Army	S. Vietnam	2-03-68
Johnson, Allen L.	Air Force	N. Vietnam	12-28-72
Johnson, August D.	Navy	S. Vietnam	2-03-67
Johnson, Bruce G.	Army	S. Vietnam	6-10-65
Johnson, Dale A.	Air Force	N. Vietnam	10-27-66
Johnson, Edward H.	Air Force	N. Vietnam	12-21-72
Johnson, Frankie B., Jr.	Army	S. Vietnam	4-21-68
Johnson, Gary L.	Army	Laos	2-18-71
Johnson, James R.	Army	S. Vietnam	8-21-66
Johnson, Randolph L.	Army	Laos	2-20-71
Johnson, Richard H.	Marine Corps	S. Vietnam	7-29-67
Johnson, Robert D.	Navy	S. Vietnam	9-01-67
Johnson, Stanley G.	Marine Corps	S. Vietnam	12-03-65
Johnson, William D.	Army	S. Vietnam	1-19-68
Johnston, Steven B.	Air Force	Laos	1-04-73
Johnstone, James M.	Army	S. Vietnam	11-19-66
Jones, Bobby M.	Air Force	S. Vietnam	11-28-72
Jones, George E.	Air Force	S. Vietnam	7-07-67
Jones, Grayland	Army	S. Vietnam	11-23-69
Jones, James E.	Army	Laos	10-03-66
Jones, James G.	Navy	S. Vietnam	11-12-66
Jones, John R.	Army	S. Vietnam	6-05-71
Jones, Johnny M.	Army	S. Vietnam	4-24-72
Jones, Louis F.	Air Force	Laos	11-29-67
Jones, Orvin C., Jr.	Air Force	N. Vietnam	4-16-72
Jones, Thomas P.	Navy	S. Vietnam	2-06-68
Jordan, Larry M.	Navy	China	4-12-66
Jourdenais, George H.	Air Force	S. Vietnam	4-01-67
Judd, Michael B.	Navy	S. Vietnam	6-30-67
Jurecko, Daniel E.	Army	S. Vietnam	5-08-68
Kahler, Harold	Air Force	Laos	6-14-69
Kane, Bruce E.	Marine Corps	S. Vietnam	8-09-69
Kane, Richard R.	Marine Corps	S. Vietnam	9-12-67
Kardell, David A.	Navy	N. Vietnam	5-09-65
Karger, Barry E.	Navy	N. Vietnam	5-14-68

Name	Military Service	Country of Casualty	Date of Incident
Karins, Joseph J., Jr.	Air Force	N. Vietnam	3-11-67
Karst, Carl F.	Air Force	S. Vietnam	11-16-68
Kasch, Frederick M.	Navy	N. Vietnam	7-02-67
Kaster, Leonard L.	Air Force	S. Vietnam	8-06-64
Kearns, Joseph T., Jr.	Air Force	N. Vietnam	6-03-67
Keefe, Douglas O.	Marine Corps	S. Vietnam	5-20-67
Keiper, John C.	Marine Corps	S. Vietnam	11-15-66
Keller, Jack E.	Navy	N. Vietnam	4-21-66
Keller, Wendell R.	Air Force	Laos	3-01-69
Kelley, Daniel M.	Army	S. Vietnam	4-25-68
Kemmerer, Donald R.	Air Force	N. Vietnam	8-06-67
Kemp, Clayton C., Jr.	Navy	N. Vietnam	1-12-67
Kemp, Freddie	Army	S. Vietnam	8-17-66
Kennedy, James E.	Army	Laos	12-22-69
Kennedy, John W.	Air Force	S. Vietnam	8-16-71
Kenney, Harry J.	Navy	S. Vietnam	11-01-68
Kent, Robert D.	Marine Corps	Laos	12-20-68
Kerns, Arthur W.	Army	S. Vietnam	12-23-66
Kerr, Ernest C., Jr.	Marine Corps	S. Vietnam	3-26-68
Kerr, Everett O.	Air Force	Laos	6-13-66
Kerr, John C.G.	Air Force	Laos	8-22-67
Ketchie, Scott D.	Marine Corps	Laos	4-09-72
Ketterer, James A.	Air Force	N. Vietnam	1-20-68
Kibbey, Richard A.	Air Force	N. Vietnam	2-06-67
Kiefel, Ernst P., Jr.	Air Force	Laos	2-10-66
Kieffer, William L., Jr.	Air Force	Laos	2-11-70
Kier, Larry G.	Army	S. Vietnam	5-06-70
Kilcullen, Thomas M.	Air Force	N. Vietnam	8-26-67
Killen, John D., III	Marine Corps	S. Vietnam	6-30-67
Kilpatrick, Larry R.	Navy	N. Vietnam	6-18-72
Kimsey, William A., Jr.	Army	N. Vietnam	1-21-68
King, Charles D.	Air Force	Laos	12-25-68
King, Donald L.	Air Force	N. Vietnam	5-14-66
King, Gerald E.	Marine Corps	S. Vietnam	5-10-68
King, Michael E.	Army	Laos	3-05-71
King, Paul C., Jr.	Army	Laos	5-04-68
King, Ronald R.	Air Force	N. Vietnam	10-03-67
Kinkade, William L.	Air Force	N. Vietnam	9-01-68
Kinsman, Gerald F.	Army	S. Vietnam	1-15-71
Kipina, Marshall F.	Army	Laos	7-14-66
Kirby, Bobby A.	Air Force	N. Vietnam	12-21-72
Kirk, Herbert A.	Air Force	Laos	3-11-68
Kirksey, Robert L.	Army	S. Vietnam	1-01-66
Klemm, Donald M.	Air Force	N. Vietnam	6-11-67

Name	Military Service	Country of Casualty	Date of Incident
Klenda, Dean A.	Air Force	N. Vietnam	9-17-65
Klimo, James R.	Army	S. Vietnam	11-04-69
Kline, Robert E.	Air Force	N. Vietnam	11-02-66
Klingner, Michael L.	Air Force	Laos	4-06-70
Klinke, Donald H.	Air Force	S. Vietnam	6-18-72
Klugg, Joseph R.	Navy	N. Vietnam	11-14-70
Klute, Karl E.	Air Force	S. Vietnam	3-14-66
Kmetyk, Jonathan P.	Marine Corps	S. Vietnam	11-14-67
Knabb, Kenneth K., Jr.	Navy	N. Vietnam	10-21-68
Knapp, Fredric W.	Navy	N. Vietnam	11-02-67
Knapp, Herman L.	Air Force	N. Vietnam	4-24-67
Knebel, Thomas E.	Air Force	Laos	5-22-68
Knight, Henry C.	Army	S. Vietnam	10-20-68
Knight, Larry C.	Navy	N. Vietnam	4-09-70
Knight, Larry D.	Air Force	S. Vietnam	10-07-66
Knight, Roy A., Jr.	Air Force	Laos	5-19-67
Knochel, Charles A.	Navy	N. Vietnam	9-22-66
Knuckey, Thomas W.	Army	Cambodia	5-27-71
Knutsen, Donald P.	Army	Laos	3-22-71
Knutson, Richard A.	Army	S. Vietnam	1-08-73
Koenig, Edwin L.	Navy	S. Vietnam	12-14-66
Kohler, Delvin L.	Navy	N. Vietnam	10-02-69
Kollman, Glenn E.	Navy	N. Vietnam	3-12-68
Kommendant, Aado	Air Force	S. Vietnam	8-08-66
Konyu, William M.	Army	S. Vietnam	4-16-69
Kooi, James W.	Marine Corps	S. Vietnam	6-11-67
Koonce, Terry T.	Air Force	Laos	12-25-67
Koons, Dale F.	Air Force	N. Vietnam	12-26-71
Kosko, Walter	Air Force	N. Vietnam	7-27-65
Koslosky, Howard M.	Navy	N. Vietnam	10-02-69
Kraner, David S.	Navy	N. Vietnam	6-05-72
Krausman, Edward L.	Marine Corps	S. Vietnam	3-16-68
Kravitz, James S.	Navy	Laos	2-17-68
Krech, Melvin T.	Navy	S. Vietnam	4-01-66
Krogman, Alva R.	Air Force	Laos	1-17-67
Krommenhoek, Jeffrey M.	Navy	N. Vietnam	10-25-67
Kroske, Harold W., Jr.	Army	Cambodia	2-11-69
Krupa, Frederick	Army	S. Vietnam	4-27-71
Krusi, Peter H.	Navy	S. Vietnam	11-03-67
Kryszak, Theodore E.	Air Force	Laos	6-03-66
Kubley, Roy R.	Air Force	Laos	1-31-67
Kuhlman, Robert J., Jr.	Marine Corps	S. Vietnam	1-17-69
Kuhlmann, Charles F.	Air Force	Laos	9-22-68
Kulland, Byron K.	Army	S. Vietnam	4-02-72

Name	Military Service	Country of Casualty	Date of Incident
Kusick, Joseph G.	Army	Laos	11-09-67
Kustigan, Michael J.	Navy	N. Vietnam	5-05-68
Kuykendall, Willie C.	Army	S. Vietnam	8-18-71
LaBohn, Garry R.	Army	Laos	11-30-68
LaGrand, William J.	Army	S. Vietnam	9-05-65
LaHaye, James D.	Navy	N. Vietnam	5-08-65
LaPlant, Kurt E.	Marine Corps	S. Vietnam	6-06-68
LaVoo, John A.	Marine Corps	N. Vietnam	9-19-68
Lacey, Richard	Army	S. Vietnam	1-31-68
Ladewig, Melvin F.	Air Force	N. Vietnam	8-24-68
Lafayette, John W.	Army	Laos	4-06-66
Laker, Carl J.	Army	Cambodia	6-17-70
Lambton, Bennie R.	Navy	N. Vietnam	6-13-66
Lamp, Arnold W., Jr.	Air Force	S. Vietnam	4-12-69
Lancaster, Kenneth R.	Army	S. Vietnam	1-03-68
Lane, Charles, Jr.	Air Force	N. Vietnam	8-23-67
Lane, Glen O.	Army	Laos	5-23-68
Lane, Mitchell S.	Air Force	S. Vietnam	1-04-69
Laney, Billy R.	Army	Laos	6-03-67
Lannom, Richard C.	Navy	N. Vietnam	3-01-68
Lapham, Robert G.	Air Force	S. Vietnam	2-08-68
Laporte, Michael L.	Navy	S. Vietnam	9-05-67
Latimer, Clarence A.	Army	S. Vietnam	3-30-69
Laureano, Lopez I.	Army	S. Vietnam	2-20-68
Lauterio, Manuel A.	Army	S. Vietnam	1-08-73
Lautzenheiser, Michael	Army	S. Vietnam	10-26-71
Lawrence, Bruce E.	Air Force	N. Vietnam	7-05-68
Lawrence, Gregory P.	Air Force	Laos	10-05-68
Laws, Delmer L.	Army	S. Vietnam	7-29-66
Laws, Richard L.	Navy	N. Vietnam	4-03-66
Lawson, Karl W.	Army	S. Vietnam	4-09-68
Leaver, John M., Jr.	Navy	N. vietnam	5-08-72
Ledbetter, Thomas I.	Army	S. Vietnam	6-19-64
Lee, Albert E.	Navy	S. Vietnam	2-16-72
Lee, Glenn H.N.	Navy	Cambodia	5-27-70
Lee, Leonard M.	Navy	N. Vietnam	12-27-67
Leeper, Wallace W.	Army	S. Vietnam	12-02-67
Leeser, Leonard C.	Air Force	N. Vietnam	1-28-70
Leet, David L.	Marine Corps	N. Vietnam	4-13-72
Leetun, Darel D.	Air Force	N. Vietnam	9-17-66
Lefever, Douglas P.	Air Force	Laos	11-05-69
Lehnhoff, Edward W.	Air Force	N. Vietnam	11-18-67
Lehrke, Stanley L.	Air Force	S. Vietnam	6-18-72
Lemcke, David E.	Army	S. Vietnam	5-21-68

Name	Military Service	Country of Casualty	Date of Incident
Lemmons, William E.	Army	S. Vietnam	6-18-67
Lemon, Jeffrey C.	Air Force	Laos	4-25-71
Leonard, Marvin M.	Army	Laos	2-15-71
Leonard, Robert B.	Navy	N. Vietnam	10-02-69
Leonor, Leonardo C.	Air Force	N. Vietnam	10-10-72
Lerner, Irwin S.	Air Force	N. Vietnam	12-20-72
Lester, Roderick B.	Navy	N. Vietnam	8-20-72
Letchworth, Edward N.	Navy	S. Vietnam	2-27-67
Levan, Alvin L.	Navy	S. Vietnam	10-25-66
Levis, Charles A.	Air Force	S. Vietnam	4-02-72
Lewandowski, Leonard J., Jr.	Marine Corps	S. Vietnam	10-19-66
Lewellen, Walter E.	Army	Laos	2-18-71
Lewis, Charlie G.	Army	S. Vietnam	5-17-67
Lewis, James W.	Air Force	Laos	4-07-65
Lewis, Larry G.	Navy	S. Vietnam	2-27-71
Lewis, Merrill R., Jr.	Air Force	N. Vietnam	7-20-66
Lillund, William A.	Air Force	N. Vietnam	10-04-67
Lilly, Carroll B.	Air Force	Laos	4-09-71
Lilly, Lawrence E.	Army	Cambodia	3-17-71
Lindahl, John C.	Navy	N. Vietnam	1-06-73
Lindbloom, Charles D.	Navy	S. Vietnam	8-20-68
Lindewald, Charles W.	Army	S. Vietnam	2-07-68
Lindsey, Marvin N.	Air Force	N. Vietnam	6-29-65
Lindstrom, Ronnie G.	Air Force	Laos	1-02-70
Lineberger, Harold B.	Air Force	Cambodia	1-29-71
Link, Robert C.	Army	S. Vietnam	4-21-68
Lint, Donald M.	Air Force	Laos	4-22-70
Little, Danny L.	Army	S. Vietnam	4-23-70
Livingston, Richard A.	Navy	N. Vietnam	10-02-69
Lloyd, Allen R.	Army	Laos	2-18-71
Locker, James D.	Air Force	S. Vietnam	6-09-68
Lockhart, George B.	Air Force	N. Vietnam	12-21-72
Logan, Joacob D.	Navy	N. Vietnam	12-02-65
Loheed, Hubert B.	Navy	N. Vietnam	2-01-66
Lomax, Richard E.	Army	S. Vietnam	3-26-68
Loney, Ashton N.	Marine Corps	Cambodia	5-15-75
Long, Carl E.	Marine Corps	S. Vietnam	12-20-69
Long, George W.	Air Force	S. Vietnam	5-12-68
Long, John H.S.	Air Force	N. Vietnam	10-18-66
Longanecker, Ronald L.	Marine Corps	S. Vietnam	7-08-66
Lono, Luther A.	Marine Corps	Laos	9-29-69
Lopez, Robert	Army	S. Vietnam	3-06-68
Lopez, Robert C.	Marine Corps	S. Vietnam	5-10-68
Lord, Arthur J.	Army	S. Vietnam	4-19-68

Name	Military Service	Country of Casualty	Date of Incident
Lovegren, David E.	Army	S. Vietnam	3-01-69
Lowry, Tyrrell G.	Air Force	S. Vietnam	6-18-65
Lucas, Larry F.	Army	S. Vietnam	12-20-66
Lucki, Albin E.	Air Force	Laos	4-23-70
Lukenbach, Max D.	Navy	N. Vietnam	12-22-65
Luker, Russell B.	Marine Corps	N. Vietnam	2-01-66
Lull, Howard B., Jr.	Army	S. Vietnam	4-07-72
Lum, David A.	Air Force	S. Vietnam	12-20-66
Luna, Carter P.	Air Force	Laos	3-10-69
Luna, Donald A.	Air Force	Laos	2-01-69
Lundy, Albro L., Jr.	Air Force	Laos	12-24-70
Lunsford, Herbert L.	Air Force	N. Vietnam	7-25-67
Luttrell, James M.	Army	S. Vietnam	5-10-71
Lynn, Doyle W.	Navy	N. Vietnam	5-27-65
Lynn, Robert R.	Air Force	N. Vietnam	12-21-72
Lyon, Donavan L.	Air Force	Laos	3-22-68
Lyon, James M.	Army	S. Vietnam	2-05-70
MacLaughlin, Donald C., Jr.	Navy	S. Vietnam	1-02-66
MacCann, Henry E.	Air Force	N. Vietnam	3-28-68
Mackedanz, Lyle E.	Army	S. Vietnam	4-21-68
Macko, Charles	Air Force	Laos	2-22-69
Maddox, Notley G.	Air Force	N. Vietnam	5-20-67
Madison, William L.	Air Force	Laos	5-15-66
Madsen, Marlow E.	Navy	S. Vietnam	1-18-67
Magee, Patrick J.	Army	S. Vietnam	1-03-71
Magee, Ralph W.	Air Force	Laos	3-23-61
Magers, Paul G.	Army	S. Vietnam	6-01-71
Magnusson, James A., Jr.	Air Force	N. Vietnam	4-04-65
Mahoney, Thomas P., III	Marine Corps	S. Vietnam	7-06-68
Mailhes, Lawrence S.	Navy	S. Vietnam	8-10-65
Mallon, Richard J.	Air Force	N. Vietnam	1-28-70
Malone, Jimmy M.	Army	S. Vietnam	5-04-66
Mamiya, John M.	Air Force	N. Vietnam	7-29-66
Mancini, Richard M.	Navy	Laos	1-11-68
Mangino, Thomas A.	Army	S. Vietnam	4-20-67
Mangus, Arlie R.	Army	S. Vietnam	11-03-70
Mann, Robert L.	Air Force	S. Vietnam	10-22-65
Manning, Ronald J.	Navy	Cambodia	5-15-75
Manor, James	Air Force	Cambodia	3-27-72
Manske, Charles J.	Air Force	S. Vietnam	5-24-69
Mape, John C.	Navy	N. Vietnam	4-13-66
Marik, Charles W.	Navy	N. Vietnam	6-25-66
Marker, Michael W.	Army	N. Vietnam	3-04-71
Marshall, Danny G.	Marine Corps	Cambodia	5-15-75

Name	Military Service	Country of Casualty	Date of Incident
Marshall, James A.	Air Force	S. Vietnam	6-18-65
Marshall, Richard C.	Air Force	S. Vietnam	9-05-65
Martin, David E.	Navy	N. Vietnam	4-04-67
Martin, Douglas K.	Air Force	Cambodia	4-18-73
Martin, Duane W.	Air Force	N. Vietnam	9-20-65
Martin, James E.	Navy	Laos	2-17-68
Martin, Jerry D.	Army	S. Vietnam	11-03-70
Martin, John B., II	Navy	S. Vietnam	10-16-70
Martin, John M.	Air Force	N. Vietnam	11-20-67
Martin, Larry E.	Air Force	N. Vietnam	7-15-68
Martin, Richard D.	Army	S. Vietnam	5-01-68
Martin, Russell D.	Air Force	Laos	6-03-66
Martin, Sammy A.	Air Force	N. Vietnam	12-27-67
Martinez-Mercado, Edwin J.	Army	S. Vietnam	11-11-67
Marvin, Robert C.	Navy	N. Vietnam	2-14-67
Mascari, Phillip L.	Air Force	Laos	5-02-69
Mason, James Phillip	Army	S. Vietnam	10-17-68
Mason, William H.	Air Force	Laos	5-22-68
Massucci, Martin J.	Air Force	N. Vietnam	10-01-65
Masterson, Michael J.	Air Force	Laos	10-13-68
Masuda, Robert S.	Army	S. Vietnam	5-13-69
Mateja, Alan P.	Air Force	N. Vietnam	4-16-72
Matejon, Joseph A.	Air Force	Laos	2-05-73
Matocha, Donald J.	Marine Corps	S. Vietnam	4-05-68
Matteson, Glenn	Air Force	Laos	3-23-61
Matthes, Peter R.	Air Force	Laos	11-24-69
Mauterer, Oscar	Air Force	Laos	2-15-66
Maxwell, Calvin W.	Army	S. Vietnam	10-10-69
Maxwell, James R.	Marine Corps	Cambodia	5-15-75
Maxwell, Samuel C.	Air Force	N. Vietnam	9-12-68
May, David M.	Army	Laos	2-20-71
May, Michael F.	Army	Cambodia	3-02-69
Meyer, Roderick L.	Navy	N. Vietnam	10-17-65
Mayercik, Ronald M.	Air Force	Laos	11-24-67
Maysey, Larry W.	Air Force	Laos	11-09-67
McAteer, Thomas J.	Navy	S. Vietnam	11-10-66
McBride, Earl P.	Navy	N. Vietnam	10-22-66
McCants, Leland S., III	Army	S. Vietnam	12-30-68
McClellan, Paul T., Jr.	Air Force	S. Vietnam	11-14-65
McConnaughhay, Dan D.	Navy	S. Vietnam	2-05-66
McConnell, Jerry	Army	S. Vietnam	9-24-68
McCormick, John V.	Navy	N. Vietnam	12-01-65
McCoy, Meril O., Jr.	Navy	N. Vietnam	12-15-70
McCrary, Jack	Air Force	N. Vietnam	12-29-67

Name	Military Service	Country of Casualty	Date of Incident
McCubbin, Glenn D.	Air Force	N. Vietnam	5-19-68
McDaniel, John L.	Air Force	S. Vietnam	4-26-68
McDaniel, Morris L., Jr.	Air Force	N. Vietnam	10-04-67
McDonald, Emmett R.	Air Force	N. Vietnam	5-31-66
McDonald, Kurt C.	Air Force	S. Vietnam	12-31-64
McDonnell, John T.	Army	S. Vietnam	3-06-69
McDonough, John R.	Navy	N. Vietnam	6-20-66
McElhanon, Michael O.	Air Force	N. Vietnam	8-16-68
McElroy, Glenn D.	Army	Laos	3-15-66
McElroy, John L.	Air Force	S. Vietnam	5-12-68
McEwen, James A.	Air Force	S. Vietnam	10-22-65
McGar, Brian K.	Army	S. Vietnam	5-31-67
McGonigle, William D.	Marine Corps	S. Vietnam	5-10-68
McGouldrick, Francis J., Jr.	Air Force	Laos	12-13-68
McGrath, James P.	Navy	S. Vietnam	8-03-67
McIntosh, Ian	Army	S. Vietnam	11-24-70
McKain, Bobby L.	Army	S. Vietnam	5-03-68
McKay, Homer E.	Navy	S. Vietnam	2-06-68
McKenney, Kenneth D.	Air Force	Laos	5-15-66
McKinley, Gerald W.	Navy	N. Vietnam	3-31-65
McKinney, Neil B.	Air Force	S. Vietnam	9-02-63
McLamb, Harry L.	Air Force	Cambodia	6-18-70
McLaughlin, Olen B.	Air Force	S. Vietnam	7-07-67
McLean, James H.	Army	S. Vietnam	2-09-65
McManus, Truman J.	Marine Corps	S. Vietnam	6-05-68
McPhail, William T.	Air Force	Laos	5-22-68
McPhee, Randy N.	Marine Corps	S. Vietnam	4-30-67
McPherson, Fred L.	Air Force	S. Vietnam	1-28-66
McVey, Lavoy D.	Marine Corps	S. Vietnam	3-02-70
McWhorter, Henry S.	Navy	N. Vietnam	8-29-65
McAndrews, Michael W.	Army	S. Vietnam	12-23-70
McCarty, James L.	Air Force	N. Vietnam	6-24-72
McCleary, George C.	Air Force	N. Vietnam	11-05-65
McCormick, Carl O.	Air Force	S. Vietnam	10-06-72
McCormick, Michael T.	Navy	N. Vietnam	1-10-73
McDonald, Joseph W.	Marine Corps	N. Vietnam	5-03-72
McDonell, R.D.	Army	S. Vietnam	3-25-71
McElvain, James R.	Air Force	N. Vietnam	12-18-72
McGarvey, James M.	Marine Corps	N. Vietnam	4-17-67
McIntire, Scott W.	Air Force	Laos	12-10-71
McKinney, Clemie	Navy	S. Vietnam	4-14-72
McKittrick, James C.	Army	S. Vietnam	6-18-67
McLaughlin, Arthur V., Jr.	Air Force	N. Vietnam	12-20-72
McLeod, Arthur E.	Army	S. Vietnam	2-12-71

Name	Military Service	Country of Casualty	Date of Incident
McLeod, David V., Jr.	Air Force	Cambodia	6-14-73
McMahan, Robert C.	Navy	N. Vietnam	2-14-68
McMican, M.D.	Navy	N. Vietnam	6-02-65
McMurray, Fred H., Jr.	Army	S. Vietnam	4-07-68
McPherson, Everett A.	Marine Corps	N. Vietnam	3-18-66
McQuade, James R.	Army	S. Vietnam	6-11-72
McRae, David E.	Navy	N. Vietnam	12-02-66
Meadows, Eugene T.	Air Force	N. Vietnam	10-13-66
Mein, Michael H.	Army	Laos	11-30-68
Meldhal, Charles H.	Army	S. Vietnam	10-20-68
Mellor, Fredric M.	Air Force	N. Vietnam	8-13-65
Melton, Todd M.	Air Force	Laos	2-05-73
Mercer, Jacob E.	Air Force	S. Vietnam	6-18-72
Meroney, Virgil K. III	Air Force	Laos	3-01-69
Metoyer, Bryford G.	Army	S. Vietnam	1-18-64
Metzler, Charles D.	Navy	N. Vietnam	6-21-71
Meyers, Roger A.	Navy	N. Vietnam	2-09-69
Mickelsen, William E., Jr.	Navy	N. Vietnam	8-10-69
Midgett, Dewey A.	Army	S. Vietnam	11-25-67
Midnight, Francis B.	Air Force	N. Vietnam	8-23-67
Milikin, Richard M. III	Air Force	N. Vietnam	8-20-66
Milius, Paul L.	Navy	Laos	2-27-68
Millard, Charles W.	Army	S. Vietnam	4-19-68
Miller, Carl D.	Air Force	N. Vietnam	9-05-67
Miller, Carleton P., Jr.	Navy	N. Vietnam	1-06-71
Miller, Curtis D.	Air Force	Laos	3-29-72
Miller, Glenn E.	Army	S. Vietnam	5-10-68
Miller, Malcolm T.	Navy	S. Vietnam	5-10-67
Miller, Michael A.	Air Force	S. Vietnam	3-28-69
Miller, Richard A.	Marine Corps	S. Vietnam	11-22-65
Miller, Robert C.	Air Force	Laos	8-28-68
Miller, Robert L.	Navy	N. Vietnam	3-07-67
Miller, Wyatt, Jr.	Army	S. Vietnam	9-13-70
Milliner, William P.	Army	Laos	3-06-71
Millner, Michael	Army	S. Vietnam	11-29-67
Mills, James B.	Navy	N. Vietnam	9-21-66
Mills, James D.	Marine Corps	S. Vietnam	1-29-68
Mims, George I., Jr.	Air Force	N. Vietnam	12-20-65
Minor, Carrol W.	Navy	S. Vietnam	12-09-68
Mirrer, Robert H.	Air Force	Laos	1-17-71
Mishuk, Richard E.	Marine Corps	S. Vietnam	10-19-66
Mitchell, Albert C	Air Force	N. Vietnam	4-25-68
Mitchell, Carl B.	Air Force	S. Vietnam	1-14-64
Mitchell, Donald W.	Marine Corps	S. Vietnam	5-10-68

Name	Military Service	Country of Casualty	Date of Incident
Mitchell, Gilbert L.	Navy	N. Vietnam	3-06-68
Mitchell, Harry E.	Navy	N. Vietnam	5-05-68
Mitchell, Thomas B.	Air Force	Laos	5-22-68
Mixter, David I.	Army	Laos	1-29-71
Miyazaki, Ronald K.	Air Force	Laos	1-31-67
Moe, Harold J.	Marine Corps	S. Vietnam	9-26-67
Mongilardi, Peter, Jr.	Navy	N. Vietnam	6-25-65
Montez, Anastacio	Army	S. Vietnam	5-24-69
Montgomery, Ronald W.	Navy	N. Vietnam	10-02-69
Moon, Walter, H.	Army	Laos	4-22-61
Mooney, Fred	Army	Laos	2-27-71
Moore, Herbert, W., Jr.	Air Force	N. Vietnam	9-03-67
Moore, James R.	Marine Corps	S. Vietnam	2-28-67
Moore, Jerry L.	Army	S. Vietnam	2-16-69
Moore, Maurice H.	Army	S. Vietnam	5-12-68
Moore, Ralph E.	Army	S. Vietnam	5-03-67
Moore, Raymond G.	Army	S. Vietnam	10-09-69
Moore, Scott F., Jr.	Navy	S. Vietnam	2-20-70
Moore, Thomas	Air Force	S. Vietnam	10-31-65
Moore, William J.	Air Force	S. Vietnam	5-18-66
Moore, William R.	Navy	N. Vietnam	10-02-69
Moran, Richard A.	Navy	S. Vietnam	8-07-66
Moreida, Manuel J.	Army	S. Vietnam	12-02-67
Moreia, Ralph A., Jr.	Army	Laos	3-05-71
Moreland, James L.	Army	S. Vietnam	2-07-68
Moreland, Stephen C.	Air Force	S. Vietnam	5-12-68
Moreland, William D.	Marine Corps	S. Vietnam	1-16-68
Morgan, Burke H.	Air Force	Laos	8-22-67
Morgan, Charles, E.	Air Force	N. Vietnam	7-06-66
Morgan, Edwin E.	Air Force	S. Vietnam	3-13-66
Morgan, James S.	Air Force	N. Vietnam	11-10-67
Morgan, Thomas R.	Air Force	S. Vietnam	1-26-67
Morgan, William J.	Army	S. Vietnam	2-25-72
Moriarty, Peter G.	Air Force	Laos	3-22-71
Morin, Richard G.	Marine Corps	Laos	12-20-68
Morley, Charles F.	Air Force	Laos	2-18-70
Morrill, David	Marine Corps	S. Vietnam	3-18-67
Morris, George W., Jr.	Air Force	S. Vietnam	1-27-73
Morrison, Glenn R., Jr.	Air Force	S. Vietnam	10-26-66
Morrison, Joseph C.	Air Force	N. Vietnam	11-25-68
Morrissey, Richard T.	Marine Corps	S. Vietnam	8-19-69
Morrissey, Robert D.	Air Force	Laos	11-07-72
Morrow, Larry K.	Army	S. Vietnam	5-29-72
Mosburg, Henry L.	Army	S. Vietnam	9-26-66

Name	Military Service	Country of Casualty	Date of Incident
Moser, Paul K.	Navy	N. Vietnam	10-02-69
Moshier, Jim E.	Marine Corps	S. Vietnam	6-11-67
Mossman, Harry S.	Navy	N. Vietnam	8-20-72
Mossman, Joe R.	Navy	N. Vietnam	9-13-65
Mowrey, Glenn W.	Marine Corps	S. Vietnam	3-26-68
Mowrey, Richard L.	Navy	S. Vietnam	12-14-66
Mulhauser, Harvey	Air Force	Laos	1-31-67
Mulleavey, Quinten E.	Army	S. Vietnam	1-29-68
Mullen, William F.	Marine Corps	Laos	4-29-66
Mullins, Harold E.	Air Force	Laos	6-03-66
Mundt, Henry G., II	Air Force	Laos	5-08-69
Munoz, David L.	Army	S. Vietnam	5-13-69
Muren, Thomas R.	Navy	N. Vietnam	4-03-72
Murphy, Barry D.	Army	Cambodia	3-18-69
Murphy, Larron D.	Army	S. Vietnam	4-23-70
Murphy, Terence M.	Navy	China	4-09-65
Murray, Joseph V.	Navy	N. Vietnam	2-18-66
Murray, Patrick P.	Marine Corps	N. Vietnam	1-19-68
Musetti, Joseph T., Jr.	Navy	S. Vietnam	9-28-67
Musil, Clinton A., Sr.	Army	Laos	5-31-71
Myers, David Gephart	Marine Corps	S. Vietnam	6-08-67
Nahan, John B., III	Marine Corps	S. Vietnam	8-03-67
Nash, John M.	Army	Laos	3-15-66
Neal, Dennis P.	Army	Laos	7-31-69
Neeld, Bobby G.	Air Force	S. Vietnam	1-04-69
Neislar, David P.	Navy	N. Vietnam	2-20-69
Nellans, William L.	Air Force	N. Vietnam	9-17-67
Nelson, David L.	Army	Laos	3-05-71
Nelson, James R.	Army	S. Vietnam	6-11-67
Nelson, Jan H.	Marine Corps	S. Vietnam	4-11-70
Ness, Patrick .	Navy	N. Vietnam	8-23-67
Neth, Fred A.	Navy	S. Vietnam	1-16-66
Netherland, Roger M.	Navy	N. Vietnam	5-10-67
Neville, William E.	Air Force	S. Vietnam	6-18-65
Newberry, Wayne E.	Air Force	Laos	9-19-68
Newburn, Larry W.	Army	S. Vietnam	8-29-67
Newell, Michael T.	Navy	N. Vietnam	12-14-66
Newman, James C., Jr.	Navy	S. Vietnam	2-06-68
Newman, Larry J.	Air Force	S. Vietnam	6-18-72
Newton, Charles V.	Army	S. Vietnam	4-17-69
Newton, Donald S.	Army	S. Vietnam	2-26-66
Newton, Warren E.	Army	S. Vietnam	1-09-68
Nichols, Hubert C., Jr.	Air Force	N. Vietnam	9-01-66
Nickerson, William B.	Navy	N. Vietnam	4-22-66

Name	Military Service	Country of Casualty	Date of Incident
Nickol, Robert A.	Army	S. Vietnam	10-26-71
Nidds, Daniel R.	Army	S. Vietnam	4-21-67
Niedecken, William C.	Navy	Laos	2-15-69
Nightingale, Randall J.	Navy	N. Vietnam	3-17-78
Nipper, David	Marine Corps	S. Vietnam	11-21-64
Norbert, Craig R.	Air Force	N. Vietnam	7-20-66
Nolan, Joseph P., Jr.	Army	S. Vietnam	5-16-71
Nopp, Robert G.	Army	Laos	7-14-66
Nordahl, Lee E.	Navy	N. Vietnam	12-20-65
Norris, Calvin A.	Army	S. Vietnam	11-03-70
Norton, Michael R.	Army	S. Vietnam	11-03-69
Nyhof, Richard E.	Air Force	S. Vietnam	6-18-72
Nyman, Lawrence F.	Navy	N. Vietnam	6-23-66
Nystrom, Bruce A.	Navy	N. Vietnam	12-02-66
Nystul, William C.	Marine Corps	S. Vietnam	4-29-75
O'Brien, John L.	Air Force	Laos	11-10-66
O'Brien, Kevin	Army	S. Vietnam	1-09-69
O'Grady, John F.	Air Force	N. Vietnam	4-10-67
O'Hara, Robert C.	Army	S. Vietnam	2-06-69
Oakley, Linus L.	Air Force	S. Vietnam	10-29-71
Ochab, Robert	Air Force	S. Vietnam	1-07-70
Oddonnell, Michael D.	Army	Cambodia	3-24-70
Oddonnell, Samuel, Jr.	Air Force	N. Vietnam	7-12-72
Offutt, Gary P.	Air Force	S. Vietnam	10-01-65
Ogden, Howard, Jr.	Marine Corps	S. Vietnam	10-18-67
Okerlund, Thomas R.	Army	S. Vietnam	1-03-71
Oldham, John S.	Marine Corps	S. Vietnam	6-11-67
Olds, Ernest A.	Air Force	N. Vietnam	3-11-68
Olmstead, Stanley E.	Navy	N. Vietnam	10-17-65
Olsen, Floyd W.	Army	S. Vietnam	4-21-68
Olson, Barry A.	Army	S. Vietnam	9-26-68
Olson, Delbert A.	Navy	Laos	1-11-68
Olson, Gerald F.	Air Force	S. Vietnam	3-13-66
Omelia, Dennis W.	Army	S. Vietnam	1-03-71
Oneill, Douglas L.	Army	S. Vietnam	4-03-72
Orell, Quinlan R.	Navy	N. Vietnam	10-13-68
Orr, Warren R., Jr.	Army	S. Vietnam	5-12-68
Osborn, Geoffrey H.	Navy	S. Vietnam	9-24-65
Osborne, Edwin N., Jr.	Air Force	N. Vietnam	12-29-67
Osborne, Rodney	Army	N. Vietnam	3-04-71
Osborne, Samuel W., Jr.	Marine Corps	S. Vietnam	4-27-67
Ostermeyer, William H.	Air Force	Laos	5-12-72
Ott, Edward L., III	Navy	S. Vietnam	9-01-67

Name	Military Service	Country of Casualty	Date of Incident
Ott, Patrick L.	Marine Corps	S. Vietnam	10-02-67
Ott, William A.	Air Force	Laos	10-08-70
Overlock, John F.	Air Force	N. Vietnam	8-16-68
Owen, Clyde C.	Navy	N. Vietnam	12-15-70
Owen, Robert D.	Army	Laos	5-23-68
Owen, Timothy S.	Army	S. Vietnam	6-29-68
Owens, Fred M.	Army	S. Vietnam	6-10-65
Owens, Joy L.	Air Force	N. Vietnam	6-07-67
Pabst, Eugene M.	Air Force	N. Vietnam	10-07-66
Packard, Ronald L.	Air Force	N. Vietnam	7-31-67
Padgett, David E.	Army	S. Vietnam	2-06-69
Padgett, Samuel J.	Army	S. Vietnam	4-10-68
Padilla, David E.	Marine Corps	S. Vietnam	5-18-68
Page, Albert L., Jr.	Air Force	N. Vietnam	8-06-67
Page, Gordon L.	Air Force	N. Vietnam	3-07-66
Painter, John R., Jr.	Navy	N. Vietnam	6-18-71
Palacios,Luis F.	Marine Corps	S. Vietnam	6-06-68
Palen, Carl A.	Army	S. Vietnam	1-03-71
Palenscar, Alexander J., III	Navy	N. Vietnam	3-27-67
Palmer, Gilbert S., Jr.	Air Force	Laos	2-27-68
Palmgren, Edwin D.	Air Force	N. Vietnam	4-22-68
Panek, Robert J., Sr.	Air Force	N. Vietnam	1-28-70
Pannabecker, David E.	Air Force	Cambodia	3-27-72
Pantall, James R.	Army	S. Vietnam	11-03-70
Parcels, Rex L., Jr.	Navy	N. Vietnam	3-09-70
Parish, Charles C.	Navy	N. Vietnam	7-25-68
Parker, Charles L., Jr.	Navy	N. Vietnam	1-21-73
Parker, David W.	Army	S. Vietnam	2-06-69
Parker, Frank C., III	Air Force	N. Vietnam	12-29-67
Parker, John J.	Navy	N. Vietnam	3-04-70
Parker, Maxim C.	Marine Corps	S. Vietnam	3-18-67
Parker, Thomas A.	Navy	S. Vietnam	4-05-67
Parker, Udon	Army	S. Vietnam	3-13-66
Parker, Woodrow W., II	Air Force	N. Vietnam	4-24-68
Parks, Joe	Army	S. Vietnam	12-22-64
Parks, Raymond F.	Army	Laos	7-14-62
Parra, Lionel	Marine Corps	S. Vietnam	7-17-68
Parsley, Edward M.	Air Force	S. Vietnam	2-03-66
Parsons, Don B., Jr.	Navy	N. Vietnam	9-19-66
Parsons, Donald E.	Army	S. Vietnam	2-06-69
Parsons, Michael D.	Army	S. Vietnam	1-03-71
Partington, Roger D.	Marine Corps	S. Vietnam	11-01-69
Paschall, Ronald P.	Army	S. Vietnam	4-02-72
Pasekoff, Robert E.	Air Force	S. Vietnam	3-13-66

Name	Military Service	Country of Casualty	Date of Incident
Pastva, Michael J.	Marine Corps	S. Vietnam	12-06-67
Pate, Gary	Air Force	Laos	5-22-68
Patterson, Bruce M.	Navy	N. Vietnam	7-27-67
Patterson, James K.	Navy	N. Vietnam	5-19-67
Pattillo, Ralph N.	Air Force	Laos	2-16-71
Patton, Kenneth J.	Army	S. Vietnam	2-02-68
Patton, Ward K.	Navy	S. Vietnam	7-27-68
Paul, James L.	Army	S. Vietnam	2-05-71
Pauley, Marshall I.	Air Force	S. Vietnam	3-13-66
Paulson, Merlyn L.	Air Force	Laos	3-29-72
Pawlish, George F.	Navy	N. Vietnam	3-08-67
Paxton, Donald E.	Air Force	Laos	2-22-69
Payne, Kylis T.	Navy	N. Vietnam	6-05-72
Payne, Norman	Army	Laos	12-29-68
Peace, John D., III	Navy	N. Vietnam	12-31-67
Peacock, John R., II	Marine Corps	N. Vietnam	10-12-72
Pearce, Dale A.	Army	S. Vietnam	5-17-71
Pearce, Edwin J.	Air Force	Laos	3-29-72
Pearson, Robert H.	Air Force	N. Vietnam	6-11-67
Pearson, Wayne E.	Air Force	Laos	2-22-69
Pearson, William R.	Air Force	S. Vietnam	4-06-72
Pederson, Joe P.	Army	S. Vietnam	6-23-70
Pender, Orland J., Jr.	Navy	N. Vietnam	8-17-72
Pennington, Ronald K.	Marine Corps	S. Vietnam	4-27-67
Pepper, Anthony J.	Marine Corps	S. Vietnam	4-06-68
Perisho, Gordon S.	Navy	N. Vietnam	12-31-67
Perkins, Cecil C.	Army	S. Vietnam	12-14-71
Perrine, Elton L.	Air Force	N. Vietnam	5-22-67
Perry, Otha L.	Army	S. Vietnam	12-14-71
Perry, Randolph A., Jr.	Air Force	N. Vietnam	12-20-72
Perry, Richard C.	Navy	N. Vietnam	8-31-67
Perry, Thomas H.	Army	S. Vietnam	5-10-68
Peters, Charles H.	Navy	N. Vietnam	7-01-66
Peterson, Delbert R.	Air Force	S. Vietnam	3-09-66
Peterson, Dennis W.	Navy	N. Vietnam	7-19-67
Peterson, Mark A.	Air Force	S. Vietnam	1-27-73
Pettis, Thomas E.	Navy	N. Vietnam	5-23-67
Pfaffmann, Charles B.	Navy	N. Vietnam	4-09-70
Pharris, William V.	Army	S. Vietnam	7-07-66
Phelps, Jesse D.	Army	S. Vietnam	12-28-65
Phelps, William	Air Force	Laos	11-23-71
Phillips, Daniel R.	Army	S. Vietnam	2-07-68
Phillips, David J., Jr.	Air Force	S. Vietnam	7-03-66
Phillips, Elbert A.	Air Force	Laos	8-28-68

Name	Military Service	Country of Casualty	Date of Incident
Phillips, Marvin F.	Army	S. Vietnam	9-26-66
Phillips, Robert P.	Army	S. Vietnam	6-23-70
Phipps, James L.	Army	S. Vietnam	1-09-68
Pick, Donald W.	Air Force	S. Vietnam	8-27-68
Pierce, Walter M.	Army	Cambodia	6-10-70
Piersanti, Anthony J., Jr.	Navy	N. Vietnam	12-15-70
Pierson, William C., III	Army	S. Vietnam	4-13-69
Pietrzak, Joseph R.	Army	S. Vietnam	2-10-71
Pietsch, Robert E.	Air Force	Laos	4-30-68
Piittmann, Alan D.	Air Force	Laos	11-16-66
Pike, Dennis S.	Navy	Laos	3-23-72
Pike, Peter X.	Air Force	Laos	7-12-69
Pilkington, Thomas H.	Navy	N. Vietnam	9-19-66
Pineau, Roland R.	Navy	S. Vietnam	10-08-67
Pirker, Victor J.	Marine Corps	S. Vietnam	11-22-65
Pirruccello, Joseph S., Jr.	Air Force	Laos	12-08-68
Pirman, Peter P.	Air Force	N. Vietnam	5-12-67
Pitt, Albert	Marine Corps	S. Vietnam	1-24-66
Pittman, Robert E.	Army	N. Vietnam	9-28-66
Pitzen, John R.	Navy	N. Vietnam	8-17-72
Plants, Thomas L.	Navy	N. Vietnam	6-02-65
Plassmeyer, Bernard H.	Marine Corps	S. Vietnam	9-11-70
Platt, Robert L., Jr.	Army	S. Vietnam	6-10-67
Pleiman, James E.	Air Force	N. Vietnam	3-14-66
Plowman, James E.	Navy	N. Vietnam	3-24-67
Plumadore, Kenneth L.	Marine Corps	S. Vietnam	9-21-67
Pogreba, Dean A.	Air Force	N. Vietnam	10-05-65
Pollin, George J.	Air Force	N. Vietnam	4-29-67
Polster, Harmon	Air Force	Laos	7-15-69
Pool, Jerry L.	Army	Cambodia	3-24-70
Poole, Charlie S.	Air Force	N. Vietnam	12-19-72
Poor, Russell A.	Air Force	N. Vietnam	2-04-67
Posey, George R.	Navy	S. Vietnam	9-05-68
Potter, William J., Jr.	Air Force	Laos	12-29-67
Potter, William T.	Air Force	Laos	2-05-68
Potts, Larry F.	Marine Corps	S. Vietnam	4-07-72
Powell, William E.	Air Force	N. Vietnam	8-17-68
Powers, John L.	Army	Laos	2-15-71
Powers, Lowell S.	Army	S. Vietnam	4-02-69
Powers, Trent R.	Navy	N. Vietnam	10-31-65
Powers, Vernie H.	Army	S. Vietnam	12-24-67
Poynor, Daniel R.	Air Force	Laos	12-19-71
Prater, Roy D.	Air Force	S. Vietnam	4-06-72
Prather, Martin W.	Marine Corps	S. Vietnam	9-05-67

Name	Military Service	Country of Casualty	Date of Incident
Preiss, Robert F., Jr.	Army	Laos	5-12-70
Prentice, Kenneth M.	Navy	N. Vietnam	10-02-69
Preston, James A.	Air Force	Laos	5-15-66
Prevedel, Charles F.	Army	S. Vietnam	4-17-69
Prevost, Albert M.	Marine Corps	N. Vietnam	2-01-66
Prewitt, William R.	Marine Corps	S. Vietnam	8-01-67
Price, Bunyan D.	Army	Cambodia	5-02-70
Price, David S.	Air Force	Laos	3-11-68
Price, William M.	Marine Corps	N. Vietnam	10-12-72
Pridemore, Dallas R.	Army	S. Vietnam	9-08-68
Primm, Severo J., III	Air Force	Laos	2-05-73
Pringle, Joe H.	Army	S. Vietnam	2-02-68
Prudhomme, John D.	Navy	N. Vietnam	12-22-65
Pruett, William D.	Air Force	N. Vietnam	1-28-70
Puentes, Manuel R.	Army	S. Vietnam	3-25-71
Puggi, Joseph D.	Army	S. Vietnam	2-02-68
Pugh, Dennis G.	Air Force	Laos	3-19-70
Purcell, Howard P.	Air Force	S. Vietnam	9-02-63
Putnam, Charles L.	Navy	N. Vietnam	3-09-67
Pyles, Harley B.	Air Force	S. Vietnam	10-18-65
Quinn, Michael E.	Navy	Laos	11-22-69
Rackley, Inzar W., Jr.	Air Force	N. Vietnam	10-18-66
Ragland, Dayton W.	Air Force	N. Vietnam	5-31-66
Ralston, Frank D., III	Air Force	N. Vietnam	5-14-66
Ramirez, Armando	Army	Cambodia	5-23-69
Ramos, Rainier S.	Army	S. Vietnam	1-09-68
Ramsay, Charles J.	Marine Corps	N. Vietnam	1-21-68
Ramsden, Gerald L.	Navy	N. Vietnam	1-23-68
Ramsower, Irving B., II	Air Force	Laos	3-29-72
Ransbottom, Frederick J.	Army	S. Vietnam	5-12-68
Rash, Melvin D.	Air Force	Laos	5-22-68
Rattin, Dennis M.	Army	Laos	10-16-69
Ratzel, Wesley D.	Air Force	N. Vietnam	5-18-72
Rausch, Robert E.	Air Force	Laos	4-16-70
Ravenna, Harry M., III	Army	S. Vietnam	11-15-66
Rawsthorne, Edgar A.	Navy	Laos	12-29-65
Ray, James M.	Army	S. Vietnam	3-18-68
Ray, Ronald E.	Army	Laos	11-13-69
Raymond, Paul D.	Air Force	N. Vietnam	9-05-67
Read, Charles H.W., Jr.	Air Force	N. Vietnam	8-24-68
Reardon, Richard J.	Navy	S. Vietnam	4-28-69
Reed, James W.	Air Force	Laos	7-24-70
Reed, Terry M.	Air Force	S. Vietnam	6-23-69
Reedy, William H., Jr.	Navy	N. Vietnam	1-16-68

Name	Military Service	Country of Casualty	Date of Incident
Reese, Gomer D., III	Air Force	Laos	4-24-70
Reeves, John H.	Marine Corps	S. Vietnam	12-23-66
Rehe, Richard R.	Army	S. Vietnam	1-09-68
Rehn, Gary L.	Marine Corps	S. Vietnam	11-09-67
Reid, Harold E.	Marine Corps	S. Vietnam	9-13-67
Reid, John E.	Army	Laos	2-20-71
Reilly, Edward D., Jr.	Army	S. Vietnam	4-26-66
Reilly, Lavern G.	Air Force	Laos	5-15-66
Reinecke, Wayne C.	Navy	N. Vietnam	1-12-67
Riter, Dean W.	Marine Corps	S. Vietnam	9-25-66
Reitmann, Thomas E.	Air Force	N. Vietnam	12-01-65
Renelt, Walter A.	Air Force	Laos	11-20-69
Reno, Ralph J.	Army	S. Vietnam	7-03-66
Rex, Robert A.	Air Force	Laos	12-08-68
Rex, Robert F.	Air Force	Laos	3-09-69
Rexroad, Ronald R.	Air Force	N. Vietnam	4-03-68
Reynolds, David R.	Army	S. Vietnam	11-21-67
Rhodes, Ferris A., Jr.	Army	S. Vietnam	1-03-71
Rice, Thomas, Jr.	Army	S. Vietnam	12-28-65
Rich, Richard	Navy	N. Vietnam	5-19-67
Richardson, Dale W.	Army	Cambodia	5-02-70
Richardson, Floyd W.	Air Force	N. Vietnam	3-03-67
Richardson, Stephen G.	Navy	S. Vietnam	11-30-65
Rickel, David J.	Air Force	N. Vietnam	5-16-68
Ricker, William E.	Navy	S. Vietnam	10-28-68
Rickman, Dwight G.	Marine Corps	S. Vietnam	12-25-72
Riggins, Robert P.	Air Force	S. Vietnam	4-22-68
Riggs, Thomas F.	Army	S. Vietnam	6-11-67
Riordan, John M.	Navy	S. Vietnam	11-10-66
Rios, Noel L.	Air Force	S. Vietnam	3-06-68
Ritchey, Luther E., Jr.	Marine Corps	S. Vietnam	10-08-63
Rittichier, Jack C.	Coast Guard	S. Vietnam	6-09-68
Rivenburgh, Richard W.	Marine Corps	Cambodia	5-15-75
Roark, James D.	Navy	N. Vietnam	11-12-67
Robbins, Richard J.	Air Force	Laos	4-19-66
Roberson, John W.	Army	S. Vietnam	6-22-69
Roberts, Gerald R.	Navy	N. Vietnam	12-02-65
Roberts, Harold J., Jr.	Air Force	S. Vietnam	6-18-65
Roberts, Michael L.	Navy	Laos	1-11-68
Roberts, Richard D.	Navy	S. Vietnam	3-25-69
Robertson, John H.	Army	Laos	5-20-68
Robertson, John L.	Air Force	N. Vietnam	9-16-66
Robertson, Leonard	Marine Corps	S. Vietnam	7-07-72
Robertson, Mark J.	Army	S. Vietnam	2-10-71

Name	Military Service	Country of Casualty	Date of Incident
Robinson, Edward	Army	S. Vietnam	3-09-70
Robinson, Floyd H.	Army	S. Vietnam	3-12-69
Robinson, Kenneth D.	Air Force	N. Vietnam	8-30-66
Robinson, Larry W.	Marine Corps	Laos	1-05-70
Robinson, Lewis M.	Air Force	Laos	6-04-67
Roby, Charles D.	Air Force	N. Vietnam	3-03-67
Rockett, Alton C., Jr.	Air Force	N. Vietnam	6-02-67
Rodriguez, Albert E.	Air Force	N. Vietnam	3-11-68
Roe, Jerry L.	Army	S. Vietnam	3-12-68
Roerich, Ronald L.	Navy	N. Vietnam	1-18-68
Rogers, Billy L.	Navy	N. Vietnam	12-01-69
Rogers, Charles E.	Air Force	Laos	5-04-67
Rogers, Edward F.	Marine Corps	S. Vietnam	3-12-68
Roggow, Norman L.	Navy	S. Vietnam	10-08-67
Romano, Gerald M.	Navy	N. Vietnam	6-02-65
Romero, Victor	Air Force	S. Vietnam	3-19-68
Romig, Edward L.	Navy	S. Vietnam	6-17-66
Roraback, Kenneth M.	Army	S. Vietnam	11-24-63
Rosato, Joseph F.	Air Force	S. Vietnam	6-02-66
Rose, Luther L.	Air Force	Laos	6-03-66
Rosenbach, Robert P.	Air Force	S. Vietnam	3-05-70
Ross, Douglas A.	Army	S. Vietnam	1-22-69
Ross, Jlynn, Jr.	Army	S. Vietnam	3-17-68
Ross, Joseph S.	Air Force	N. Vietnam	8-01-68
Rossano, Richard J.	Army	S. Vietnam	3-25-71
Roth, Billie L.	Air Force	S. Vietnam	6-27-65
Rowley, Charles S.	Air Force	Laos	4-22-70
Rozo, James M.	Army	S. Vietnam	6-23-70
Rucker, Emmett, Jr.	Air Force	S. Vietnam	5-24-68
Rudolph, Robert D.	Navy	N. Vietnam	9-08-65
Rumbaugh, Elwood E.	Air Force	Cambodia	5-15-75
Runnels, Glyn L., Jr.	Marine Corps	S. Vietnam	6-30-67
Rupinsky, Bernard F.	Navy	N. Vietnam	6-16-68
Rusch, Stephen A.	Air Force	Laos	3-07-72
Russell, Donald M.	Air Force	Laos	12-05-67
Russell, Peter J.	Army	S. Vietnam	8-01-68
Russell, Richard L.	Air Force	S. Vietnam	4-26-72
Ryan, William C., Jr.	Marine Corps	S. Vietnam	5-11-69
Ryder, John L.	Air Force	S. Vietnam	6-09-70
Rykoskey, Edward J.	Marine Corps	S. Vietnam	8-18-66
Saavedra, Robert	Navy	N. Vietnam	4-28-68
Sabog, Mateo	Army	S. Vietnam	2-25-70
Sadler, Mitchell O., Jr.	Air Force	Laos	6-30-70
Saegaert, Donald R.	Army	S. Vietnam	6-10-65

Name	Military Service	Country of Casualty	Date of Incident
Sage, Leland C.C.	Navy	Laos	6-23-69
Salazar, Fidel G.	Navy	N. Vietnam	10-02-69
Sale, Harold R., Jr.	Air Force	N. Vietnam	6-07-67
Salley, James, Jr.	Army	S. Vietnam	3-31-71
Salzarulo, Raymond P., Jr.	Air Force	N. Vietnam	9-04-66
Sampson, Leslie V.	Air Force	Laos	3-23-61
Sanchez, Jose R.	Marine Corps	S. Vietnam	6-06-68
Sanderlin, William D.	Army	S. Vietnam	12-02-69
Sanders, William S.	Air Force	Laos	6-30-70
Sandner, Robert L.	Air Force	Cambodia	6-07-66
Sandoval, Antonio R.	Marine Corps	Cambodia	5-15-75
Sands, Richard E.	Army	S. Vietnam	5-12-68
Sansone, James J.	Navy	N. Vietnam	8-10-72
Sargent, James R.	Marine Corps	S. Vietnam	5-10-68
Sause, Bernard J., Jr.	Navy	S. Vietnam	2-27-67
Savoy, M.J.	Navy	S. Vietnam	6-17-66
Sayre, Leslie B.	Army	S. Vietnam	3-20-68
Scaife, Kenneth D.	Navy	S. Vietnam	1-03-73
Schaneberg, Leroy C.	Air Force	Laos	6-30-70
Scharf, Charles J.	Air Force	N. Vietnam	10-01-65
Schell, Richard J.	Army	S. Vietnam	8-24-67
Scherdin, Robert F.	Army	Cambodia	12-29-68
Scheurich, Thomas E.	Navy	N. Vietnam	3-01-68
Schiele, James F.	Army	S. Vietnam	7-12-67
Schimberg, James P.	Army	S. Vietnam	1-09-66
Schimmels, Eddie R.	Navy	N. Vietnam	2-18-69
Schmidt, Peter A.	Army	Laos	8-15-70
Schmidt, Walter R., Jr.	Marine Corps	S. Vietnam	6-09-68
Schmittou, Eureka L.	Navy	N. Vietnam	5-23-67
Schoderer, Eric J.	Navy	S. Vietnam	11-10-66
Schoeppner, Leonard J.	Navy	N. Vietnam	3-09-70
Scholz, Klaus D.	Army	Laos	11-30-68
Schoonover, Charles D.	Navy	S. Vietnam	1-16-66
Schott, Richard S.	Army	S. Vietnam	4-07-72
Schreckengost, Fred T.	Marine Corps	S. Vietnam	6-07-64
Schroeffel, Thomas A.	Navy	N. Vietnam	2-18-66
Schuler, Robert H., Jr.	Air Force	N. Vietnam	10-15-65
Schultz, Ronald J.	Army	S. Vietnam	7-21-70
Schultz, Sheldon D.	Army	Laos	1-05-68
Schumann, John R.	Army	S. Vietnam	6-16-65
Schworer, Ronald P.	Army	S. Vietnam	4-09-67
Scott, Dain V.	Navy	N. Vietnam	8-21-67
Scott, David L.	Army	S. Vietnam	4-25-68
Scott, Martin R.	Air Force	N. Vietnam	3-15-66

Name	Military Service	Country of Casualty	Date of Incident
Scott, Mike J.	Army	Laos	5-13-69
Scott, Fincent C., Jr.	Air Force	Laos	4-22-69
Schrivener, Stephen R.	Air Force	Laos	3-16-71
Scull, Gary B.	Army	S. Vietnam	3-12-70
Scungio, Vincent A.	Air Force	N. Vietnam	11-04-66
Scurlock, Lee D.	Army	Laos	12-21-67
Seablom, Earl F.	Army	S. Vietnam	7-18-68
Seagraves, Melvin D.	Navy	N. Vietnam	4-30-72
Searfus, William H.	Navy	N. Vietnam	11-25-67
Seeley, Douglas M.	Air Force	Laos	3-16-71
Sennett, Robert R.	Navy	N. Vietnam	1-22-66
Serex, Henry M.	Air Force	S. Vietnam	4-02-72
Setterquist, Francis L.	Air Force	N. Vietnam	8-23-68
Sevell, John W.	Air Force	N. Vietnam	6-06-72
Seward, William H.	Marine Corps	S. Vietnam	3-06-68
Sexton, David M.	Army	S. Vietnam	3-15-71
Seymour, Leo E.	Army	Laos	7-03-67
Shafer, Philip R.	Army	S. Vietnam	4-19-68
Shanks, James L.	Air Force	S. Vietnam	5-24-68
Shanley, Michael H., Jr.	Army	S. Vietnam	12-02-69
Shannon, Patrick L.	Air Force	Laos	3-11-68
Shark, Earl E.	Army	S. Vietnam	9-12-68
Sharp, Samuel A., Jr.	Marine Corps	S. Vietnam	5-10-67
Shaw, Edward B.	Navy	N. Vietnam	9-05-65
Shaw, Gary F.	Army	S. Vietnam	11-11-67
Shay, Donald E., Jr.	Air Force	Laos	10-08-70
Shea, James P.	Navy	N. Vietnam	4-20-65
Shea, Michael J.	Marine Corps	S. Vietnam	4-29-75
Shelton, Charles E.	Air Force	Laos	4-29-65
Sherman, John B.	Marine Corps	S. Vietnam	3-25-66
Sherman, Peter W.	Navy	N. Vietnam	6-10-67
Shewake, John D., Jr.	Army	S. Vietnam	11-03-70
Shimek, Samuel D.	Army	S. Vietnam	12-09-68
Shine, Anthony C.	Air Force	N. Vietnam	12-02-72
Shingledecker, Armon D.	Air Force	N. Vietnam	5-31-66
Shinn, William C.	Air Force	N. Vietnam	1-28-70
Shoneck, John R.	Air Force	N. Vietnam	10-18-66
Shorack, Theodore J., Jr.	Air Force	N. Vietnam	6-09-66
Shriver, Jerry M.	Army	Laos	4-24-69
Shue, Donald M.	Army	Laos	11-03-69
Shumway, Geofrey R.	Navy	N. Vietnam	6-25-72
Siegwarth, Donald E.	Navy	S. Vietnam	6-17-66
Sigafoos, Walter H., III	Air Force	Laos	4-25-71
Silva, Claude A.	Air Force	N. Vietnam	1-29-67

Name	Military Service	Country of Casualty	Date of Incident
Silver, Edward D.	Air Force	N. Vietnam	7-05-68
Simmons, Robert E.	Air Force	Laos	3-29-72
Simpson, Joseph L.	Army	S. Vietnam	5-12-68
Simpson, Max C.	Army	S. Vietnam	1-24-67
Simpson, Robert L.	Air Force	S. Vietnam	8-28-62
Simpson, Walter S.	Army	S. Vietnam	5-21-67
Singleton, Daniel E.	Air Force	Laos	1-26-69
Siow, Gale R.	Navy	Laos	1-11-68
Sisson, Winfield W.	Marine Corps	S. Vietnam	10-18-65
Sitek, Thomas W.	Navy	N. Vietnam	8-23-67
Sittner, Ronald N.	Air Force	N. Vietnam	8-23-67
Sizemore, James E.	Air Force	Laos	7-08-69
Skarman, Orval H.	Marine Corps	S. Vietnam	1-15-68
Skeen, Richard R.	Navy	S. Vietnam	5-16-70
Skibbe, David W.	Marine Corps	S. Vietnam	3-02-70
Skiles, Thomas W.	Army	Cambodia	12-19-71
Skinner, Owen G.	Air Force	Laos	12-12-70
Skivington, William E., Jr.	Army	S. Vietnam	5-12-68
Small, Burt C., Jr.	Army	S. Vietnam	3-06-67
Smallwood, John J.	Air Force	Cambodia	6-16-73
Smiley, Stanley K.	Navy	Laos	7-20-69
Smith, Carl A.	Marine Corps	S. Vietnam	5-01-67
Smith, David R.	Army	S. Vietnam	3-16-69
Smith, Dean, Jr.	Navy	N. Vietnam	3-15-67
Smith, Edward D., Jr.	Air Force	Laos	3-29-72
Smith, Gene A.	Navy	N. Vietnam	6-27-66
Smith, George C.	Air Force	N. Vietnam	4-03-65
Smith, Hallie W.	Air Force	S. Vietnam	1-08-68
Smith, Harding E., Sr.	Air Force	Laos	6-03-66
Smith, Harold V.	Air Force	N. Vietnam	3-07-66
Smith, Harry W.	Air Force	Laos	11-12-69
Smith, Herbert E.	Air Force	N. Vietnam	7-29-66
Smith, Howard H.	Air Force	N. Vietnam	9-30-68
Smith, Joseph S.	Air Force	Cambodia	4-04-71
Smith, Lewis P., II	Air Force	Laos	5-30-68
Smith, Richard D.	Air Force	S. Vietnam	3-11-65
Smith, Robert N.	Marine Corps	N. Vietnam	8-19-69
Smith, Roger L.	Army	S. Vietnam	10-03-68
Smith, Ronald E.	Army	Cambodia	11-28-70
Smith, Victor A.	Air Force	Laos	1-17-69
Smith, Warren P., Jr.	Air Force	Laos	6-22-66
Smith, William A., Jr.	Army	S. Vietnam	9-27-68
Smith, William M.	Army	S. Vietnam	3-03-69
Smith, William W.	Air Force	S. Vietnam	7-23-66

Name	Military Service	Country of Casualty	Date of Incident
Smoot, Curtis R.	Army	Cambodia	3-10-71
Snider, Hughie F.	Army	S. Vietnam	4-28-70
Soucy, Ronald P., Sr.	Navy	N. Vietnam	5-23-67
Soulier, Duwayne	Marine Corps	S. Vietnam	5-01-67
Soyland, David P.	Army	S. Vietnam	5-17-71
Sparenberg, Bernard J.	Navy	S. Vietnam	2-05-66
Sparks, Donald L.	Army	S. Vietnam	6-17-69
Sparks, Jon M.	Army	Laos	3-19-71
Spencer, Dean C., III	Army	S. Vietnam	6-07-68
Spengler, Henry M., III	Army	S. Vietnam	4-05-72
Spilman, Dyke A.	Air Force	N. Vietnam	9-27-66
Spindler, John G.	Marine Corps	S. Vietnam	4-21-68
Spinelli, Domenick A.	Navy	N. Vietnam	9-30-68
Spinler, Darrell J.	Air Force	Laos	6-21-67
Spitz, George R.	Air Force	Laos	2-05-73
Sprague, Stanley G.	Air Force	Laos	9-12-66
Sprick, Doyle R.	Marine Corps	S. Vietnam	1-24-66
Springsteadah, Donald K.	Air Force	Laos	3-11-68
Springston, Theodore, Jr.	Air Force	N. Vietnam	6-03-67
Sprott, Arthur R., Jr.	Air Force	S. Vietnam	1-10-69
Squire, Boyd E.	Air Force	N. Vietnam	7-12-67
St. Pierre, Dean P.	Air Force	N. Vietnam	5-22-68
Stacks, Raymond C.	Army	Laos	11-30-68
Staehli, Bruce W.	Marine Corps	S. Vietnam	4-30-68
Stafford, Ronald D.	Air Force	S. Vietnam	11-21-72
Stancil, Kenneth L.	Army	S. Vietnam	12-28-65
Standerwick, Robert L.	Air Force	Laos	2-03-71
Stanley, Charles I.	Army	S. Vietnam	2-06-69
Stanley, Robert W.	Air Force	S. Vietnam	4-01-67
Stanton, Ronald	Army	S. Vietnam	10-20-68
Stark, Willie E.	Army	Laos	12-02-66
Staton, Robert M., Jr.	Army	S. Vietnam	11-11-67
Steadman, James E.	Air Force	Laos	11-26-71
Stearns, Roger H.	Air Force	Laos	9-11-69
Steen, Martin W.	Air Force	N. Vietnam	5-31-66
Stegman, Thomas	Navy	N. Vietnam	2-28-68
Steimer, Thomas J.	Navy	S. Vietnam	5-08-67
Stephensen, Mark L.	Air Force	N. Vietnam	4-29-67
Stephenson, Howard D.	Air Force	Laos	3-29-72
Stephenson, Richard C.	Navy	N. Vietnam	2-05-70
Stevens, Larry J.	Navy	Laos	2-14-69
Stevens, Phillip P.	Navy	Laos	1-11-68
Stewart, Jack T.	Army	S. Vietnam	3-24-67
Stewart, Paul C.	Army	Laos	2-08-71

Name	Military Service	Country of Casualty	Date of Incident
Stewart, Peter J.	Air Force	N. Vietnam	3-15-66
Stewart, Robert A.	Air Force	N. Vietnam	5-12-67
Stewart, Virgil G.	Air Force	Laos	5-17-69
Stickney, Phillip J.	Air Force	N. Vietnam	5-31-66
Stine, Joseph M.	Air Force	N. Vietnam	9-27-66
Stinson, William S.	Army	S. Vietnam	1-08-73
Stoddard, Clarence W., Jr.	Navy	N. Vietnam	9-14-66
Stolz, Lawrence G.	Air Force	N. Vietnam	12-26-71
Stone, James M.	Army	S. Vietnam	1-07-68
Stonebaker, Kenneth A.	Air Force	N. Vietnam	10-28-68
Story, James C.	Army	S. Vietnam	6-13-69
Stoves, Merritt, III	Army	S. Vietnam	1-10-67
Stow, Lilburn R.	Air Force	S. Vietnam	4-26-68
Stowers, Aubrey E., Jr.	Air Force	Laos	3-21-68
Strait, Douglas F.	Army	S. Vietnam	10-18-70
Straley, John L.	Army	S. Vietnam	1-18-64
Strange, Floyd W.	Army	S. Vietnam	12-02-67
Stratton, Charles W.	Air Force	Laos	1-03-71
Strawn, John T.	Army	N. Vietnam	3-04-71
Stride, James D., Jr.	Army	Laos	10-05-68
Stringer, John C., II	Army	S. Vietnam	11-30-70
Stringham, William S.	Navy	S. Vietnam	2-03-73
Strobridge, Rodney L.	Army	S. Vietnam	5-11-72
Strohlein, Madison A.	Army	S. Vietnam	6-22-71
Strong, Henry H., Jr.	Navy	N. Vietnam	5-25-72
Stroven, William H.	Air Force	N. Vietnam	10-28-68
Stuart, John F.	Air Force	N. Vietnam	12-20-72
Stubberfield, Robert A.	Air Force	N. Vietnam	5-06-65
Stubbs, William W.	Army	Laos	10-20-69
Stuckey, John S., Jr.	Army	S. Vietnam	11-11-67
Stuifbergen, Gene P.	Air Force	Cambodia	11-27-68
Stuller, John C.	Army	S. Vietnam	5-12-68
Suber, Randolph B.	Army	Laos	11-13-69
Sulander, Daniel A.	Army	Laos	12-02-66
Sullivan, John B., III	Air Force	N. Vietnam	6-21-66
Sullivan, Martin J.	Navy	S. Vietnam	2-12-67
Sullivan, Robert J.	Army	Laos	7-12-67
Sutter, Frederick J.	Air Force	Laos	12-31-71
Sutton, William C.	Air Force	N. Vietnam	1-28-70
Suydam, James L.	Army	S. Vietnam	10-09-69
Swanson, John W., Jr.	Air Force	N. Vietnam	6-15-67
Swanson, Jon E.	Army	Cambodia	2-26-71
Swanson, Roger W.	Army	S. Vietnam	10-31-68
Swanson, William E.	Navy	Laos	4-11-65

Name	Military Service	Country of Casualty	Date of Incident
Swigart, Paul E., Jr.	Navy	S. Vietnam	2-05-69
Switzer, Jerrold A.	Marine Corps	S. Vietnam	3-18-68
Swords, Smith, III	Air Force	Laos	12-30-67
Sykes, Derri	Army	S. Vietnam	1-09-68
Szeyller, Edward P.	Navy	N. Vietnam	4-04-67
Tadios, Leonard M.	Army	S. Vietnam	12-11-64
Talken, George F.	Navy	N. Vietnam	8-02-69
Talley, James L.	Army	S. Vietnam	6-19-64
Tapp, John B.	Navy	S. Vietnam	3-23-66
Tapp, Marshall L.	Air Force	Laos	5-15-66
Tatum, Lawrence B.	Air Force	N. Vietnam	9-10-66
Taylor, Danny G.	Army	S. Vietnam	9-28-66
Taylor, Edd D.	Navy	N. Vietnam	8-29-65
Taylor, Edmund B., Jr.	Navy	N. Vietnam	5-08-72
Taylor, Fred	Army	S. Vietnam	7-13-65
Taylor, James H.	Army	Laos	2-15-71
Taylor, James L.	Army	S. Vietnam	3-10-66
Taylor, Neil B.	Navy	S. Vietnam	9-14-65
Taylor, Phillip C.	Army	Cambodia	5-27-71
Taylor, Ted J.	Army	S. Vietnam	7-15-71
Taylor, Walter J., Jr.	Army	S. Vietnam	12-06-70
Templin, Erwin B., Jr.	Navy	N. Vietnam	1-22-66
Teran, Refugio T.	Army	S. Vietnam	5-06-70
Terla, Lothar G. T.	Air Force	Laos	3-09-70
Terrell, Keavin L.	Navy	N. Vietnam	10-02-69
Terrill, Philip B.	Army	S. Vietnam	3-31-71
Terry, Oral R.	Army	S. Vietnam	5-03-68
Terry, Ronald T.	Army	S. Vietnam	1-29-66
Terwillinger, Virgil B.	Marine Corps	S. Vietnam	3-13-67
Thackerson, Walter A.	Army	S. Vietnam	5-21-66
Thomas, Daniel W.	Air Force	Laos	7-06-71
Thomas, Darwin J.	Navy	N. Vietnam	10-14-66
Thomas, Harry E.	Navy	N. Vietnam	8-13-65
Thomas, James C.	Marine Corps	S. Vietnam	4-03-68
Thomas, James R.	Air Force	S. Vietnam	11-25-71
Thomas, Leo T., Jr.	Air Force	Laos	12-19-71
Thompson, Benjamin A.	Army	S. Vietnam	10-25-68
Thompson, David M.	Navy	N. Vietnam	8-12-72
Thompson, Donald E.	Navy	N. Vietnam	2-04-67
Thompson, George W.	Air Force	Laos	5-15-66
Thompson, Melvin C.	Navy	S. Vietnam	2-06-68
Thompson, William J.	Air Force	N. Vietnam	8-01-68
Thompson, William J.	Navy	N. Vietnam	1-16-68
Thoreson, Donald N.	Navy	Laos	1-11-68

Name	Military Service	Country of Casualty	Date of Incident
Thorne, Larry A.	Army	S. Vietnam	10-18-65
Thornton, Larry C.	Air Force	Laos	12-24-65
Thornton, William D.	Army	S. Vietnam	1-28-67
Thurman, Curtis F.	Navy	Laos	2-17-68
Tice, Paul D.	Marine Corps	S. Vietnam	9-25-66
Tiderman, John M.	Navy	N. Vietnam	3-21-66
Tiffin, Rainford	Air Force	N. Vietnam	7-21-66
Tigner, Lee M.	Air Force	S. Vietnam	8-22-72
Timmons, Bruce A.	Navy	S. Vietnam	11-15-66
Tipping, Henry A.	Air Force	S. Vietnam	7-02-68
Todd, Larry R.	Air Force	S. Vietnam	4-26-68
Todd, Robert J.	Marine Corps	S. Vietnam	5-09-67
Todd, William A.	Air Force	Laos	3-29-72
Tolbert, Clarence O.	Navy	N. Vietnam	11-06-72
Toms, Dennis L.	Navy	S. Vietnam	11-21-65
Toomey, Samuel K., III	Army	Laos	11-30-68
Towle, John C.	Air Force	Laos	4-22-70
Townsend, Francis W.	Air Force	N. Vietnam	8-13-72
Trampski, Donald J.	Army	S. Vietnam	9-16-69
Traver, John G., III	Army	Laos	3-22-71
Travis, Lynn M.	Navy	S. Vietnam	2-06-68
Treece, James A.	Air Force	S. Vietnam	10-07-66
Trembley, J. Forrest G.	Navy	N. Vietnam	8-21-67
Trent, Alan R.	Air Force	Cambodia	5-13-70
Trimble, James M.	Marine Corps	S. Vietnam	4-06-68
Trimble, Larry A.	Air Force	N. Vietnam	4-15-72
Tritt, James F.	Navy	N. Vietnam	7-07-67
Trivelpiece, Steve M.	Army	S. Vietnam	4-04-68
Tromp, William L.	Navy	N. Vietnam	4-17-66
Trowbridge, Dustin C.	Navy	S. Vietnam	12-26-69
Trudeau, Albert R.	Army	S. Vietnam	10-26-71
Trujillo, Joseph F.	Marine Corps	S. Vietnam	9-03-66
Trujillo, Robert S.	Army	S. Vietnam	1-07-68
Tubbs, Glenn E.	Army	S. Vietnam	1-13-70
Tucci, Robert L.	Air Force	Laos	11-12-69
Tucker, Edwin B.	Navy	N. Vietnam	4-24-67
Tucker, James H.	Air Force	N. Vietnam	4-26-66
Tucker, Timothy M.	Air Force	Laos	12-24-71
Tunnell, John W.	Navy	N. Vietnam	6-20-66
Turner, Frederick R.	Marine Corps	S. Vietnam	11-06-68
Turner, James H.	Army	S. Vietnam	10-09-69
Turner, Kelton R.	Marine Corps	Cambodia	5-15-75
Turose, Michael S.	Air Force	N. Vietnam	9-17-72
Tycz, James N.	Marine Corps	S. Vietnam	5-10-67

Name	Military Service	Country of Casualty	Date of Incident
Tye, Michael J.	Navy	N. Vietnam	10-02-69
Tyler, George E.	Air Force	N. Vietnam	10-24-68
Uhlmansiek, Ralph E.	Army	S. Vietnam	6-11-67
Underwood, Paul G.	Air Force	N. Vietnam	3-16-66
Underwood, Thomas W.	Marine Corps	Laos	3-21-70
Upner, Edward C.	Army	S. Vietnam	12-05-65
Urquhart, Paul D.	Army	S. Vietnam	5-28-71
Utley, Russel K.	Air Force	Laos	1-26-69
Vaden, Woodrow W.	Air Force	S. Vietnam	12-10-64
Van Artsdalen, Clifford D.	Army	S. Vietnam	5-09-68
Van Buren, Gerald G.	Air Force	N. Vietnam	12-29-67
Van Campen, Thomas C.	Army	S. Vietnam	6-24-65
Van Cleave, Walter S.	Air Force	Laos	4-22-69
Vanbendegom, James L.	Army	S. Vietnam	7-12-67
Vandegeer, Richard	Air Force	Cambodia	5-15-75
Vanden Eykel, Martin D., II	Army	S. Vietnam	12-02-69
Vanrenselaar, Larry J.	Navy	N. Vietnam	9-30-68
Varnado, Michael B.	Army	Cambodia	5-02-70
Vaughan, Robert R.	Navy	N. Vietnam	10-14-67
Vennik, Robert N.	Army	S. Vietnam	8-26-71
Versace, Humberto R.	Army	S. Vietnam	10-29-63
Viado, Reynaldo R.	Navy	N. Vietnam	10-02-69
Villeponteaux, James H., Jr.	Marine Corps	S. Vietnam	5-11-66
Vinson, Bobby G.	Air Force	N. Vietnam	4-24-68
Visconti, Francis	Marine Corps	S. Vietnam	11-22-65
Vlahakos, Peter G.	Marine Corps	N. Vietnam	2-01-66
Vogt, Leonard F., Jr.	Navy	N. Vietnam	9-18-65
Wadsworth, Dean A.	Air Force	S. Vietnam	10-08-63
Wagener, David R.	Air Force	Laos	10-20-66
Wagner, Raymond A.	Air Force	Cambodia	3-27-72
Wald, Gunther H.	Army	Laos	11-03-69
Walker, Bruce C.	Air Force	S. Vietnam	4-07-72
Walker, Kenneth E.	Air Force	S. Vietnam	10-02-64
Walker, Lloyd F.	Air Force	Laos	1-31-67
Walker, Michael S.	Air Force	Laos	7-15-69
Walker, Orien J.	Army	S. Vietnam	5-23-65
Walker, Samuel F., Jr.	Air Force	Laos	12-13-68
Walker, Thomas T.	Air Force	Laos	4-07-66
Walker, William J.	Marine Corps	S. Vietnam	4-20-68
Wall, Jerry M.	Air Force	S. Vietnam	5-18-66
Wallace, Arnold B.	Army	S. Vietnam	1-25-67
Wallace, Charles F.	Marine Corps	N. Vietnam	8-28-67
Wallace, Hobart M., Jr.	Marine Corps	N. Vietnam	1-19-68
Wallace, Michael J.	Army	S. Vietnam	4-19-68

Name	Military Service	Country of Casualty	Date of Incident
Wallace, Michael W.	Navy	Laos	3-28-68
Waller, Therman M.	Air Force	S. Vietnam	2-03-66
Walling, Charles M.	Air Force	S. Vietnam	8-08-66
Walsh, Richard A., III	Air Force	Laos	2-15-69
Walters, Donovan K.	Air Force	N. Vietnam	12-21-72
Walters, Tim L.	Army	Laos	3-09-69
Walters, William	Army	S. Vietnam	5-10-69
Walton, Lewis C.	Army	S. Vietnam	5-10-71
Walton, Wilbert	Army	S. Vietnam	1-03-70
Wann, Donald L.	Army	S. Vietnam	6-01-71
Wanzel, Charles J., III	Air Force	Laos	3-29-72
Ward, Neal C.	Air Force	Laos	6-13-69
Ward, Ronald J.	Air Force	N. Vietnam	12-18-72
Ware, John A.	Army	S. Vietnam	11-04-69
Warren, Arthur L.	Air Force	N. Vietnam	12-05-66
Warren, Ervin	Air Force	Laos	6-03-66
Warren, Gray D.	Air Force	Laos	10-26-69
Washburn, Larry E.	Air Force	S. Vietnam	6-17-66
Waterman, Craig H.	Marine Corps	S. Vietnam	7-30-67
Watkins, Robert J., Jr.	Army	S. Vietnam	10-08-69
Watson, Frank P.	Air Force	S. Vietnam	6-18-65
Watson, Jimmy L.	Army	S. Vietnam	3-13-68
Watson, Ronald L.	Army	Laos	2-18-71
Wax, David J.	Air Force	S. Vietnam	12-20-65
Weaks, Melvin L.	Army	S. Vietnam	8-18-71
Weaver, George R., Jr.	Navy	S. Vietnam	11-01-66
Weger, John, Jr.	Air Force	S. Vietnam	10-22-65
Weimorts, Robert F.	Navy	N. Vietnam	4-22-66
Weisner, Franklin L.	Army	S. Vietnam	10-10-69
Weissmueller, Courtney E.	Air Force	Laos	2-12-67
Weitkamp, Edgar W.	Army	Laos	3-23-61
Weitz, Monek	Marine Corps	S. Vietnam	5-25-69
Welch, Robert J.	Air Force	N. Vietnam	1-16-67
Wellons, Phillip R.	Air Force	S. Vietnam	8-17-70
Wells, Robert J.	Army	S. Vietnam	7-22-66
Welsh, Larry D.	Army	S. Vietnam	1-07-69
Welshan, John T.	Air Force	S. Vietnam	3-03-68
Wenaas, Gordon J.	Air Force	N. Vietnam	12-29-67
Werdhoff, Michael R.	Army	S. Vietnam	4-19-68
West, John T.	Air Force	Laos	1-02-70
Westbrook, Donald E.	Air Force	Laos	3-13-68
Westcott, Gary P.	Army	S. Vietnam	3-30-72
Wester, Albert D.	Air Force	Laos	10-05-68
Weston, Oscar B., Jr.	Air Force	Laos	3-23-61

Name	Military Service	Country of Casualty	Date of Incident
Westwood, Norman P., Jr.	Navy	N. Vietnam	5-17-70
Wheeler, Eugene L.	Marine Corps	S. Vietnam	4-21-70
Wheeler, James A.	Air Force	S. Vietnam	4-18-65
White, Charles E.	Army	Cambodia	1-29-68
White, Danforth E.	Navy	Laos	3-31-69
White, James B.	Air Force	Laos	11-24-69
Whited, James L.	Army	Laos	11-19-66
Whitesides, Richard L.	Air Force	S. Vietnam	3-26-64
Whitford, Lawrence W., Jr.	Air Force	Laos	11-02-69
Whitmire, Warren T., Jr.	Army	S. Vietnam	5-01-68
Whitt, James E.	Air Force	Laos	3-23-72
Whitteker, Richard L.	Air Force	N. Vietnam	3-27-68
Whittemore, Frederick H.	Navy	N. Vietnam	4-11-68
Whittle, Junior L.	Army	S. Vietnam	9-24-66
Wickham, David W., II	Navy	S. Vietnam	12-16-65
Widdis, James W., Jr.	Air Force	Laos	3-23-68
Widdison, Imlay S.	Army	S. Vietnam	5-12-68
Widener, James E.	Marine Corps	S. Vietnam	6-11-67
Widner, Danny L.	Army	S. Vietnam	5-12-68
Widon, Kenneth H.	Navy	Laos	1-11-68
Wiechert, Robert C.	Air Force	S. Vietnam	11-16-68
Wiehr, Richard D.	Navy	N. Vietnam	1-21-73
Wilbrecht, Kurt M.	Marine Corps	S. Vietnam	6-07-70
Wilburn, John E.	Army	S. Vietnam	4-19-68
Wilburn, Woodrow H.	Air Force	N. Vietnam	2-04-67
Wiles, Marvin B.	Navy	N. Vietnam	5-06-72
Wiley, Richard D.	Army	S. Vietnam	6-12-72
Wilke, Robert F.	Air Force	N. Vietnam	1-17-68
Wilkins, Calvin W.	Marine Corps	S. Vietnam	2-08-69
Wilkins, George H.	Navy	N. Vietnam	7-11-66
Wilkinson, Clyde D.	Army	S. Vietnam	2-12-71
Willett, Robert V., Jr.	Air Force	Laos	4-17-69
Williams, Billie J.	Air Force	N. Vietnam	12-09-72
Williams, David B.	Marine Corps	N. Vietnam	5-03-72
Williams, David R.	Air Force	Laos	4-01-67
Williams, Eddie L.	Army	Laos	10-03-66
Williams, Edward W.	Army	S. Vietnam	4-03-72
Williams, Howard K.	Air Force	N. Vietnam	3-18-68
Williams, James E.	Air Force	Laos	5-15-66
Williams, James R.	Air Force	N. Vietnam	12-29-67
Williams, Leroy C.	Marine Corps	S. Vietnam	5-25-69
Williams, Robert C.	Air Force	N. Vietnam	7-01-66
Williams, Robert J.	Army	S. Vietnam	5-11-72
Williams, Roy C.	Army	S. Vietnam	5-12-68

Name	Military Service	Country of Casualty	Date of Incident
Williams, Thaddeus E.	Army	S. Vietnam	1-09-66
Williamson, Don I.	Air Force	N. Vietnam	7-07-65
Williamson, James D.	Army	Laos	1-05-68
Willing, Edward A.	Marine Corps	S. Vietnam	7-21-68
Wills, Francis D.	Army	S. Vietnam	2-26-66
Wilson, Claude D., Jr.	Navy	N. Vietnam	12-14-66
Wilson, Gordon S.	Air Force	N. Vietnam	11-22-66
Wilson, Harry T.	Marine Corps	Laos	6-04-70
Wilson, Marion E.	Army	S. Vietnam	2-03-68
Wilson, Mickey A.	Army	S. Vietnam	1-08-73
Wilson, Peter J.	Army	Laos	10-19-70
Wilson, Richard, Jr.	Army	S. Vietnam	6-14-71
Wilson, Robert A.	Air Force	S. Vietnam	6-18-72
Wilson, Roger E.	Marine Corps	N. Vietnam	6-11-72
Wilson, Wayne V.	Marine Corps	S. Vietnam	7-02-67
Windeler, Charles C., Jr.	Army	S. Vietnam	4-05-72
Winkler, John A.	Navy	S. Vietnam	11-22-65
Winters, Darryl G.	Air Force	S. Vietnam	7-19-66
Winters, David M.	Army	S. Vietnam	4-21-67
Wiseman, Bain W., Jr.	Army	S. Vietnam	12-23-70
Wistrand, Robert C.	Air Force	Laos	5-09-65
Wogan, William M.	Army	S. Vietnam	2-16-69
Wolfe, Donald F.	Navy	S. Vietnam	10-08-67
Wolfe, Thomas H.	Air Force	Laos	6-28-66
Wolfkeil, Wayne B.	Air Force	Laos	8-09-68
Woloszyk, Donald J.	Navy	N. Vietnam	3-01-66
Wolpe, Jack	Marine Corps	S. Vietnam	8-03-67
Wong, Edward P., Jr.	Army	S. Vietnam	3-27-72
Wonn, James C.	Navy	Laos	2-17-68
Wood, Don C.	Air Force	Laos	1-16-66
Wood, Patrick H.	Air Force	N. Vietnam	2-06-67
Wood, Rex S.	Navy	N. Vietnam	6-02-67
Wood, Walter S.	Navy	N. Vietnam	5-02-66
Wood, William C., Jr.	Air Force	Laos	9-02-72
Woods, David W.	Army	S. Vietnam	11-03-70
Woods, Gerald E.	Army	Laos	2-18-71
Woods, Lawrence	Army	Cambodia	10-24-64
Woods, Robert F.	Air Force	N. Vietnam	6-26-68
Woodworth, Samuel A.	Air Force	N. Vietnam	4-17-65
Worchester, John B.	Navy	N. Vietnam	10-19-65
Worley, Don F.	Air Force	Laos	3-11-68
Worst, Karl E.	Air Force	Laos	3-02-66
Worth, James F.	Marine Corps	S. Vietnam	4-01-72
Wortham, Murray L.	Air Force	Laos	12-30-67

Name	Military Service	Country of Casualty	Date of Incident
Worthington, Richard C.	Army	S. Vietnam	5-06-70
Wozniak, Frederick J.	Air Force	N. Vietnam	1-17-67
Wright, Arthur	Army	S. Vietnam	2-21-67
Wright, David I.	Air Force	N. Vietnam	11-13-70
Wright, Donald L.	Air Force	Laos	11-24-69
Wright, Frederick W.	Navy	N. Vietnam	11-10-72
Wright, Gary G.	Air Force	N. Vietnam	1-17-67
Wright, Jerdy A., Jr.	Air Force	N. Vietnam	3-07-66
Wright, Thomas T.	Air Force	Laos	2-27-68
Wrobleski, Walter F.	Army	S. Vietnam	5-21-67
Wrye, Blair C.	Air Force	N. Vietnam	8-12-66
Xavier, Augusto M.	Marine Corps	S. Vietnam	3-10-66
Yeakley, Robin R.	Army	S. Vietnam	6-11-72
Yeend, Richard C. J.	Air Force	S. Vietnam	6-09-68
Yonan, Kenneth J.	Army	S. Vietnam	4-24-72
Young, Barclay B.	Air Force	Laos	3-29-72
Young, Charles L.	Army	S. Vietnam	5-17-68
Young, Jeffrey J.	Army	S. Vietnam	4-04-70
Young, Robert M.	Army	Cambodia	5-02-70
Zavocky, James J.	Navy	N. Vietnam	8-25-67
Zempel, Ronald L.	Navy	S. Vietnam	2-27-67
Zerbe, Michael R.	Navy	S. Vietnam	4-15-66
Zich, Larry A.	Army	S. Vietnam	4-03-72
Zimmer, Jerry A.	Marine Corps	S. Vietnam	8-29-69
Zissu, Andrew G.	Navy	S. Vietnam	10-08-67
Zollicoffer, Franklin	Army	S. Vietnam	4-24-72
Zook, David H., Jr.	Air Force	S. Vietnam	10-04-67
Zook, Harold J.	Air Force	N. Vietnam	5-31-66
Zorn, Thomas O., Jr.	Air Force	N. Vietnam	9-17-72
Zubke, Deland D.	Army	S. Vietnam	3-01-71
Zukowski, Robert J.	Air Force	Laos	2-11-69
Zutterman, Joseph A., Jr.	Marine Corps	S. Vietnam	4-20-68

CIVILIANS MISSING IN SOUTHEAST ASIA

Name	Country of Casualty	Date
Ackley, James H.	Laos	3-07-73
Bailon, Rubin	S. Vietnam	12-25-65
Blewett, Allan L.	Laos	7-12-62
Blood, Henry F.	S. Vietnam	2-01-68
Chenye, Joseph C.	Laos	9-05-63
Cocheo, Richard N.	S. Vietnam	1-31-68
Dean, Charles	Laos	9-10-74
DeBruin, Eugene H.	Laos	9-05-63
Degnan, Jerry L.	S. Vietnam	8-28-67
Dolan, Edward V.	S. Vietnam	3-08-75
Driver, Clarence N.	Laos	2-07-73
Duffy, Charles J.	Laos	1-13-61
Duke, Charles R.	S. Vietnam	5-30-70
Eby, Robert G.	S. Vietnam	8-21-67
Erskine, Jack D.	S. Vietnam	11-13-68
Flynn, Sean L.	Cambodia	4-06-70
Gerber, Daniel A.	S. Vietnam	5-30-62
Grainger, Joseph W.	S. Vietnam	8-08-64
Grzyb, Robert H.	S. Vietnam	12-10-67
Hangen, Welles	Cambodia	5-31-70
Hart, Thomas T.	Laos	12-21-72
Herrich, Charles G.	Laos	9-05-63
Hertz, Gustav	S. Vietnam	2-02-65
Kalil, Tanos E.	S. Vietnam	2-08-69
Mark, Kit T.	S. Vietnam	5-30-70
Miller, George C.	S. Vietnam	3-08-75
Mitchell, Archie E.	S. Vietnam	5-30-62
Morales, Frank A.	S. Vietnam	12-05-68
Niehouse, Daniel L.	S. Vietnam	11-15-66
Olsen, Betty A.	S. Vietnam	2-01-68

Name	Country of Casualty	Date
Rallings, James	S. Vietnam	1-03-75
Reynolds, Terry L.	Cambodia	4-26-72
Ritter, George L.	Laos	12-27-71
Seidl, Robert	S. Vietnam	3-08-75
Shimkin, Alex	S. Vietnam	7-12-72
Simpson, James E.	S. Vietnam	11-05-68
Stone, Dana	Cambodia	4-06-70
Tavares, John R.	S. Vietnam	5-18-65
Townley, Roy F.	Laos	12-27-71
Vietti, Eleanor A.	S. Vietnam	5-30-62
Walsh, Brian	Cambodia	4-25-75
Weissenback, Edward	Laos	12-27-71
Yim, John S.	Cambodia	4-25-75

Remains Returned

Name	Military Service	Date Returned
Abbott, John	Navy	3-13-74
Ammon, Glendon L.	Air Force	8-23-78
Arroyo-Baez, Gerasimo	Army	3-20-85
Atterberry, Edwin L.	Air Force	3-13-74
Biediger, Larry W.	Air Force	6-3-83
Bowling, Roy H.	Navy	3-18-77
Brand, Joseph W.	Air Force	9-30-77
Brooks, Nicholas G.	Navy	2-3-82
Brown, Donald H., Jr.	Navy	8-14-85
Buckley, Jimmy L.	Navy	12-16-75
Burdett, Edward B.	Air Force	3-6-74
Cameron, Kenneth R.	Navy	3-6-74
Cannon, Francis E.	Army	8-14-85
Capling, Elwyn R.	Air Force	3-18-77
Chesnutt, Chambless M.	Air Force	3-20-85
Chwan, Michael D.	Air Force	3-20-85
Clark, Donald E., Jr.	Air Force	9-30-77
Cobeil, Earl G.	Air Force	3-6-74
Connell, James J.	Navy	3-6-74
Connelly, Vincent J.	Air Force	7-17-84
Dawson, Clyde D.	Air Force	9-30-77
Dennison, Terry A.	Navy	3-6-74
Diamond, Stephen W.	Air Force	3-18-77
Dickens, Delma E.	Air Force	2-21-85
Diehl, William C.	Air Force	3-6-74
Doby, Herb	Air Force	9-30-77
Dodge, Ronald W.	Navy	7-8-81
Dodge, Ward K.	Air Force	3-13-74
Doyle, Michael W.	Navy	8-14-85
Ducat, Bruce C.	Air Force	3-18-77
Dudash, John F.	Air Force	3-6-83

Name	Military Service	Date Returned
Elliott, Robert T.	Air Force	2-21-85
Estes, Walter O.	Navy	9-30-77
Fanning, Hugh M.	Marine Corps	7-17-84
Fantle, Samuel	Air Force	9-30-77
Fenter, Charles F.	Air Force	2-21-85
Ferguson, Walter L.	Air Force	8-23-78
Finch, Melvin W.	Army	8-14-85
Finney, Arthur T.	Air Force	8-14-85
Fitton, Crosley J.	Air Force	12-21-75
Ford, Randolph W.	Navy	8-14-85
Frederick, John W.	Marine Corps	3-13-74
Frye, Donald P.	Navy	10-14-82
Fryer, Ben L.	Air Force	9-30-77
Fuller, James R.	Air Force	2-21-85
Golberg, Lawrence H.	Air Force	9-30-77
Goodrich, Edwin R., Jr.	Air Force	8-14-85
Goss, Bernard J.	Air Force	8-23-78
Gougelmann, Tucker P.E.	Civilian	9-30-77
Graham, Alan U.	Air Force	9-30-77
Graham, James S.	Navy	8-14-85
Graustein, Robert S.	Navy	12-4-85
Griffin, James L.	Navy	3-13-74
Grubb, Wilmer N.	Air Force	3-13-74
Hagerman, Robert W.	Air Force	12-4-85
Haifley, Michael F.	Navy	8-14-85
Hardy, Arthur H.	Air Force	9-20-83
Harris, Cleveland S.	Air Force	3-20-85
Hartman, Richard D.	Navy	3-6-74
Heggen, Keith R.	Air Force	3-13-74
Hockridge, James A.	Air Force	9-30-77
Jackson, William B.	Navy	10-14-82
Johnson, Guy D.	Navy	3-18-77
Jones, William E.	Air Force	8-14-85
Judge, Darwin L.	Marine Corps	2-22-76
Killian, Melvin J.	Air Force	3-20-85
Klenert, William B.	Navy	3-18-77
Klinck, Harrison H.	Air Force	8-14-85
Kolstad, Thomas C.	Navy	3-18-77
Kott, Stephen J.	Marine Corps	7-17-84
Kroboth, Stanley N.	Air Force	2-21-85
Kwortnik, John C.	Air Force	8-14-85
Lagerwall, Harry R.	Air Force	2-21-85
Lecornec, John G.	Civilian	8-14-85
Lee, Charles R.	Navy	6-3-83

Name	Military Service	Date Returned
Liles, Robert L., Jr.	Air Force	2-21-85
Lindland, Donald F.	Navy	6-3-83
Lodge, Robert A.	Air Force	9-30-77
MacDonald, George D.	Air Force	2-21-85
McGrane, Donald P.	Navy	10-14-82
McGrath, William D.	Navy	12-4-85
McMahon, Charles, Jr.	Marine Corps	2-22-76
Means, Arthur S.	Air Force	9-30-77
Meder, Paul O.	Air Force	2-21-85
Menges, George B.	Air Force	9-80
Metz, James H.	Air Force	3-18-77
Meyer, William M.	Air Force	8-14-85
Minnich, Richard W., Jr.	Navy	12-4-85
Monroe, Vincent D.	Navy	8-23-78
Moorberg, Monte L.	Air Force	8-14-85
Morrill, Merwin L.	Air Force	6-3-83
Morris, Robert J., Jr.	Air Force	9-30-77
Morrow, Richard D.	Navy	8-23-78
Musselman, Stephen O.	Navy	7-8-81
Nelson, Richard C.	Navy	7-17-84
Nelson, William H.	Air Force	9-30-77
Newsom, Bejamin B.	Air Force	3-6-74
Paul, Craig A.	Air Force	9-30-77
Pemberton, Gene T.	Air Force	3-6-74
Perry, Ronald D.	Air Force	12-21-75
Petersen, Gaylord D.	Air Force	8-23-78
Port, William D.	Army	8-14-85
Powell, Lynn K.	Air Force	6-3-83
Pugh, Kenneth W.	Navy	12-16-75
Reaid, Rollie K.	Air Force	2-21-85
Rissi, Donald L.	Air Force	3-18-77
Roark, William M.	Navy	3-18-77
Ruffin, James T.	Navy	6-3-83
Sansone, Dominick	Army	7-17-84
Sather, Richard C.	Navy	8-14-85
Schmidt, Norman	Air Force	3-6-74
Shank, Gary L.	Navy	7-1-84
Sherman, Robert C.	Marine Corps	3-20-85
Sijan, Lance P.	Air Force	3-13-74
Singer, Donald M.	Air Force	9-30-77
Smith, Homer L.	Navy	3-13-74
Spencer, Warren R.	Air Force	9-30-77
Stamm, Ernest A.	Navy	3-13-74
Storz, Ronald E.	Air Force	3-06-74

Name	Military Service	Date Returned
Sullivan, Farrell, Jr.	Air Force	6-3-83
Sullivan, James E.	Navy	8-14-85
Taylor, Jesse, Jr.	Navy	12-21-75
Teague, James E.	Navy	9-30-77
Thomas, Kenneth D., Jr.	Air Force	8-14-85
Thomas, Robert J.	Air Force	8-23-78
Thum, Richard C.	Navy	9-30-77
Trier, Robert D.	Air Force	10-14-82
Van Dyke, Richard H.	Air Force	7-8-81
Vescelius, Milton J.	Navy	8-14-85
Wade, Barton S.	Navy	12-04-85
Walsh, Francis A., Jr.	Air Force	2-21-85
Walters, Jack	Navy	3-13-74
Waters, Samuel E.	Air Force	3-18-77
Weatherby, Jack W.	Air Force	8-23-78
Weskamp, Robert L.	Air Force	3-6-74
Wiggins, Wallace L.	Air Force	8-24-78
Wilkinson, Dennis E.	Air Force	8-23-78
Williams, Richard F.	Army	8-14-85
Wimbrow, Nutter J.	Air Force	9-30-77
Winningham, John Q.	Air Force	2-21-85
Winston, Charles C., III	Air Force	9-30-77
Worrell, Paul L.	Navy	8-14-85
Wright, James J.	Navy	8-23-78
Wynne, Patrick E.	Air Force	3-18-77
Yarbrough, William P., Jr.	Navy	8-14-85
Zawtocki, Joseph S., Jr.	Marine Corps	8-14-85

INDEX

Please send **First Heroes.**

Shipping Charges for Prepaid Orders

____ Copies at $19.95 each = _____
____ Leather-bound Copies
         at $90 each= _____
         Shipping = _____
(New York State Residents
   add 8.25% Sales Tax = _____

         Total = _____

☐ Fourth Class: $1.75 for the first book;
   $.50 for each additional book.

☐ First Class: $2.50 for the first book;
   $1.00 for each additional book.

☐ UPS: Same charge as for First Class;
   requires a street address.

____ Visa ____ MasterCard ____ Check or Money Order

Card Number _____ Expires ____/____ Signature_____

To _____ *Irvington Publishers, Inc.*
_____ *740 Broadway*
_____ *New York, N.Y. 10003*
_____ Zip _____

Phone_____

Prices subject to change without notice.

— —
Please clip or photocopy this order form

Special, limited, leather-bound editions of *First Heroes*, numbered and signed by the author, are available from Irvington Publishers for $90. See order form above.

QUANTITY PURCHASES
Organizations, associations, corporations and other groups may qualify for special discounts when ordering more than twenty-four copies of *First Heroes*. Please specify quantity desired, and discount information will be sent to you.
Write Special Sales Department, Irvington Publishers, Inc., 740 Broadway, New York, NY 10003

Please send **First Heroes.**

Shipping Charges for Prepaid Orders

____ Copies at $19.95 each = _____
____ Leather-bound Copies
         at $90 each= _____
         Shipping = _____
(New York State Residents
     add 8.25% Sales Tax = _____

           Total = _____

☐ Fourth Class: $1.75 for the first book;
     $.50 for each additional book.

☐ First Class: $2.50 for the first book;
     $1.00 for each additional book.

☐ UPS: Same charge as for First Class;
     requires a street address.

____ Visa ____ MasterCard ____ Check or Money Order

Card Number _____ Expires ___/___ Signature _____

To _____ *Irvington Publishers, Inc.*
_____ *740 Broadway*
_____ *New York, N.Y. 10003*
_____ Zip _____

Phone _____

Prices subject to change without notice.

— —

Please clip or photocopy this order form

Special, limited, leather-bound editions of *First Heroes*, numbered and signed by the author, are available from Irvington Publishers for $90. See order form above.

QUANTITY PURCHASES
Organizations, associations, corporations and other groups may qualify for special discounts when ordering more than twenty-four copies of *First Heroes*. Please specify quantity desired, and discount information will be sent to you.
Write Special Sales Department, Irvington Publishers, Inc., 740 Broadway, New York, NY 10003